Wings Across the Pacific

Wings Across

The Courageous Aviators Who Challenged

the Pacific

and Conquered the Greatest Ocean

TERRY GWYNN-JONES

ORION BOOKS / NEW YORK

Copyright © 1991 by Terry Gwynn-Jones

Published by Orion Books, a division of Crown Publishers, Inc., 201 East 50th Street, New York, New York 10022. Member of the Crown Publishing Group.

ORION and colophon are trademarks of Crown Publishers, Inc.

Manufactured in the United States of America

Library of Congress Cataloging-in-Publication Data

Gwynn-Jones, Terry, 1933–
    Wings across the Pacific : Terry Gwynn-Jones.—1st ed.
       p. cm.
    1. Aeronautics—Pacific Area—History. 2. Transpacific
flights—
  History. I. Title.
  TL530.A1G86 1990
  629.13′0915—dc20   90-31673
                                          CIP

ISBN 0-517-56968-X

10 9 8 7 6 5 4 3 2 1

Design by Leonard Henderson

First Edition

To my son
STEPHEN GWYNN-JONES,
who arrived mid *Wings Across the Pacific*

Contents

Acknowledgments

My fascination with the Pacific Ocean goes back to my childhood. My dear father, the late Norman Gwynn-Jones, was a Marconi (radio) operator on an armed merchant cruiser and sailed the Pacific during World War I. His vivid yarns and photographs of numerous voyages between San Francisco and Sydney, and of the tropical islands they visited en route, left a deep impression. Indeed his tales of California and Australia, and of the great ocean between, were probably the catalyst behind my decision to spend most of my life in those Pacific places he loved so dearly. In 1961 I emigrated to San Francisco and four years later moved to Australia.

The idea for this book goes back to 1975, when my friend Denys Dalton and I flew the Pacific during an around-the-world record flight in a Beechcraft Duke. Although previously I had spent many hours over the North Sea flying an R.A.F. Gloster Meteor, this was my introduction to real transoceanic flying.

Our personal conquest of the Pacific was achieved in a relatively sophisticated and extremely reliable modern aircraft. Furthermore we had the benefit of a superb Bendix radio compass, twin V.O.R.s, distance measuring equipment, weather radar, and trustworthy short- and long-range radios. Nevertheless I still recall the anxiety, nine hours out from Brisbane, Australia, watching for a sign that the radio compass was receiving the beacon at Tarawa, and the relief when we finally reached the tiny atoll ten minutes ahead of E.T.A. Nor will I forget the storms of the intertropical front, the hours of dead reckoning navigation far beyond radio compass range, the tension of those overloaded takeoffs in our flying fuel tank, or the fuel-critical, lonely 2,400-mile leg from Hawaii to San Jose, California.

To help pass the long hours above the Pacific Denys and I discussed the flights of the early pioneers . . . the first crossing by the *Southern Cross* and Pan Am's fabled flying boat service. Names on our charts prompted memories of other flights. Near Tarawa we angled across the course followed by Amelia Earhart and Fred Noonan heading for Howland Island and mystery. Our first sight of Oahu reminded Denys of Charles Ulm desperately searching for signs of the Hawaiian islands as his *Stella Australis* ran out of fuel. The marathon from Hawaii to California prompted discussion about the U.S. Navy and Army fliers of the 1920s who ventured across in the days when 50 hours without repairs was a remarkable engine performance, and of those lost in the disastrous Dole Pacific Air Race. When we landed in San Jose, California, we had not only crossed the Pacific but had also time-traveled back through much of its aviation history.

As we headed on toward the Atlantic, I recall telling Denys that the history of Pacific aviation would make a fascinating book. "Well, now that you have some idea of what they faced, you better write it," Denys replied. I agreed, but somehow other book projects got in the way. Two years ago Denys died suddenly, and I was asked to ferry his record-breaking Beechcraft *Duke of Broadbeach* to Brisbane

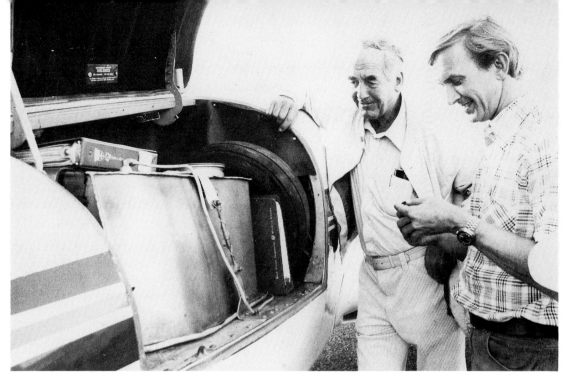

The late Denys Dalton (left) and the author check one of the long-range fuel tanks of their Beechcraft B.60 *Duke of Broadbeach* for the transpacific leg of their around-the-world record flight. (Queensland Newspapers)

where it is now permanently displayed in the Queensland Museum. That last flight in our wonderful Beechcraft reawakened my desire to write about the Pacific, and the remarkable fliers that played a part in its conquest.

Besides my lifelong gratitude to Denys Dalton for the opportunity to be involved in an around-the-world record, there are many others I must thank. Their generosity and support have contributed immeasurably to this book. First I must thank my eldest son, Anthony, who spent many nights producing most of the prints that illustrate this book. In the United States I received invaluable assistance from the staff at Washington's extraordinary National Air and Space Museum. Their unselfish assistance enabled me to locate the reference material and photographs that form the backbone of this book. In particular am indebted to Robert Mikesh, Ronald E. G. Davies, E. Tim Wooldridge, Larry Wilson, Dale Hrabak, and Melissa Keiser. Nor must I neglect to mention long-term support and encouragement given to me by Claudia M. Oakes, Tom D. Crouch, von D. Hardesty, and former museum director Walter J. Boyne. In Australia the library staff at Queensland Newspapers and the State Library of New South Wales have assisted in the search for photographs. In New Zealand Erik Adank of New Zealand Post and Shayne Niblok of Whites Aviation helped locate photographs. The problem of finding rare Japanese illustrations was solved by Fujiko Teramoto who took time from her job as Qantas Promotions Officer in Tokyo. The Federal Airports Corporation in Brisbane and Sydney assisted me greatly with the illustrations of the *Southern Cross*.

Finally I must thank my wife, Susan, for her patience and support while I spent months on research in Washington. And for her gift of our son Stephen, who arrived mid *Wings Across the Pacific*.

Research Note

A variety of different weights and measures was disclosed during my research for this book. This posed a problem as in world aviation today distance is measured in nautical miles, speed is expressed in knots (nautical miles per hour), and weight is measured in kilograms as well as pounds.

Statute miles, miles per hour, and short tons (2,000 pounds) were the most commonly used measurements in the period, and much of the geographic area, embraced by *Wings Across the Pacific*. Also, as they will be more easily understood by readers outside the aviation industry, I have elected to use them as the standard for this book.

The fuel figures I extracted from early reports and news clippings were generally expressed in U.S. gallons. However, some reports appear to have used Imperial gallons and, for the purpose of consistency, I have converted these to U.S. gallons. In those cases where I was unable to establish which standard of fuel measurement was used, I have settled on the more common U.S. gallon.

Wings Across the Pacific

"Beyond That Sunset Lies Cathay…"

Through four long centuries, man heard no signal bell to spur him on to higher, bolder ventures than that which sent him out across the vast Pacific. Nowhere on the face of the globe was there a stage of such proportions, so fit for vivid pageantry. Upon that stage, before that background of an ocean that covers half the world's dimensions, ventured the proud Magellan leading his tiny caravels across an endless sea . . . freebooting Drake fled homewards with the plunder of a mystic continent . . . roving whalers sought out siren islands of undreamed peace and loveliness . . . courageous explorers, great men of war, bold men of peace dipped in and out of forbidden ports, sped homewards with tales of magic lands still hid behind the sunset. Tall-masted Yankee clipper ships, with billowing sails and decks awash, raced halfway 'round the globe to win a trade near fable in richness. Then steam had come and clumsy craft, smoke belching from their towering stacks, ploughed the trackless miles to sweep forever from the seas the proud old clipper ships. Great ocean liners followed—and here the saga was to end. The islands of Hawaii lay no farther from our western coast than Europe from our east. And even far-off China was scarcely three weeks distant. Men said that half a world of sea could surely shrink no less than this! Yet even as they spoke, a winged generation was moving onto the stage. They had already shrunk the continents to a third their former size. Three weeks to China? World markets and modern industry separated by three costly weeks just because nine thousand miles of ocean intervened? Three weeks was ample time to circle the globe—if only wings were strong enough and man could learn to guide them across that ocean barrier! . . . In all the stirring history of the great Pacific there can be no more thrilling chapter.

Pan American Airways brochure . . . 1939

Pan American Airways brochure—1939. (NASM)

On final approach the crew of a Qantas Flight QF/11 Boeing 747 SP prepare for
a night landing at Sydney's Kingsford-Smith Airport. (Qantas)

Prologue

In the Wake of Magellan

Qantas Flight QF/11 takes fourteen hours and forty minutes to cross the Pacific Ocean. Its 7,530-mile, nonstop route from Sydney, Australia, to Los Angeles, California, is the longest overwater airway in the world.

During the flight the Boeing 747 SP's four Pratt & Whitney jet engines consume 156 tons of fuel. Its 204 passengers and 19 crew members can devour 1,500 pounds of food, helped down by hundreds of cans of soft drink—if they care to eat the galleys bare. For those with a different thirst, the bars are stocked with a large enough range of spirits, champagnes, wines, and beers to satisfy the most discriminating tippler.

QF/11 is just one of the scores of jet airliners that daily carry thousands of passengers across the Pacific. Like the Atlantic Ocean, where two decades earlier the jet age opened the door on mass intercontinental air travel, the Pacific is today crisscrossed by an aerial network linking the Americas with the nations of the ocean's Asian and Australasian seaboards. For the passengers on board QF/11, names like Hawaii, Guam, Midway, Fiji, Tahiti, the Solomons . . . roll off the tongue as easily as those of the larger nations around the Pacific rim. It was not always so.

Barely two centuries have passed since most of the world was unknown to the general public. In the eighteenth century travel was by foot or horse and most people's world was encompassed by a radius of about 10 miles. For the few who ventured overseas to wage war, conduct business, or search for new lands, the distance between continents meant months at sea at the mercy of the fickle wind.

Maps of the world showed the outline of most of the continents but, other than Europe, their interiors were depicted by blank areas or wildly inaccurate guesswork. The world was still mostly unexplored and Australia and Antarctica were not yet on the map. The sketchy details of the west

1

coast of the Americas was based on the descriptions of the Spanish adventurers who battled around Cape Horn or marched overland to colonize the Pacific regions of the New World. Little was known of China and its great empire other than the words of Marco Polo. Less still of mysterious Japan.

The vast Pacific and its myriad islands were unimaginable to all but a few well-read scholars. Spanning a third of the world, the ocean's remoteness and sheer size were forbidding. Twice the expanse of the Atlantic, in places it is deep enough to submerge Mount Everest. Little wonder that few sailing ships found a reason to voyage eastward beyond the Indies, or venture west through the terrible storms of Cape Horn into the great uncharted ocean. The few that did—and survived—brought home tales of terrible hurricanes, savage island tribes, ship-eating creatures, and mysterious disease-ridden continents.

El mar Pacifico, the Pacific Ocean, was named by the first to cross its expanse, Portuguese mariner Fernao de Magalhaes, better known as Ferdinand Magellan. Sailing westward in search of the fabled riches of the "spice islands" of the East Indies he ended his epic voyage at Mactan, in the Philippines, when he was killed in 1521. Spanish explorers followed in search of the gold said to abound in a great southern continent. Sailing from Peru in 1567, Alvaro de Mendana made landfall on a group of islands he named after King Solomon's fabled gold mine. Short of food, and with his men tortured by scurvy, Mendana was forced to turn back. On a later voyage he tried without success to relocate the Solomon Islands. With the primitive navigation instruments and techniques of the time, two centuries were to pass before they were rediscovered.

The Spanish were joined by Dutch seamen seeking to expand the trading power of the powerful Dutch East India Company. New Zealand, the New Hebrides, Tonga, and Fiji were added to the maps. Several expeditions made landfall on parts of the Australian coastline, but it was not until 1770—when Britain's great navigator Captain James Cook charted its eastern shores—that the great southern continent finally took shape.

Five years later Cook was to discover the Hawaiian Islands, and by the beginning of the nineteenth century a reasonably accurate map of the great ocean began to emerge. Knowledge of the Pacific and its people increased when, in 1854, America's Commodore Matthew Calbraith Perry blithely sailed his fleet into Japan's secretive empire, opening its doors to the Western world.

By the turn of the twentieth century the world's major powers had substantial interests in the Pacific region. America's centered on its new territory of Hawaii and the Philippines which had been ceded from Spain in 1898. The colonial empires of Great Britain, France, Spain, Portugal, Germany, and Holland had spread to the Pacific islands, and the British colonies of the great southern island continent had united into 'the Commonwealth of Australia. Most of the European powers maintained Pacific fleets to patrol their island colonies and watch over the growing numbers of merchant ships that cruised the great ocean. Clippers, their sails billowing in the trade winds, were steadily being replaced by coal-burning merchant ships. Ocean liners carried colonial officials, immigrants, and the first wide-eyed tourists.

In 1903, the first flight of the Wright brothers —thousands of miles away on the east coast of the United States—caused little more than a ripple of interest out across the Pacific. Certainly the news made interesting reading. But who could have foreseen that the strange little machine that staggered for 12 seconds across the sands of Kill Devil Hill, North Carolina, would one day revolutionize world transportation.

The world's first powered flight had covered a mere 120 feet—barely half the wingspan of Qantas Flight QF/11's Boeing 747! Even Orville and Wilbur Wright could not have dreamed that within sixty years, jumbo-jet descendants of their flimsy *Flyer* would replace the great ocean liners and long-distance railway trains; that airplanes carrying hundreds of passengers would shrink the oceans and continents until the far ends of the earth were but a day apart. Sadly, Wilbur Wright would die in 1912 before the aerial revolution really began. His brother Orville, however,

Much of the Pacific detail of this eighteenth-century French map was pure guesswork. Notice that California is shown as an island and the expanse of the North Pacific is greatly exaggerated. (TGJ)

would witness all but the final chapter of that miraculous transformation. Before his death in 1948 he would see the airplane cross countries . . . then continents . . . the Mediterranean . . . the Atlantic . . . and finally span the vast Pacific Ocean.

The story of the aerial conquest of the Pacific embraces more than just the great transoceanic flights. For nearly two decades before the first crossing, fliers from nations around its rim were taking small hesitant steps out over its water. In machines of the Wright *Flyer*'s vintage they first would cross the beach and venture out over the surf. Then, as aircraft design and reliability slowly improved, pioneering pilots crossed their fingers and island-hopped . . . 12 miles across Cook Strait separating New Zealand's North and South islands . . . 70 miles from Japan's main island Honshu to Shikoku . . . 90 miles from Hawaii to Maui . . . farther and faster as courage, confidence, and aircraft reliability increased.

Around the fringes of the Pacific, visionary pi-

lots speculated that one day they would find an aircraft with the range to set out across the ocean and a sponsor with money to make it possible. In 1925, after a team of U.S. Army aircraft had in effect crossed the North Pacific by a land-hugging Alaskan route, U.S. Navy fliers took the first serious step toward spanning the Pacific Ocean—via the natural westward steppingstone of Hawaii. Their gallant but unsuccessful flight proved that aviation was still not equal to the task.

Following Lindbergh's epochal transatlantic flight in 1927, the conquest of the Pacific would become aviation's last great ocean challenge. The stage was set for nine years of pioneering before the first airline passengers made the crossing.

Aviation's conquest of the Pacific—from the first faltering flights over the surf to Pan American Airways' fabled Clipper flying boat service—involved the pilots of many nations. Heroes and heroines, the famous and the forgotten, flying fools and aviation's great pioneers, they all played a part. This is their remarkable story.

Calbraith Perry Rodgers completed his transcontinental flight by dipping the wheels of his Wright Model EX in the Pacific Ocean at Long Beach. (NASM)

1

Venture the Pacific Surf

Narrabeen Heads, Australia, December 9, 1909

Asteady breeze blew in from the Tasman Sea lifting gently over the sand hills of Narrabeen Heads, near Sydney. It was an ideal day for gliding. Stretched across the lower wing of his biplane glider, *Punch* cartoonist and secretary of Australia's newly formed Aerial League George Augustine Taylor felt the sea breeze lifting his aircraft. On his command friends manning the slip ropes let it rise into the air like a giant kite. Once well clear of the ground and with the breeze clearly supporting his home-built craft, Taylor yelled for them to let go.

Dipping and curving above the sand, the Australian cartoonist flew more than 250 yards before splashing to a landing in the surf. Later in the day the exultant airman's wife, Florence, and his three other helpers all made flights. Heavier than air flight had finally arrived down under.

Aviation had come late to Australia. Six years had passed since the Wright brothers' first flight. Even though Taylor's friend, the brilliant inven-

tor Lawrence Hargrave, had solved the problem of lift and stability sixteen years earlier, Australia lagged behind the rest of the world. Like early European designers Gabriel Voisin, Alberto Santos Dumont, Henri Farman, and Samuel Cody, Taylor had been greatly influenced in his wing design by Hargrave's kite experiments.

Hargrave was an astronomer and also an experienced engineering draftsman. He had "retired" at thirty-three years of age to devote his life to finding a solution to heavier-than-air manned flight. But, after inventing the box kite in 1893 and finding it a stable vehicle capable of producing great lift, the pioneer was unable to capitalize on his ingenuity.

Instead of using his invention to produce a fully controllable man-carrying glider as a stepping-stone to powered flight—the natural progression followed by the Wright brothers—Hargrave spent the next eleven years, and most of his assets, building models and twenty-six unsuccessful engines. His attempt to leapfrog from man-lifting

5

A trio of Australian pilots, (from left) Charles Kingsford-Smith, Cyril Maddocks, and Valentine Rendle, were determined to enter the 1919 England-Australia air race. When Kingsford-Smith was barred from taking part, he moved to California in search of a transpacific sponsor. (TGJ)

box kite to powered aircraft was doomed to failure.

Powered flight eventually arrived down under in March 1910 when a young Australian airman, Fred Custance, and America's Eric Weiss, better known to his adoring fans around the world as the Great Houdini, battled for the honor of being the first to make a successful flight. Their flights were less than a day apart, and it is unclear who won, although it was the American escapologist's brief flirtation with flight that captured Australian headlines. Flying a lumbering Voisin biplane, whose wings were evolved from Hargrave's box kite, the American made three successful flights at Digger's Rest near Melbourne. Following his final landing Houdini leapt from the aircraft and, striking a theatrical pose, shouted: "I can fly, I can fly."

Australia continued to lag behind Europe and the United States until World War I when Australian pilots, mostly trained in England, displayed remarkable skills and tenacity in combat. Some suggested their ability as horsemen gave the Australians a natural aptitude for controlling their fractious aerial mounts.

Following the Armistice in 1918, Australia's visionary Prime Minister W. "Billy" Hughes, seeing the possibilities for aircraft as a future transport solution for his vast and isolated country, offered £10,000 for the first Australians to fly from England to Australia. Many Australian military airmen still in England awaiting demobilization applied to make the flight in their military aircraft. One who applied, but was turned down through lack of navigation experience, was Lt. Charles Kingsford-Smith, Australian Flying Corps. Bitterly disappointed, Kingsford-Smith headed instead for California. By 1920, when a Vickers Vimy bomber flown by Australians Ross and Keith Smith won Billy Hughes's prize, Kingsford-Smith was already planning another way home. For him aviation's future lay across the Pacific.

The sheer distance did not deter him. Nor did he suffer from the paranoid fear most fliers shared of flight over water. Young Smithy had already experienced and survived his first dramatic meeting with the great ocean. Eleven years earlier at Bondi Beach, just 2 miles from where George Taylor had splashed down in the surf, ten-year-old Charles Kingsford-Smith had made his own headlines. BOY SAVED FROM DROWNING, they read. The fearless ten year-old and a swimming companion, foolishly ignoring the dangerous riptide, had been swept out to sea. Rescuers thought Charles was dead when he was eventually brought back to the beach. It took thirty minutes of artificial respiration and a "miracle" to bring the youngster "back from the dead."

For more than a year Lieutenant Kingsford-Smith planned, and pestered Californian businessmen. Finally accepting that it was impossible to find a sponsor, or a suitable airplane, the young Australian returned home by sea—aware that he must curb his impatience until design caught up with his dreams. Nevertheless, he knew it was only a matter of time.

In 1920 Kingsford-Smith hoped to fly the Pacific in a Vickers Vimy, similar to this one flown across the Atlantic by Britain's John Alcock and Arthur Whitten Brown in 1919. (NASM)

Long Beach, California, April 3, 1912

Seven thousand spectators thronged the shore at Long Beach, California, craning their necks to watch as the little Wright biplane swooped overhead. Most had never seen an airplane before. The pilot, a former college football star named Calbraith Perry Rodgers, buzzed the amusement park, then headed across the sands toward the Pacific breakers.

In California, as in the rest of the world, the airplane was still a novelty and people gladly paid to see one fly. Great crowd pullers at state fairs and city race tracks, they also attracted tens of thousands to special air shows held in major cities. In Chicago and New York some top European fliers were the new matinee idols, commanding $1,000 for a brief joy flight. Profligate socialites happily paid up—clinging precariously to their heroes' new-fangled flying machines. But these fliers were the exception to the rule. Most early pilots lived a hand-to-mouth existence.

The flamboyant cigar-chomping Rodgers epitomized the public's perception of this new breed of hero. A genial six-foot-four-inch giant who, despite being almost deaf, could turn a phrase as neatly as his Wright biplane, he was the great grandson of Commodore Matthew Perry—the naval hero who had opened the door on modern Japan. Cal Rodgers had learned to fly the previ-

ous year at the Wright brothers' school in Dayton, Ohio. Shortly after completing his training he had become a national hero by making the first coast-to-coast flight across the United States. Nevertheless, like most of his contemporaries, Rodgers was having trouble making ends meet and relied on performing demonstration flights for a living. He was making his first appearance at Long Beach since ending his coast-to-coast flight there four months earlier.

Rodgers had made his epic transcontinental flight in an effort to win the then staggering sum of $50,000 offered by California newspaper tycoon William Randolph Hearst. Whether Hearst's challenge was merely another of his news-making stunts or a genuinely patriotic effort to further the course of American aviation is unclear. But there is no doubt that since 1908 the pioneering Wright brothers had squandered America's aviation supremacy by becoming involved in a series of patent squabbles while European aircraft builders and pilots, particularly the French, had leapt into the lead.

While most of America's growing band of professional fliers concentrated on demonstration and stunt flying in outdated designs, their European counterparts were setting an array of speed and distance records and refining the aircraft from a plaything to a machine with military and

An embroidered scarf recalls aviation's first international overwater flight. Louis Blériot's 1909 conquest of the English Channel gave the world a glimpse of the transcontinental possibilities of the airplane. (NASM)

transportation potential. By 1910 Blériot monoplanes had doubled the 34-mph record set the previous year by a Wright biplane, and a Farman biplane had increased Wilbur Wright's 1908 distance record of 77.5 miles by almost tenfold.

International competition between European fliers had been the spur. Forty-three airplanes representing six nations had contested the 1,000 mile European Circuit air race. Nineteen had set off to fly a similar distance in the Circuit of Britain. Air races had linked Paris with Rome and Madrid and, in 1909, Louis Blériot had made the first great overwater flight spanning the 22-mile-wide English Channel.

The catalyst for much of Europe's aviation activity had been the huge cash prizes offered by European newspapers. Britain's Baron of Fleet Street, Lord Northcliffe, had offered £1,000 ($5,000) for the cross-Channel flight. On seeing the unprecedented public interest, not to mention the newspaper sales, generated by Blériot's epochal flight, Northcliffe upped the prize money for the Circuit of Britain to £10,000 ($50,000)—a fortune in those days. His early interest would turn into a lifelong crusade during which he almost single-handedly strove to promote the advancement of British aviation.

In the fall of 1910 Hearst, already noted for his knack of making headline news, had followed Lord Northcliffe's lead by promoting America's first transcontinental flight. However, his prize required the winner to link the Atlantic and Pacific oceans by air within thirty days. The chance of success was so remote that America's professional airmen dismissed the offer as another news-making gimmick and it was not until September 1911—a month before the offer expired—that a novice Wright pilot named Robert Fowler had set off eastward from San Francisco.

Fowler gave up when his radiator boiled as he tried to negotiate the Donner Pass. A second contestant, ex-jockey Robert Ward, heading westward in a Curtiss biplane never got past the boundaries of New York State. In the meantime Calbraith Rodgers had set off in his Wright *Vin Fiz,* named for a soft drink produced for the Armour Company of Chicago. J. Ogden Armour had agreed to sponsor the flight to the tune of five dollars for every mile Rodgers covered and to supply a special three-car train to follow the flier. It consisted of a Pullman car and day coach for Rodgers's wife and mechanics and a specially equipped "hangar car" that carried a backup aircraft, an assortment of spare parts, gasoline, oil,

Calbraith Perry Rodgers is seen here taking off at Sheepshead Bay, New York, on his marathon flight across the United States on September 17, 1911. (NASM)

tools, and even a special racing car to get to Rodgers quickly in case of an accident. Rodgers's long-suffering support crew were to get plenty of work.

His progress westward along the railway line became a succession of short stop-and-go hops—sixty-nine in all. Besides five serious crashes, which each required a major rebuild, the flight was punctuated with minor mishaps. Broken landing skids, spark plugs working loose in flight, spectators souveniring parts of his machine, storms, swooping eagles, engine failures, all combined to slow his progress and his hopes of winning the $50,000.

At Chicago, with only two days of Hearst's time limit remaining, and still only a third of the way across the continent, Rodgers had told reporters: "Prize or no prize I am bound for California," then, chomping firmly on his cigar, he continued on his heroic odyssey. On November 3, soon after crossing the Californian border, Rodgers was injured when an exploding engine cylinder drove shards of steel into his arm. Two days later, following temporary repairs to pilot and plane, *Vin Fiz* limped into Pasadena to be greeted by 10,000 cheering Californians. Officially the flight was over and had already exceeded the time limit by nineteen days. However Rodgers, insisting that his goal had literally been to fly to the edge of the Pacific Ocean, took off again a week later to fly the final 20 miles to the coast. He had covered just 8 miles when the newly reconditioned engine failed once again and he crashed in a ploughed field, suffering internal injuries and a broken ankle.

Shortly after recovering consciousness from his accident the indefatigable Rodgers lit a cigar and proclaimed: "I am going to finish that flight and finish it with that same machine." It mattered little that only the rudder and oil drip pan remained of the original aircraft. A month later the determined airman left the hospital and hobbled once more aboard his rebuilt machine, strapped his crutches to the wings, and flew on to the sands at Long Beach. Fifty thousand cheered

from the boardwalk as, still puffing at a cigar, Rodgers rolled the Wright's wheels in the Pacific surf. He had flown 4,250 miles in the epic 84-day journey to the Pacific Ocean.

Rodgers had made no money from his odyssey. The funds from his sponsor had been expended in repairing his aircraft. However, the publicity had made him a "famous aviator"—a fact confirmed by the 7,000 who had paid to watch him demonstrate his skill over Long Beach that afternoon in 1912.

For many of the crowd it was their first sight of an airplane and they watched enthralled as Rodgers left the safety of the beach and flew out across the ocean. He headed toward a large flock of seagulls feeding off a shoal of sardines. Putting on a show for the crowd Rodgers was seen to turn

Glenn L. Martin's 1912 floatplane was a far cry from the magnificent M-130 flying boats he would eventually produce for Pan American Airways. (NASM)

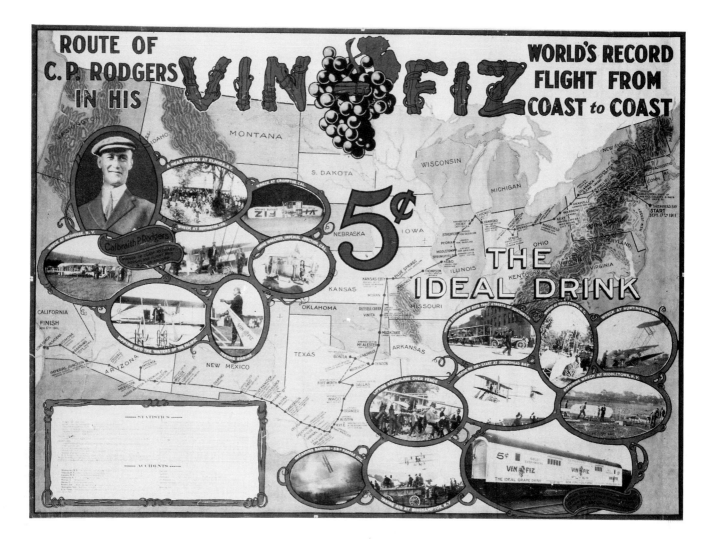

Shortly after Rodgers's sponsor produced this poster promoting their soft drink and his flight, the pioneer airman died when he crashed in the Pacific. (NASM)

and dive into the wheeling flock of birds, apparently intent on scattering them. As the biplane passed through the flock one gull struck the machine. It wedged between the tail and rudder, causing a control wire to break and sending the plane out of control into the ocean. Swimmers quickly reached the scene and pulled Rodgers from the wreckage, but it was too late. He had died of a broken neck. The Pacific Ocean had claimed its first aerial victim. On his tombstone they carved: "I endure—I conquer," an epitaph that would be equally fitting for others who would die as aviation reached out across the Pacific.

Five weeks later another showman, dubbed the "Flying Dude" for his stylish black leather aviator's clothing, was attracting the attention of Los Angelians. A former garage owner and car salesman, Glenn Luther Martin made demonstration flights to help finance the tiny aircraft manufacturing company he had started in an abandoned church four years earlier. Now occupying an old cannery and employing an assistant, Martin had just built his first seaplane—a float-equipped pusher biplane.

On May 10, 1912, the daring young airman used it to make a 60-mile return flight over the

Pacific to Catalina Island, thus accomplishing the first tentative island-hopping flight out across the Pacific. It was a minuscule step compared with the transpacific flights that were to be made by Martin aircraft twenty-seven years hence.

Fired by the enthusiasm of a young airline builder named Juan T. Trippe, the Martin name would become synonymous with Pacific aviation and one of the world's most successful flying boats.

Auckland Harbor, New Zealand, December 16, 1919

Pilot George Bolt could hardly contain his excitement as the bags containing 825 letters and 25 pounds of newspapers were loaded into the New Zealand Flying School's launch. Minutes later they were transported into the middle of Auckland Harbor where his seaplane was moored. At last he was going to demonstrate the commercial capabilities of his beloved Boeing seaplanes.

For more than a year the school had waited patiently for the Postal Department to accept their offer of a demonstration air mail service. Even though thirty years earlier New Zealand had boasted the first official "airmail" when carrier pigeons had been used, postal officials were loath to trust their precious mail to airplanes. Flying machines, they said, were "very tricky." They preferred the slow-but-safe steamers that carried the mails to the numerous isolated villages and settlements dotted around the coast of New Zealand.

The New Zealand Flying School's two Boeing B & W seaplanes, also called Model 1s, had been built in 1916 by William Boeing and Comdr. G. Conrad Westervelt, U.S.N. They were the first two airplanes built by the company that was to become the world's largest manufacturer of transport aircraft. Half a century later their descendants, Boeing 747 jumbo jets, would revolutionize the airline industry, bringing air travel within the reach of the masses.

William Boeing had constructed the two B & W biplanes in his boathouse on Lake Union, in the heart of Seattle, Washington, hoping to attract the interest of the U.S. Navy. Their success encouraged him to establish Pacific Aero Products company, which in 1917 became the Boeing Airplane Company. Although the Navy did not pur-

chase the Model 1s, Boeing was eventually given an order for fifty Model 5 trainers. The two B & Ws had been sold to the New Zealand government in 1919 and became the pride of the New Zealand Flying School.

Following World War I many New Zealand pilots had returned home eager to find a way to use their new-found skill. A few, like George Bolt, found work giving joy flights and instruction but most found it necessary to return to their old jobs. Bolt was certain that aircraft had a commercial future in his South Pacific homeland and, on this warm, clear southern summer morning, was about to prove his case.

At 10:15 A.M., right on schedule, Bolt took off from Auckland Harbor. His destination was Dargaville—a town 100 miles to the north. A crowd of 2,000 cheered as he climbed steadily, hugging the Pacific coastline as he gained height over the water: "Due to the unreliability of engines in those days, we never cared to go very far away from the water and the route was arranged up the east coast," Bolt recalled years after. An hour and a half later, after crossing over to the west coast at a narrow neck of land, Bolt brought the Boeing down on the river at Dargaville. The return flight was equally uneventful. "The pioneer aerial Royal Mail of New Zealand was carried from Auckland to Dargaville without a hitch in the arrangements," the *New Zealand Herald* stated.

However, the news reports were very different a couple of months later when Bolt hit a log while landing at Dargaville, bringing about a rescue that would be joked about for years after. As the damaged float filled with water, Bolt and a companion climbed onto the wingtip and used their weight to prevent the crippled seaplane from roll-

Bolt's Boeing B & W alongside the beach at Pahi in 1921, following a flight from Auckland carrying the New Zealand prime minister, Gordon Coates.
(M. Sterling)

ing over. A railway track ran close to the water's edge near where the Boeing was listing dangerously.

Realizing that the seaplane was likely to sink, the driver of the Dargaville post office motor launch quickly carried a line to the shore, where he flagged down a passing steam locomotive. The line was secured and the locomotive shunted slowly backward, dragging the sinking Boeing up onto the beach. When the news got out that an airplane had been rescued by a railway train, journalists—and the wags in the local bars—had a field day at Bolt's expense. It was an aviation "first" the airman would have rather forgone.

Due to its extreme isolation from the rest of the world, New Zealand, like Australia, had been slow to take a constructive interest in aviation. New Zealand had also possessed its own early aviation pioneer whose experiments, though not as significant as Lawrence Hargrave's, might have given his country an early lead.

Richard Pearse, a farmer with a brilliant engineering mind, lived in a remote little settlement on New Zealand's South Island. Like his Australian counterpart Lawrence Hargrave, Pearse worked in isolation from others around the world who were studying the problems of flight. Just four months after the Wright brothers, Pearse

tested a flying machine. It was the culmination of his first attempt "to solve the problem of aerial navigation," which he had started in 1900.

Little more than a flying wing, spanning about 45 feet and with a 15-foot chord, the contraption looked like a huge barn door mounted on steerable tricycle landing gear. The pilot's seat was suspended below the wing, perilously close to the metal propeller he had shaped from an old farm drum that had once contained sheep dip. It was powered by an extremely light, four-cylinder engine, which the gifted farmer had designed and built himself. Though totally unlike the Wright's machine, it bore a striking resemblance to today's powered hang gliders.

How well it flew was another matter. Witnesses, who helped Pearse wheel it to a grassed track near the Waitohi schoolhouse in March 1904, maintained the strange monoplane clearly left the ground. It rose to about 12 feet but, after a hundred or so yards, veered to the left and settled on top of a high gorse hedge. Years later in a letter to a newspaper, Pearse stated that although he had been airborne, he had been unable to control his machine, which had subsequently carried him only as far and as high as it had chosen to go. Nevertheless it was a remarkable achievement. Pearse had solved the problem of lift and built a crude, but practical, engine and propeller. Had he perfected the control system—which resembled modern ailerons—the New Zealander would have achieved controlled flight only months after the Wright brothers.

George Bolt, after retiring from airline flying, meticulously researched Pearse's experiments and wrote: "All things have small beginnings, and this was so with New Zealand long-distance flights. If Pearse did not make a cross-country flight, he at least got off the ground in one place and landed somewhere else."

New Zealand airmail pioneer George Bolt and one of the Boeing seaplanes. Note the rolled-up trousers and bare feet—the trademark of a true seaplane pilot. (Whites Aviation)

Prior to World War I a handful of itinerant aerial showmen had made the long voyage across the Tasman from Australia. Generally they had done little to promote the cause of aviation. One was Arthur "Wizard" Stone, an American circus daredevil who had turned from motorcycles to a Blériot monoplane. His Auckland performance, marred by high winds, ended with a spectacular crash and the "Wizard" being castigated by the angry crowd. One of the spectators was a young apprentice chemist, J. William Scotland. Undaunted by the public's reaction to the unfortunate American's accident, he made up his mind to become a pilot.

In 1914, after learning to fly in England, Scotland made many impressive exhibition flights in his Caudron Type C biplane. His efforts generated great public enthusiasm for airplanes. One performance at Otaki, 50 miles north of Wellington, New Zealand's capital, was attended by crowds of native Maori people. Spellbound by their first sight of an airplane, they made Scotland their idol. "Him t' good fellow. Him like t' big hawk," they chanted.

The Maoris were equally impressed by Bolt and his mail service five years later when he flew to Whatakane, on the Bay of Plenty. Landing in a natural harbor, safe from the big Pacific rollers, he tied up to a rock. He was totally unaware of its significance in Maori legend. Centuries earlier one of the first Maori canoes to reach New Zealand after voyaging across the Pacific was said to have anchored to the same rock. The canoe had carried Chief Toroa and his people.

A Maori who paddled out to help Bolt secure the Boeing declared himself a direct descendant of Toroa. The Maori was so delighted the first aircraft he had ever seen should moor at the historic rock that he named the airman "Chief Toroa the Second" after the great New Zealand chief. As the flights continued the Maoris of the coastal settlements hero-worshipped Bolt and his Boeing, calling him "Captain of the Big Bird." Writing to his mother, the airman said: "The Maoris treat us as though we come from another world and it was embarrassing, in a way, when some of them kneel down as we walk along the road. In some places, these people have never seen a car, let alone an aeroplane."

In 1919 white New Zealanders had been caught up in the excitement generated by John Alcock and Arthur Whitten-Brown's nonstop Atlantic flight. The following year an Australian-crewed Vickers Vimy flew from London to Darwin, bringing a vision of long-distance flights almost to New Zealand's doorstep. Pilots began talking about flights across the Tasman Sea linking New Zealand and Australia.

It was still too soon to even consider the possibility that aircraft might one day retrace the routes across the Pacific first traveled by the ancestors of New Zealand's Maori people. Except, perhaps, in the Maori settlements where Chief Toroa the Second and his Big Bird seemed capable of any miracle.

Hilo Bay, Hawaii, August 13, 1921

Charlie Stoffer really looked the part of a flamboyant flier: knee boots, riding britches, white shirt, and bow tie. His sporty outfit was topped off with goggles perched on a peaked cap—peak turned backward in true intrepid-aviator style.

Two passengers were jammed in the front cockpit of the Curtiss N 9 seaplane that Hawaiians had affectionately nicknamed "Charley's Crate." Hilo resident Ed Searle and Van Dyke Johns, a visiting Stanford, California, tennis player, were about to travel on the maiden flight of Stoffer's interisland air service. Their destination was Oahu, 180 air miles and three island hops away.

Stoffer, a former World War I Army flying instructor, had come to the islands at the invitation of a former student, W. "Ben" Stoddard. In December 1919, after finding his native California flooded with would-be barnstormers, Stoddard had started a small flying business in Honolulu and employed another discharged military instructor, Charles Fern. Stoffer and his Curtiss had joined the company when Fern resigned. Since March 1920, when Fern had used the company's Curtiss JN4D Jenny to make a 90-minute flight to Maui (the 90-mile trip took 12 hours by overnight steamer), Honolulu businessmen had been talking about the need for an interisland air service. Stoffer and his seaplane seemed set to fill that need.

Charley's Crate was launched from a seaplane ramp the U.S. Navy had installed at Hilo. Despite brushing against a lava ledge while preparing to take off, everything went well as Stoffer hugged the coast and climbed to 5,000 feet for the 28-mile overwater crossing to Maui. He recalled the crossing and how one of his passengers saved them from almost certain death: "The flight had progressed to approximately midway between Hawaii and Maui when the auxiliary fuel tank ran dry, and when I attempted to turn on the main supply the bronze handle on the main line sheared."

Stoffer put the Curtiss into a shallow glide, desperately trying to find a way to open the fractured fuel cock. The only way to reach the stub of the shaft was through a small panel located on the outside of the fuselage between the two open cockpits. Unable to leave the controls, Stoffer shouted to his passengers, explaining the problem. One of them, displaying tremendous courage, reacted immediately, as Stoffer related:

Ed Searle, who luckily had a pair of pliers in his pocket, climbed out of the cockpit and opened a small inspection door adjacent to the valve and attempted to twist the small remaining portion of the valve handle. At about 75 feet above the waves, he had opened it sufficiently so that I could power glide, and at approximately 25 feet it was open sufficiently to ascend again.

Despite almost sinking at its moorings at Maui, and an unscheduled overnight stop on Molokai island due to high winds, Charley's Crate finally

BUD MARS AND THE CURTIS AEROPLANE
MANILA CARNIVAL FEB. 22, 1911.

Hawaii's first flight took place on December 31, 1910, when J. C. "Bud" Mars (pictured here in the Philippines) made an exhibition flight in a Curtiss P 18 from the Moanalua Polo Field. (NASM)

reached Honolulu. Stoffer eventually converted the Curtiss into a land plane and over the next few years ran Hawaii's most popular and most successful aviation company.

Aviation in Hawaii went back to 1889 when Joseph Van Tassell of Salem, Ohio, flew over Honolulu perched on a trapeze suspended below a balloon. Guaranteeing to ascend to "the dizzy height of one mile" or to refund the fifty cents admission, the aerial showman ascended near Diamond Head before parachuting safely to the ground. The first airplane flight was made in December 1910 by J. C. "Bud" Mars in a Curtiss P 18 from the Moanalua Polo Field, near Honolulu. Thousands of Hawaiians witnessed his four flights, many of them calling out: "Aloha, Mokulele [skyboat]!"

Yet to the Hawaiian Islanders, Mars and his airplane, though immensely exciting, were nothing totally new. They had been brought up on tales of their own legendary Polynesian airman Maui, "the Quick One," who had used the first Mokulele to fly from island to island around the Pacific. Indeed, one of Hawaii's island chains was named for the god Maui, who had built a "birdcraft" of "rootlets, ti leaves, and feathers." Even as far away as New Zealand, the Maoris knew of the pan-Polynesian sky hero and his amazing flights.

World War I prompted the U.S. War Department to station the 6th Aero Squadron, Army Air Service, on Ford Island in Pearl Harbor for the "aerial coastal defense" of Oahu. In 1919 the Army fliers were joined by a U.S. Naval Aviation Unit. During the early 1920s most of Hawaii's interisland flying was conducted by the military. Stoffer, who returned to California in 1924 to fly for the movies, had made infrequent interisland flights. However, no regular service had been established by 1927 when a new company, Lewis

17

When Hawaiian pineapple magnate James Dole challenged fliers to link the islands with California, Honolulu-based pilot Martin Jensen was Hawaii's only contender. Like most 1920s pilots Jensen did anything to stay solvent. Here his wife says farewell as he prepares to leave on a crazy promotional tour for M.G.M. Studios. (NASM)

Air Tours, employed as its pilot an ex-naval flier named Martin Jensen.

A World War I veteran, Jensen was working toward establishing a proper interisland service when, in the wake of Lindbergh's Atlantic flight, an air race between California and Hawaii was announced. Its promoter, Hawaiian pineapple magnate James D. Dole, had decided to focus world attention on Hawaii. Even though there were few aircraft with the range or reliability for such a flight, with prize money of $35,000 there was no shortage of wildly optimistic entrants from the mainland. In Honolulu, Martin Jensen decided to represent Hawaii in the Dole challenge.

To those seriously concerned for the future of aviation and its public image of death and danger, the race between California and Hawaii had far-reaching implications. The 2,400 miles also represented the longest overwater leg on any future island-hopping transpacific route. Before any airline could contemplate a service between America and the Orient, it must first safely make the giant leap onto the Hawaiian steppingstone. Such a flight required meticulous preparation, a highly-qualified crew, and a long-range multi-engine aircraft. Instead, hard on the heels of Lindbergh's hard-won success, it appeared that the future of transpacific aviation was about to be placed in the hands of a band of ill-prepared aerial cowboys. Fliers were so dazzled by hard cash and glory, they would cheerfully gamble their lives in an assortment of overloaded single-engine airplanes. Short of a miracle, American aviation faced a disaster.

Charles Lindbergh's epochal transatlantic flight was the catalyst for a decade of Japanese interest in conquering the Pacific. Within two months of Lindbergh's flight, Japan's Imperial Aeronautic Association announced a project to fly nonstop across the Pacific. (Don Tuma)

Tokyo, Japan, July 1927

In Japan, Lindbergh's flight also acted as a catalyst for a Pacific flight. However, unlike James Dole's challenge, the Imperial Aeronautic Association's project was cautiously structured. Rather than rely on unsuitable aircraft and ill-prepared pilots, it called on Japanese aircraft manufacturers to design a special long-range airplane and train its crew. The association's ambitious plan was to stun the world with a nonstop flight across the Pacific.

The leading industrial nation in Asia, Japan sought the honor and international attention such an epic flight would bring. The Japanese had long realized that the airplane was an ideal means of rapid travel around its expanding island empire. As early as 1920 three Japanese army planes and three naval seaplanes had successfully crossed the Sea of Japan to Korea. In May 1921 three Yokosho floatplanes of the Sasebo Naval Air Corps had ranged down the eastern edge of the Pacific, making a 750-mile flight across the

East China Sea to Taiwan. The same month, possibly trying to upstage the navy fliers, army pilot Lieutenant Kawaida made a more lighthearted contribution to Japanese aviation history by completing a world-record 456 consecutive loops in his Sopwith fighter.

Competitions sponsored by the Imperial Aeronautical Association encouraged rapid advances in civil aviation. In 1922 seaplanes operated the first scheduled interisland airmail service, and a year later Japan Air Lines had been formed to serve a holiday resort on Kyushu Island. Despite the devastation caused by the great earthquake in September 1923, J.A.L. and a second airline, Tozai Teiki Kokukwai, were operating four interisland passenger services by mid-1925.

The same year, inspired by the arrival in Japan of American and European pilots attempting to circumnavigate the world, the *Asahi Shimbun* newspaper sponsored a flight to Europe by two Japanese Breguet XIX biplanes. Touring the capitals of Europe, their crews flew 10,813 miles in 116 flying hours. In 1926 Japanese airmen pioneered another future Pacific route when two Kawanishi K-7 floatplanes crossed the East China Sea on a 950-mile flight from Osaka to Shanghai. On the return flight one of the K-7s ditched in the sea and its crew clung to a float for six hours before being rescued by a passing cargo ship. Nevertheless it was now clearly only a matter of time and the right aircraft before Japan's airlines would commence services linking its islands with the east Pacific mainland.

Japan's growing aviation industry, though financially secure, still relied heavily on foreign designs. As early as 1910, when a Japanese military officer made his country's first successful flight in a Henri Farman biplane, the embryo aircraft-building industry was at work. In 1911 a would-be airman named Narahara constructed a biplane that carried him a distance of 75 yards. Quick to sense the future military importance of airplanes, both the army and navy appointed their first flying officers by 1912. However, during World War I Japan's military air wings relied on an armada of foreign types: Farmans, Sopwiths, Nieuports, SPADSs, Shorts, and Breguets. Following the war, most commercial aircraft were imported from overseas. It was not until 1926, when an army evaluation team chose aircraft designed by Mitsubishi and Kawasaki, that there was a significant growth in Japanese aircraft production. Even then the larger companies employed foreign technical specialists, and designs tended to mirror European and American aircraft.

Thus it is not surprising that when the Imperial Aeronautic Association announced its transpacific project, Japanese designers looked first toward other aircraft that had completed similar flights. While the world still celebrated Lindbergh's Atlantic crossing, representatives of a Tokyo newspaper visited the Ryan Airlines Company's tiny factory in a fish cannery on the San Diego waterfront. After talking to owner T. Claude Ryan and designer Donald Hall, they placed an order for Ryan NYP-2. The unknown sister ship of Lindbergh's *Spirit of St. Louis* might just help Japan conquer the Pacific.

Opposite: The little-known sister ship of the Ryan NYP *Spirit of St. Louis*. Shortly after Lindbergh's Atlantic flight, the Ryan Airlines Company built this copy of the NYP monoplane for a Japanese newspaper. (NASM)

Lindbergh's immortal *Spirit of St. Louis* today hangs above the Wright brothers' *Flyer* in the National Air and Space Museum in Washington, D.C. (TGJ)

2

Around the North Pacific Rim

The first aircraft to link North America and Asia did so as a part of a much greater adventure—the first aerial circumnavigation of the world. The flight was carried out in 1924 by a team of United States Army Air Service pilots. Its significance as the starting point of transpacific aviation has long been overshadowed by its more obvious global achievement.

The Army's Pacific crossing was achieved by a land-hugging route that followed the coastlines and islands of the ocean's northern rim rather than an attempt to fly a direct, transoceanic path. Nevertheless this was the first vital step toward the aerial conquest of the great ocean.

Maj. Gen. Mason Patrick, chief of the Army Air Service, was Brig. Gen. "Billy" Mitchell's superior. Patrick readily approved the formation of a special World Flight. (NASM)

Six years had passed since the end of the Great War and in terms of aviation progress, little had happened in the United States. The Army Air Corps had been blooded on the western front in the dying moments of aviation's first holocaust. But with the coming of peace and the mad roaring twenties, there was little government and public interest in the new branch of the military. World War I had been the war to end all wars, and there seemed little future need for air forces. They were expensive and no longer had any *raison d'être*.

It was against this background that Maj. Gen. Mason Patrick, chief of the newly formed Air Service, and his outspoken deputy, Brig. Gen. Billy Mitchell, had decided to publicly promote military aviation. A self-appointed champion of "air power," Mitchell wanted to see the Army absorb the Navy's infant air arm into a single independent national air force. While Patrick worked quietly behind the scenes, Mitchell became a belligerent promoter. Besides battling with the Navy, there was the task of attracting the support of President Calvin Coolidge and his government. Funds were desperately needed to preserve and eventually expand the Army Air Service, whose pilots had already been relegated to such mundane tasks as flying the nation's mail.

Besides upsetting admirals and his old-school Army superiors, Mitchell was a genius at making headlines as he strove for funds and new equipment. To keep the service in the public eye, he encouraged his men to fly their old crates into the limelight. Flights around the boundaries of the United States, to Alaska, and setting a series of transcontinental speed records all helped. A breakthrough came when Mitchell was finally given a small appropriation to purchase two new aircraft for experimental development.

He chose the Dutch Fokker T-2, a military version of Anthony Fokker's extremely successful line of civilian transport aircraft. In May 1923 the mammoth single-engine monoplane was used by Lieutenants O. G. Kelly and J. A. Macready to make the first nonstop crossing of the United States. The press went wild, hailing the flight as "the greatest record of all"—something of an overstatement, perhaps, since both British and American teams had crossed the Atlantic four years earlier.

Nevertheless it was just the sort of response that Patrick and Mitchell had wanted. Two months later, with the nation still bubbling over the Army's success, they gained approval from the War Department to mount a flight around the world. Their submission stated that the flight would demonstrate that international flight was practical and would be a valuable test of the effects of varying climatic conditions on aircraft operations.

Funds were allocated for a small aircraft manufacturer named Donald Douglas to tailor-make four special aircraft in his converted movie studio factory in Santa Monica, California. Based on an earlier naval design, his new biplane was of tubular steel and wood construction, covered with fabric, and powered by a 420-hp Liberty engine. The airplanes were designed so that wheels or floats could be installed for various stages of the world flight. The extremely reliable Liberty engine had been one of the success stories of America's wartime manufacturing industry. It gave the Douglas DWC/0-5 World Cruiser a maximum speed of about 100 mph and a range of 2,100 miles, although fully loaded with crew and supplies and equipped with floats, its range was more than halved and the most economical cruising speed was closer to 80 mph.

With typical military precision, a special group called the "World Flight" was formed. The planners had quickly realized that whereas a single aircraft had little chance of success, a flight by four aircraft with adequate ground support had excellent prospects of completing the 28,500-mile journey.

Though the odds for the group may have looked good, the picture was not so bright for the individual crews. The distance to be covered did not bear thinking about, nor did the fact that greater portion of the route lay over some of the most desolate parts of the globe. Not only would they cross vast uninhabited deserts and jungles of Asia and the Middle East but also two great oceans. The Atlantic crossing was planned via Iceland and Greenland. The Pacific flight would be achieved by skirting around its rim along the coast of Canada and Alaska, then crossing the Bering Sea via the Aleutian Islands and following a ribbon of Russian islands to Japan. Although the longest overwater leg was only about 650 miles, the whole area was notorious for foul and unpredictable weather.

"It's one hell of a gamble," the airmen decided as they scanned the orders calling for volunteers. Predictably, however, there was no shortage of bright-eyed young men prepared to stake their lives against the chance of a moment in history. Maj. Frederick Martin, a tall, broad-shouldered career officer of forty, was chosen to command the flight. The three other pilots were lieutenants: Leigh Wade had learned to fly with the Royal Air Force in Canada and had commanded a squadron on the western front in 1917, Lowell H. Smith had been the engineering officer of Mexican revolutionary Pancho Villa's three-plane

Maj. Frederick Martin (second from right), pictured here with six of the World Flight crewmen, was commanding officer of the airborne detachment until he crashed in Alaska. (NASM)

air force before joining the U.S. Army in 1917, and Erik Nelson had established a reputation for long-distance flying in numerous flights and had won the *Detroit News* Aerial Mail Trophy in 1922. Their flight engineers were Lt. Leslie Arnold, an observation pilot during World War I; Sgt. Henry Ogden, whose hobbies included wing walking and jumping between aircraft in flight; Sgt. Alva Harvey, whose great physical strength would be put to the test; and 2d Lt. John Harding, an ex–kitchen hand, ditch digger, and auto mechanic who had become an engineering genius.

The preflight planning and logistics were unparalleled for that time. Advance parties were dispatched to set up seventeen refueling and

servicing depots along the route. In addition, permission was gained to use facilities at many of the fifty-two planned stops in the twenty-nine countries they would visit. Britain's Royal Air Force granted the use of their facilities at out-of-the-way parts of the British Empire. As a further precaution, U.S. Navy and Coast Guard vessels were fanned out to stand guard along the route during the two ocean crossings. A total of 91,800 gallons of fuel and 11,650 gallons of oil were purchased and scattered at various points along the World Flight route.

Every possible loophole that could be closed was closed. But there were still vast areas of their route where help might as well have been a mil-

Capt. Lowell H. Smith figured in a number of the Army's promotional flights and during his career set sixteen world speed and endurance records. He took over command when Martin crashed. (NASM)

Two of the Douglas DWC/0-5 World Cruisers on display at Clover Field, Santa Monica, California, before flying to Seattle, Washington, where they were equipped with floats for the North Pacific crossing. (NASM)

lion miles away. If the airmen came down in these places they had little chance of survival. The aircraft were not radio equipped—airborne radios were still notoriously unreliable and, besides, would have been of little use over the vast uninhabited regions of their route. As the aircraft were to be equipped with floats on the overwater legs, it was decided not to carry life rafts or life preservers. Nobody seemed concerned that if an aircraft came down in anything other than a calm sea the floats would be little use—waves of more than three feet would eventually batter the machines to pieces.

Coincidentally with the American preparations, fliers from England, France, Portugal, Argentina, and Italy announced their intentions of circling the globe. The six nations were vying for the honor of awakening the world public to the global potential of the airplane. Though not a race in the sense of being an organized event, each team was striving to be first. The prize would be a nation's pride of achievement and the applause of the world.

The four World Cruisers were flown from Douglas's Santa Monica factory to Seattle, Washington, in March 1924. On arrival their wheeled landing gear was removed and floats for the Pacific crossing were installed by the Boeing Airplane Company. The aircraft were test-flown in their new seaplane configuration. This gave their pilots a chance to gain a little more experience in floatplane operations—their previous seaplane experience had been limited to a brief training course a few months earlier.

The aircraft were christened *Seattle, Chicago, Boston,* and *New Orleans* before they set out from Seattle, Washington, on April 6, 1924. They were a day late following an abortive start the previous morning when flight commander Major Martin had damaged his propeller and a float making numerous attempts to get his heavily laden *Seattle* off the water. It had been repaired and lightened, and this time Martin had no trouble taking off. Nor had two of the others. However, Lieutenant Wade, flying the *Boston,* experienced similar problems to his commander and finally got away 40 minutes late after offloading rifles, boots, and a bundle of personal gear.

Each of the eight crewmen had a rabbit's foot tucked into a pocket of his bulky flying suit. They were going to need their share of luck. The airmen experienced their first taste of bad weather in the beginning of the trip on the 650-mile flight to Prince Rupert, British Columbia. North of Vancouver they struck thick fog and were forced to skim the wave tops for 2 hours. Like all aircraft of that era, the Douglas biplanes were not equipped with blind-flying instruments nor were their pilots trained to fly in cloud. Thus it was vital that they either flew in sight of the ground or above the clouds where they had a clear horizon. At this stage of the flight they had little option but to stay low, for their navigation to Alaska and through the Aleutians relied on their following the coastline and islands.

Things did not improve as the fog gave way to pouring rain. As they progressed farther north, sleet and snow drove into their open cockpits. After eight torturous hours they reached the little Canadian outpost in the midst of a snowstorm and Major Martin, blinded by snow, misjudged his approach. Leveling off 30 feet too high, his aircraft stalled into the water. The impact snapped the *Seattle*'s left wing struts and broke the rigging wires. With a yell of disgust one of its crew flung his "lucky" rabbit's foot into the freezing ocean. Moments later they were greeted by the mayor of the tiny town. The white-whiskered, snow-encrusted Canadian, who reminded the airmen of Santa Claus, announced: "Gentlemen, you have arrived on the worst day in ten years."

Chatting around the fire that night and recalling the day's events, one topped the list. It was the hectic moment when the group, forced down to wave-top height, had narrowly missed colliding with a steamer that had loomed out of the fog. Discussion then turned to the repairs to Martin's aircraft. The pilots and their mechanics had been trained to conduct their own servicing and repairs during the flight. All the materials they required were on board except the wood to make new wing struts. Martin's flight now hinged on the local carpenter and his stock of hardwood.

The repairs to the *Seattle* eventually took four days, and it was April 10 before the formation set out on the next leg to Seward—930 miles away on the southwest coast of Alaska. Strong head winds forced an unscheduled landing in the bay at Sitka where a furious storm blew up. The *Boston* and the *New Orleans* were almost lost when they dragged their anchors in the high wind. It was two days before the weather improved sufficiently for the formation to carry on to Seward. Throughout the 600-mile flight they were again forced low by clouds and snow. For long periods the driving snow obscured the shoreline and the pilots resorted to navigating along the white crests of the breakers. Landing at Seward the World Flight had reached the most northerly point of its Pacific crossing.

Trouble continued to plague Martin in the cantankerous *Seattle*. When the formation headed off again the next day, the team leader was having trouble keeping up and eventually dropped back out of sight. When the three remaining aircraft reached the next staging point at Chignik, on the Alaskan peninsula, Lieutenant Smith used the settlement radio to request the destroyers *Hull* and *Corey* to search for his commander. He recorded in his official diary:

> On several occasions the *Seattle* dropped far to the rear and upon these occasions, although it was being closely watched by the remaining personnel, it was seen to swing over toward Portage Bay. At this time the other planes were flying directly into very strong head winds and did not have enough fuel to return and still reach Chignik. They are still uncertain as to whether the *Seattle* really landed in difficulty or is following in the rear. The three remaining planes landed in a poorly protected harbor at Chignik at 4:25 P.M.

The *Seattle* had suffered a ruptured engine crankcase and had force-landed in a bay near Cape Igvak. Martin and Harvey spent an uncomfortable night adrift, preventing drifting ice from damaging the floats of their World Cruiser. The next day they were located by the *Hull*, which towed the crippled aircraft to the beach at Kanatak for repairs. A new engine was shipped to them from Dutch Harbor aboard a Coast Guard cutter.

Once it appeared that their commander would soon be following, the rest of the formation carried on to the little port of Dutch Harbor, in the Aleutians. There they waited for Martin and Harvey to join them, taking the opportunity to check and overhaul their aircraft. A thorough mechanical inspection disclosed that the *Boston*'s engine needed changing. It had run for just over 35 hours since leaving Seattle and was the first of an additional sixteen engines that would be replaced during the epic flight—most averaging around 70 hours of operation before they wore out.

The weather became progressively worse and winds would have prevented the formation from taking off even had the stragglers arrived. The men waited two weeks before an alarming signal arrived from General Patrick. Besides ordering Smith to take command, it read: "Do not delay longer waiting for Major Martin to join you. [I will] See everything possible done to find him. Planes number 2,3, and 4 to proceed to Japan at earliest possible moment. Patrick."

Due to lack of radio communications in Alaska, the men had not known that their commander was missing. Nearly a week earlier Martin and Harvey had repaired the *Seattle*. The pair had reached Chignik safely, then vanished on the 370-mile flight to Dutch Harbor. On May 2, as the three remaining crews prepared to continue the flight, U.S. Coast Guard cutters were commencing a fruitless search of the coast for their missing comrades, and in San Francisco an airborne relief expedition was being organized.

The wreck of the *Seattle* in fact lay well inland, on the side of a mountain. Martin had struck bad weather soon after leaving Chignik but, desperate to catch up, had elected to head inland in an effort to avoid the storm. Trapped in cloud and blowing snow he became lost and had flown straight into the side of a mountain. Miraculously, the two airmen survived the impact. On recovering consciousness they found themselves lying in the shattered remains of their Douglas. Martin crawled from the wreckage and found his only injuries were cuts and bruises to his face. To his amazement he found that Harvey had sur-

Martin's *Seattle* was forced down by engine problems and towed to Kanatak, Alaska, for repairs. (NASM)

While attempting to catch up with the other aircraft, Martin became lost in cloud cover and crashed the *Seattle* into the side of a mountain. (NASM)

vived the crash without a scratch. Undoubtedly the deep snow had helped cushion the impact and prevent an explosion. Furthermore, they had struck a part of the mountain where the face was not steep.

Gathering as many items as they could carry, the pair headed south toward the coast. Within minutes a blanket of cloud descended on the mountain and wind-blown snow caused a complete "whiteout." There was no horizon, and without even a clear view of nearby terrain, they became completely disoriented. After two agonizing hours walking and crawling in white confusion, they saw an object looming ahead. To their utter amazement they realized that they had covered a big circle and were back at the wreckage.

Exhausted, the two airmen crawled into the remains of the aircraft's luggage locker, where they spent a cold and cramped night. The next day they built a snow shelter and were a little more comfortable as they waited for the weather to improve. By their fourth day on the mountain there had been little improvement. But with their emergency rations running low, both knew that they would soon become too weak to travel. They set off in blowing snow, stumbling slowly southward down the mountain.

On May 5, near exhaustion and with their rations all but gone, they sighted a small hut. It was uninhabited, but as is the custom in the polar regions, its owner had left a small cache of food for any lost traveler. The unknown Alaskan saved their lives. They rested there for two days before covering the last 25 miles to the tiny settlement of Port Moller. Though bitterly disappointed to be out of the flight, both men knew they were lucky to be alive.

While Martin and Harvey had been struggling across the Alaskan wilderness, their comrades had also had a tortuous journey traversing the Aleutians. The legendary spring williwaws (storms) that batter the island chain provided the worst operating conditions of the entire world flight. The three crews had left Dutch Harbor on May 3 and were pelted by rain, sleet, and snow on the 365-mile hop to Nazan.

The following morning, waves on the wind-whipped harbor made it impossible for the crews to board their aircraft, let alone get airborne again. As the storm worsened, their support ship, the Coast Guard cutter *Haida,* was forced to put to sea to avoid being blown aground. Six days passed before the storm abated sufficiently for the aircraft to carry on toward Attu, the last island in the Aleutian chain. Even then howling head winds reduced their groundspeed to 70 mph on the 555-mile flight.

Arriving at Attu they were greeted by Lt. Clifford Nutt. He had established a supply base on the tiny island, one of the seventeen fuel, supply, and spare part depots that had been positioned around the World Flight route. It was the team's final staging point for its planned 700-mile crossing of the North Pacific to Paramashiru, in the Japanese-controlled Kurile Islands. At Attu they were grounded by weather for a further six days. Smith related: "Attu, even in mid-May, was the bleakest of imaginable places. At that time the island was inhabited by only one man and thirty-seven women, the rest of the men being away fishing."

When plans had been formalized for the first long overwater leg across the North Pacific, a decision was made to provide the fliers with a bolt-hole in Russian-controlled territory. To the north of their track lay the Komandorskiye Islands, and even though no diplomatic clearance to land had been sought from the Soviet government, a U.S. Bureau of Fisheries vessel had been positioned nearby. Its task was to act as lighthouse and fuel depot should the aircraft need to divert.

The planning paid off when the three airplanes were yet again slowed by strong head winds. The problems were exacerbated when the aircraft flew into icing conditions and became encrusted in ice. The extra weight of the ice and the drag it produced—one crewman estimated it added half a ton to the aircraft—further reduced the planes' speed and range. Wisely the crews decided to risk diplomatic displeasure rather than run out of fuel. After averaging only 64 mph over the 350 miles, the formation landed in a snowstorm in the harbor of the little island settlement of Nicholski.

The spartan instrumentation of the World Cruisers was suitable only for fair-weather flying. Flight attitude information was gleaned from the primitive variometer and a skid ball visible just above the control wheel. (NASM)

Close by, their supply ship lay at anchor. A group of the town's fishermen rowed out to meet the fliers and courteously, but firmly, advised that they could not come ashore unless permission was granted from Moscow.

The next morning, as the airmen prepared to leave, a message arrived from the Soviet government requesting that the expedition depart immediately. Taking off in heavy swells, the formation headed across open sea for Paramashiru. By heading directly to the closest point of land they were able to reduce the distance over the open Pacific to 600 miles. Once reaching the safety of the coast, they headed south and followed it to their destination. Even so the weather remained poor and they continually changed cruising levels to avoid clouds and snowstorms. Seven hours after leaving Russian waters they landed at Paramashiru amid a severe rainstorm. That night they wined and dined aboard a U.S. Navy destroyer positioned to meet them.

The airmen made an additional five stops as they flew for more than 2,000 miles down the islands of Japan. They received an unprecedented reception as crowds lined the shores and every child seemed to be waving American or Japanese flags. Lieutenant Arnold recalled: "The shore was black with people. It was an inspiring scene." At Hitokappu children sang the Ameri-

can anthem. At Kushimoto the fliers were greeted with a feast spread out on tables in a hangar at a nearby Japanese army air service base. The meal included chestnuts, signifying triumph, and dried fish, signifying good luck. In his welcoming speech the service's commander, General Yasumitsu, said: "It is a great honor to welcome the aviators representing the American Army, who have just accomplished the great task of linking the hemispheres and establishing an aerial tie between friendly nations." Referring to Commodore Matthew Perry, who negotiated the first treaty between the two nations in 1854, the general concluded: "You have already gained a name comparable to Perry."

At Kasumigaura the crews, who had planned to carry out major servicing of their aircraft, had trouble finding the time, as Lieutenant (later Major General) Wade recalled: "Much to our dismay, twenty-eight days of receptions had been planned. We compromised and boiled everything down to three days to give us time for engine changes and repairs."

Attending a formal reception in Tokyo, Lieutenant Smith was introduced to Colonel T. E. Broome, the one-man advance party for British pilot Squadron Leader Stuart MacLaren, who was the British challenger in the round-the-world stakes. Broome had just heard that his man had

Stuart MacLaren (standing in cockpit) checks his Vickers Vulture. To cross the North Pacific the British pilot planned to fly the reverse of the route taken by the American Army fliers. (NASM)

crashed in Burma, wrecking his Vickers Vulture flying boat. Broome had a replacement aircraft in Tokyo but was having trouble finding a ship bound for Burma. Despite the fact that MacLaren was competition, Smith sportingly arranged for the U.S. Navy to transport the replacement machine to the grounded airman. "Hats off to the Stars and Stripes for real sportsmanship," cabled MacLaren when he heard of the Americans' chivalrous gesture.

While in Japan, Smith requested that the crew's lone noncom, Sergeant Ogden, be granted an instant commission so that he might receive equal honors and treatment from their hosts. General Patrick promoted the delighted Ogden immediately.

Although they had linked America and Japan, there was a feeling that the trans-Pacific flight was not really over until they reached mainland Asia. This involved a 550-mile hop over the East China Sea to Shanghai departing from Kagoshima, at the southern tip of the Japanese islands. On June 4 the *Boston* and the *New Orleans* got away safely, but the *Chicago* was unable to get airborne despite several attempts. The airborne pair carried on. For the first time since leaving Seattle, the fliers experienced a full day's good weather and made the crossing in 4½ hours. To their relief the *Chicago* arrived the following day. Its floats had been damaged the previous day, and mechanics on U.S. repair ship *Black Hawk* had worked all night to replace the ruptured skin.

That night the six airmen celebrated in Shanghai. They had safely crossed the Pacific from continent to continent. As guests of Chinese aviation leaders, they feasted on shark fins, hundred-year-old eggs, and bird's nest soup.

During the following week they headed south along the Pacific rim toward the coastal city of Haiphong in French Indochina (today North Vietnam). Between Shanghai and Hong Kong they passed the Breguet XIX biplane flown by Capt. Peltier D'Oisy, the French contender who was making his world flight in the opposite direction. Though originally planning only to show the flag as far as Tokyo, since leaving Paris the French flier had stated his intention of continuing on around the world. Soon afterward, the unfortunate D'Oisy wrecked his aircraft landing at Shanghai. He eventually reached Tokyo in a borrowed Chinese aircraft and proceeded no farther.

Before reaching the British crown colony the Americans battled through a coastal typhoon. However, on the 7-hour flight to Haiphong the weather was excellent. They landed in the river and were greeted with the news that the Portuguese team had crashed in Burma, but was hoping to continue in a borrowed machine.

The next morning none of the aircraft was able to get airborne off the river. The lack of wind and the performance-robbing heat made it impossible. The three World Cruisers were forced to taxi slowly to the river mouth and eventually took off at midday. Once airborne they turned inland and headed across the jungles for Saigon, leaving behind the Pacific Ocean.

The remainder of their epic journey around the world was a long, enervating grind punctuated by moments of tremendous public acclaim and high drama. During its second great ocean crossing the *Boston* was wrecked in a salvage operation following a successful forced landing in the Atlantic. On September 28, 1924, the *Chicago* and the *New Orleans* finally arrived back at Seattle. They were accompanied by Wade and Ogden, who had rejoined the flight in Canada in a spare Douglas christened *Boston II*. The first aerial circumnavigation of the world had taken six months. During the 371 hours and 11 minutes actual flying time, the World Flight had touched down in twenty-nine countries, survived five forced landings, lost two planes and worn out

seventeen engines. It had flown 27,553 miles at an average speed of approximately 74 mph.

There was little doubt that the critical stage of the flight had been the Pacific crossing, as Smith stated: "We knew the transpacific leg would be the worst of our flight, but it was ten times worse than we expected. Fog, snow, hail, wind, and more fog conspired to prevent us crossing the Pacific. The natives in the Aleutian Islands said it was the worst winter in ten years, and we believed them."

Of the other would-be contenders, none completed the flight and only one, the gallant Mac-Laren, got as far as the Pacific. He had eventually reached Tokyo in his replacement Vickers and commenced a west-east Pacific crossing. Flying a reverse route of the American team, the British flier was island-hopping toward the Aleutians when he was forced down in the sea by impenetrable rain and fog. His seaplane was damaged by the waves and MacLaren taxied to the closest island. With the nearest spare parts in Canada and the northern winter setting in, the unfortunate Briton was forced to give up.

The Americans' success had been the result of superb planning and highly organized ground support. This fact was emphasized by the fate of the other teams, which attempted the flight with little or no backing. In 1924 aircraft were still too imperfect for a lone, unsupported machine to make such a flight. Nowhere was this more obvious than in the sweeping leg across the Pacific.

The transpacific flight from Seattle to the first stop on the home islands of Japan had taken more than five weeks to complete. Even though the crews took advantage of coastlines and islands, they had neither the range nor the reliability to conduct such a flight without a massive land and sea support system. The seven officers of the World Flight Committee, and countless noncoms also involved in organizing the logistic support, had spent months in preparation.

Nowhere had their preparations been more intensive than the 5,715-mile Pacific sector. Fuel, oil, spare parts, and food supplies had been transported to five special depots established on the route. Spare engines had been located at key

They Go Smiling Round The World

A composite photograph produced by the U.S. Army shows the land-hugging route taken by the World Flight airmen across the North Pacific and the six men who completed the flight. (NASM)

positions—four were consumed during the Pacific crossing. Numerous U.S. Navy destroyers, cruisers, and tenders, Coast Guard cutters, and Bureau of Fisheries vessels had been positioned to nurse the team through the remote stretches of their route. Besides their search and rescue role, the ships provided weather information, carried ground members of the support parties, transported supplies, and offered shelter to the airmen.

Clearly the cost of mounting such a mission was far beyond the resources of any individual. The Pacific, indeed the world, had been conquered, but in an experimental rather than a practical fashion. When announcing the proposed flight in 1923, General Patrick had stated that, besides bringing to America the honor of being the first to circle the globe, one of the flight's aims was "to point the way for all nations to develop aviation commercially." This his pilots had achieved. They had given the world a glimpse of aviation's long-distance potential. But there was still a long way to go before the public would be enticed into the air—particularly across the great oceans. Until airplanes were built with range, reliability, speed, and comfort, intercontinental travelers would continue to travel by the world's great ocean liners.

MacLaren being welcomed in Tokyo. Later, when forced to land in the North Pacific, his Vickers was damaged but he managed to taxi to an island. (NASM)

Following their triumphant return to America, the Army fliers had landed at Washington's Bolling Field to receive the congratulation of President Calvin Coolidge. Delayed by bad weather, the airmen were three hours late. Nevertheless the President and his cabinet refused to budge. "I'll wait all day," Coolidge said. After shaking their hands, the President told the airmen:

It has been your skill, your perseverance, and your courage that have brought great honor to our country. In what is probably the greatest opportunity for future scientific development of transportation, your enterprise has made America first. I trust the appreciation of your countrymen will be sufficient so that in this field America will be kept first.

Three months later the President's words must have had a hollow ring for the men of the Air Service. Their tireless commander General Patrick was again pleading for increased appropriations and highlighting the plight of American aviation. He stated: "There is today in the United States no commercial aviation deserving of the name, and the aeronautical manufacturing industry is unprepared to meet the demand of quantity production in the event of an emergency."

Even though the world flight had not solved the military's immediate problems, there had been one real winner. The success of Donald Douglas's rugged World Cruisers put his infant company on the road to becoming one of the world's great aircraft manufacturers.

In 1924, while General Patrick's World Flight pilots had been hammering home the Army's air superiority, the Navy was desperately searching for a similarly spectacular flight to promote its cause—and block General Mitchell's attack on the fleet's air arm. With Naval Aviation firmly established at its base on Ford Island in Pearl Harbor, the admirals finally chose a transpacific flight to Hawaii as their proving ground. The scene was set for a succession of events that would make Hawaii the staging post for the conquest of the Pacific.

35

3

Hawaii-Bound
A Matter of Navy Pride

In 1925 the Pacific Ocean became the scene of a battle for American military air power between the Navy and the Army when two Navy flying boats attempted to make the first non-stop flight to Hawaii. The drama that was to surround this flight would ultimately help establish American naval aviation and bring about the downfall of its severest Army critic, Gen. William "Billy" Mitchell.

An outspoken architect of air power, General Mitchell had been battling for an autonomous air force since 1919. Besides promoting the cause of army aviation, he had publicly denigrated the Navy and its token fleet air arm. The Navy's air wing was purely defensive and consisted of bumbling biplane flying boats, scout planes, and an ineffective little aircraft carrier, the U.S.S. *Langley*—a converted collier.

General William "Billy" Mitchell was the severest critic of American naval aviation. (NASM)

Following bombing demonstrations in 1921, when his Army pilots had easily sunk three captured German warships and the outdated battleship U.S.S. *Alabama*, Mitchell had declared that the Navy was obsolete. It was an overstatement at the time. However there were many men, including naval officers who had openly wept while witnessing the *Alabama*'s death throes, who perceived that airpower would eventually replace the battle fleet as the bulwark of the nation's defenses. Mitchell was less concerned with the future of the fleet than with seeking to incorporate the Navy's air arm into his envisioned air force. Privately many military men agreed with his vision, if not with his methods of dealing with the powerful, old-school generals and admirals. Ultimately it was a power struggle with neither the Army nor the Navy wanting to lose control of its air wing.

Mitchell's naval opponent, Rear Adm. William Moffett, had been appointed chief of the Navy's new Bureau of Aeronautics in 1921. An equally tireless proponent of aviation, Moffett agreed with Mitchell's concept of air power. However, unlike Mitchell he was tactful and politic. As a contemporary wrote: "Mitchell tried to stir up a revolution; Moffett was trained in orderly development. Mitchell attacked personally all who disagreed with him; Moffett was a diplomat."

Moffett's diplomacy did not include Mitchell, whom he perceived as hellbent on destroying the Navy if it served his purpose. "We've got a fight on our hands to keep Mitchell from sinking the Navy, and the country with it," he warned his superiors. Later, after the pair had clashed violently at a conference, he told the press that the volatile general was "suffering from delusions of grandeur or mental aberrations."

Since 1923 Moffett had been searching for a spectacular way to match the publicity gained in recent years by Mitchell's far-ranging Army flyers. In April 1924, as all America focused on the Army World Flight airmen battling around the rim of the North Pacific, the Navy settled on an attempt to fly nonstop from the mainland to Hawaii. To fly 2,400 miles over open ocean was then considered a bold and imaginative idea. If successful it would gain world attention and demonstrate that the Navy was capable of matching the Army's efforts.

It was appropriate that naval aircraft should pioneer the Pacific Ocean. In 1919 the U.S. Navy's NC-4 flying boat had made the first Atlantic crossing from Newfoundland to Portugal, and even though it had landed twice en route and two accompanying flying boats were forced down, the epic flight had made world headlines. There was also speculation that, if successful, the Navy fliers might later continue on to the Philippines via America's Pacific island bases.

However, Moffett was still faced with one major hurdle. The Navy's best long-range flying boat, the PN7, did not have the range to get even halfway to Hawaii. Clearly a totally new and radically improved machine was needed, and in June 1924 the Naval Air Factory in Philadelphia was instructed to build two modified versions of the PN7. To be called PN8, the machines were to make extensive use of duralumin—a new alloy of

Rear Adm. William F. Moffett was appointed chief of the Navy's new Bureau of Aeronautics in 1921. (NASM)

aluminum, copper, manganese, and magnesium. The revolutionary metal compared in strength with mild steel but was much lighter. This would enable designers to reduce the new flying boats' empty weight, allowing them to carry more fuel.

To enhance their chances of success, the Navy also placed an order with the Boeing Company for a considerably larger flying boat designated the PB-1. Boeing nicknamed their new design the "Flying Dreadnaught"—the airframe was to be virtually all metal with only the upper section of the hull incorporating wood. To be powered by a pair of tandem-mounted 800-hp Packard engines, the 25,000-pound biplane was designed to carry 1,700 gallons of fuel and cruise at 94 mph.

To cover the 2,400 miles to Honolulu, the Navy required that the flying boats have thirty hours endurance at a still-air cruising speed of 80 mph.

America took a lead in seaplane design in 1914 when Curtiss built a twin-engine flying boat to cross the Atlantic. Here British pilot John Porte christens the machine *America*. When war intervened, Britain purchased fifty machines for antisubmarine patrol. Five years later, America's Navy-Curtiss NC-4 flying boat made the first transatlantic flight. (NASM)

Although this left no margin for error, they were confident of tail winds for much of the flight. Their only other safety buffer was the fact that they would actually reach the coast of Hawaii Island 70 miles before Honolulu. It was a small margin indeed.

Moffett chose one of the Navy's most respected officers to lead the venture, Comdr. John Rodgers. The son of an admiral, by a peculiar quirk of fate John Rodgers was also a cousin of Calbraith Perry Rodgers—the flamboyant transcontinental flier who had lost his life in the Pacific breakers off Long Beach, California, in 1912. In 1911 John Rodgers had been the second Navy officer trained to fly, and the first to be instructed by the Wright brothers. His flying had been curtailed a year later when his more famous cousin was killed. Both were descendants of Navy hero Commodore Matthew Perry and, concerned for the safety of another member of the famous family, the Navy reassigned the young lieutenant to submarines!

However, he had returned to aviation in 1922 as the commanding officer of Hawaii's Ford Naval Air Station. Besides being overall commander of the mission, Rodgers decided to undertake the critical task of navigating one of the aircraft.

Early in 1925 the Naval Air Factory advised Moffett's office that the Wright engines of the new PN8 flying boat would not produce the necessary range. Moffett, who had widely publicized that the flight would take place late in August, advised the N.A.F. that it had until mid-May to solve the problem. The obstacle seemed to be overcome when the two flying boats were reequipped with much lighter, 525-hp Packard 1A-1500 engines. On May 1 the first completed machine, redesignated PN9-1, set a new world endurance record of 28 hours and 36 minutes. Though it was hailed in the press, the result was a disaster for Moffett and his men. The aircraft had failed to meet its 30-hour endurance target by nearly 1½ hours. This meant that on a flight to

On April 3, 1925, the first completed PN9 flying boat stands on the ramp outside
the Naval Aircraft Factory in Philadelphia. (NASM)

Hawaii, without tail winds, the aircraft would come down more than 100 miles short of its destination. At Packard's suggestion the engines were returned to the factory for minor modifications to the carburetors and ignition systems. It was late July before the PN9-1 was again ready for further testing and its sister ship, the PN9-3, was completed. At last all seemed to be going according to plan, until it was discovered that the flying boats' radiators leaked "like sieves."

The Boeing PB-1 was also behind schedule. On its first test flight early in August, a radiator burst and serious design flaws were found in its engine mounts. On its delivery flight from Seattle to the team's starting point in San Francisco Bay, the PB-1 was forced down when severe engine vibration ruptured an oil line. The PN9-1 also had a similar problem on its flight from San Diego. Only the PN9-3, which left San Diego at the same time, managed to complete a nonstop flight.

Despite a frenzy of work on the PB-1, as the target day of August 31 approached it became obvious that only the two PN9s were likely to be ready on time—and even they were doubtful starters. There was insufficient time to conduct extended flight tests of the new machines, which had been plagued by continuing mechanical problems. By August 30, when the maximum-load takeoff trials were scheduled, no tests had been conducted to establish the fuel consumption rate of the reworked engines. With no intention of calling off its heavily publicized flight, the Navy had already decided to trust its aviation future to the vagaries of the wind. Weather experts had predicted that the fliers would reach Hawaii provided they were pushed along by the normally prevailing east Pacific trade winds.

Huge crowds lined the shore to watch the full-load takeoff trials in San Pablo Bay, at the northern end of San Francisco Bay. Despite the assistance of strong head winds and choppy water, both the PN9s failed three times to get airborne. The aircraft merely ploughed across the water throwing up great plumes of spray which drenched the crews and streamed through the propellers. Before making a fourth run, Lt. Allen P. Snody, command pilot of the PN9-3, decided to offload three sailors who had been acting as ballast. Relieved of their 500 pounds he just managed to get the flying boat to break water. Almost immediately Snody was forced to cut the throttles when he detected vibration caused by a water-damaged propeller. Commander Rodgers on board the PN9-1 chose to retain his human ballast and ordered his pilot, Lt. Byron J. Connell, to try again. When they eventually managed to lift a few feet off the water, Rodgers was satisfied and signalled Connell to land.

Both aircraft returned to their moorings to top up the fuel tanks and replace their human ballast with final provisions for the flight. Each received forty ham sandwiches, two dozen oranges, twenty one-quart canteens of water, fifteen pints of coffee, and two and a half pints of hot soup. They were also equipped with three days' emergency rations of biscuits and corned beef. By the time loading was completed, each PN9 weighed 19,300 pounds, including its five-man crew. Empty the aircraft weighed only 9,100 pounds, and thus was lifting a load greater than its own weight—a remarkable design achievement. By far the greatest part of the load was the 1,350 gallons of fuel and 50 gallons of oil each machine carried.

The following afternoon an armada of spectator craft lined the takeoff area on San Pablo Bay. The day was fine and only light winds rippled the water—not ideal for overloaded takeoffs. The crews had been on board their aircraft since mid-morning making final preparations. Shortly after 2 P.M. Commander Rodgers's aircraft made the first takeoff run, but after a mile and a half had failed to lift off. With the engines overheating, pilot Connell aborted the attempt. Lieutenant Snody in the PN9-3 had similar problems as the plane charged across the water in the takeoff configuration but unable to liftoff. Snody yelled for crewmen to move aft to bring the bow up, and moments later the stately flying boat lifted slowly from the water.

Before commencing a second takeoff run Rodgers also ordered his crewmen to move as far back as possible to help the pilot's task of lifting his nose-heavy machine. For 6 miles the PN9-1 roared across the bay; then, just as Rodgers was also scrambling toward the tail, it too lumbered slowly into the air. Both machines staggered slowly past Alcatraz Island clawing for height. Snody was still only at 100 feet as he pierced the narrow opening of the Golden Gate. Connell managed to reach about 150 feet. It was as well for both crews that San Francisco's famed bridge was still ten years away.

The takeoff had been the first major hurdle of the flight. Now the ten Navy fliers faced an even greater worry. Would the predicted trade winds develop? With a cruising airspeed of around 80 mph, they required tail winds that would boost their speed over the water to an average of 85 mph throughout the flight. Already they were punching into a slight head wind as they approached the Farallon Islands, their final landfall before Hawaii, and the favoring northeast trade wind was not forecast to appear until they were

41

The Boeing PB-1 had a virtually all-metal airframe and was nicknamed the "Flying Dreadnaught." However, it was plagued by mechanical problems that were not overcome in time for the flight to Hawaii. (Carl Apollonio)

Senator Hiram Bingham, chairman of the Senate Military Affairs Committee, dons helmet and parachute for the press while inspecting one of the PN9 flying boats in San Diego. (NASM)

Bringing the PN9s ashore for maintenance required many hands to maneuver the flying boats onto wheeled dollies. When secured, they were towed up specially constructed slipways. (Carl Apollonio)

This view of the PN9-1 taken during preparation in San Diego shows the crew's rear observation hatch. (NASM)

The PN9-1 being prepared for the flight. Crew members display the drums of fuel required for the trans-pacific attempt to Hawaii. (NASM)

The PN9-3 in flight. (NASM)

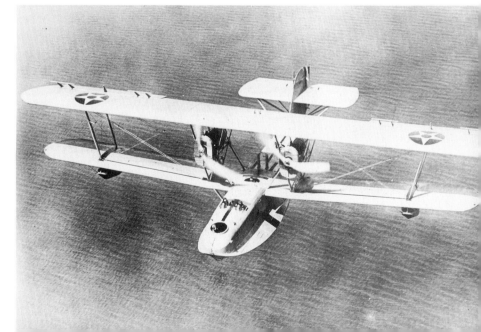

about 450 miles out. It was a real cross-the-fingers time, although they gained some comfort from the knowledge that strung out ahead at strategic 200-mile intervals ten Navy ships marked their transpacific route. If the winds did not develop, at best they could land alongside one of the ships and take on extra fuel. At worst they could ditch alongside and hope to be rescued. As flying boats were not constructed for midocean landing in anything but gentle conditions, ditching loomed as a real possibility.

The planned purpose of the Navy ships was to assist in navigation. By day their smoking funnels would act as visual beacons. At night their searchlights would turn them into lighthouses. They would also provide a radio link and take radio bearings on the two flying boats. If either aircraft came down off track, or in the intervening 200 miles, the ships' final role was to steam to the rescue.

Two hundred miles out, the first guardship, the U.S.S. *William Jones*, saw both aircraft pass. The PN9-1 established radio contact but no report came from the PN9-3, which had already lost its wind-driven generator and was unable to transmit. However this was the least of Snody's problems, for he was more concerned with severe vibrations which no amount of throttle jockeying would overcome. It was a legacy of the propeller damage sustained the previous day during the takeoff trials. Inexplicably, the crew had decided that the damage had not warranted a propeller change—even though a spare had been available. Now they were paying the penalty as Snody was forced to throttle back to reduce the dangerous vibrations the ailing propeller caused throughout the whole aircraft.

About 100 miles past the *William Jones*, the PN9-3's mechanic, C.P.O. Charles Sutter, climbed out along the lower wing to make his first night inspection of the engines. In the beam of his flashlight he saw oil leaking from the port engine but was unable to locate the source. Soon after Sutter reported to Snody, the oil pressure gauge had dropped to zero. There was no way the flying boat would remain in the air on one engine, and Snody decided to make an immediate

forced landing before the failing engine seized. Despite the darkness and heavy seas, Snody managed to get his seaplane down in one piece. However, the initial impact and those that followed as the PN9-3 charged through five massive waves threw men and equipment violently around the hull. When the aircraft finally wallowed to a stop, its once rectangular fuel tanks had been bulged into cylinders, the right wing float buckled, and the right tail plane supports torn from the fuselage.

Although there was no hope of taking off again, the crew gained some comfort from the knowledge that the hull had sprung no leaks. An inspection by Sutter revealed that the oil leak had come from fractured feed lines caused, he believed, by the vibrations from the damaged propeller. They were soon repaired and the engines were restarted to prevent the aircraft from drifting as they awaited rescue.

When the PN9-3 failed to report at the next guardship, the *William Jones* was dispatched to search along the route. After six hours wallowing in the Pacific, Snody and his crew were located and taken in tow. For twenty-nine hours they bounced along behind the *William Jones* before arriving exhausted back in San Francisco.

Throughout the night, while the drama was being played out on the ocean behind them, Rodgers and his crew were reporting like clockwork to ships along the route. Early the next morning they passed the carrier U.S.S. *Langley*. Although now 1,200 miles out from San Francisco, they had picked up only a miserable 3-mph tail wind. The situation had worsened by the time they passed the U.S.S. *Reno*, 1,400 miles out, and discovered that their fuel consumption was worse than during the setting of the May endurance record. It was obvious that they could not reach Hawaii without refueling, and Rodgers sent a radio message advising he would land and refuel alongside the seaplane tender U.S.S. *Aroostook*—1,800 miles out and just 600 miles short of Honolulu.

As the PN9-1 came within radio range of the *Aroostook*, Rodgers began receiving a series of confusing radio bearings from the ship's opera-

An early type of sight, used in conjunction with smoke bombs, for measuring aircraft drift. Knowing the drift enabled fliers to calculate the wind and make corrections to remain on course. This was vital in transoceanic flying with no ground features to keep a check on flight progress. (NASM)

tor. They indicated he was running south of his planned track. Rodgers's navigation plot showed that he was slightly north of track—which subsequent events were to prove correct. Nevertheless, as the fliers closed on the seaplane tender, additional messages from the ship indicated they were still south and moving farther away.

Rodgers's years of navigational experience told him that his own position was correct. If the ship's radio operator was using his equipment correctly, the only solution seemed to be that the *Aroostook* was itself north of its planned position. In fact the ship was still ahead, just off their nose, when Rodgers succumbed to the mounting pressure and banked hard right in response to the incoming radio messages that the aircraft was "bearing 181 degrees." With fuel critically low, Rodgers had elected to fly 001 degrees, running along the bearing line given by the *Aroostook*. In fact he had unwittingly turned away from the ship. As he later related stoically:

We flew down a radio bearing, and chased around for about an hour, following different radio bearings, and finally the gasoline gave out, and so naturally the engine wouldn't run anymore and we came down. The landing was made under very difficult circumstances, since there was no power. That means that we only had one chance. The pilot, Lieutenant Connell, was at the wheel, and did it perfectly. He had been sitting in the pilot's seat all during the flight.

When the PN9-3 touched down at sea, about 50 miles north of the *Aroostook*, it had flown at an average speed of 73 mph for 2,119 miles, establishing a new world's nonstop distance record for seaplanes. However, such matters were of little interest to its exhausted crew as they prepared to wait the arrival of the *Aroostook*. Connell had indeed done a fine job. The aircraft was undamaged and it seemed all they had to do was refuel from the seaplane tender and take off again for Honolulu—which lay a mere 365 miles away.

Hawaii and the mainland were sobered by the news, especially when it was reported that one of the last messages sent by radio operator Otis Stantz had stated: "Guess it will be goodnight if we have to land in this rough sea with no motors." As ships raced toward the area where they thought the plane had landed, the world waited for news. Unfortunately the search centered on an area south of the downed airmen. On their battery-powered receiver the frustrated crew of the PN9-3 were able to hear the messages between searching ships. However, as their transmitter would run only on the aircraft's wind-powered generator, they were unable to radio that they were located only 30 miles north of the area being searched. On their second day afloat the men tried unsuccessfully to run the transmitter using one of the hand-driven starter motors.

The following morning they saw smoke on the horizon and it seemed certain they would be rescued when a merchant ship came in view. But despite their frantic signaling the ship passed along the horizon without spotting the downed seaplane. Shortly after the ship steamed away the fliers' depression deepened when they intercepted a radio message announcing the loss of the U.S. Navy airship *Shenandoah* and fourteen of her crew. The giant dirigible had been sent on a public relations exercise showing the flag over crowds at state fairs in America's midwestern states—despite her commander's concern about severe thunderstorm activity in the area.

The situation became grave later in the day when other messages the airmen intercepted indicated that the search was moving farther away. By now Rodgers realized that they were unlikely to be found and must sail the flying boat to the nearest land. Gathering together the remains of the food and water, he instituted strict rationing. Rodgers wrote:

We stripped the fabric off the lower wing and rigged them up for sails between the wings, and we started the sails for Nawiliwili, Hawaii. That was the last stopping place [the most

northerly point in the island chain] in the Hawaiian Islands; and we had to pick that out, because the wind blew in that direction. We would have had a pleasant trip of it, but we didn't have much water. We had two quarts apiece when we started.

Billy Mitchell was among the millions of Americans who read the dramatic headlines of September 4, 1925. They painted a gloomy picture for the naval aviation. HOPE IS DIMINISHING, headlined a story about the missing flying boat. PRIDE OF THE NAVY IS NOW A TANGLED WRECK, blared another concerning the *Shenandoah* disaster. A few months earlier Mitchell had not been reappointed to his post as assistant chief of Air Service. Embarrassed by his continued grandstanding, the Army brass had posted him to an air base in Texas where he had reverted to his permanent rank of colonel. Asked by the press to comment, the still-crusading Mitchell saw a golden opportunity to attack the administration and spent the night writing a 6,000-word statement. It was a damning indictment of American military aviation which, it is generally agreed, was intended to provoke a court-martial to give him a forum to bring the whole matter of air power into the open.

It contained this explosive sentence concerning the *Shenandoah* and transpacific debacles: "These accidents are the direct results of the incompetency, criminal negligence and almost treasonable administration of the National Defense by the Navy and War Departments." It was followed by detailed criticism of the planning, execution, and reasons for the two ventures and asserted: "The *Shenandoah* was going west on a propaganda mission for the Navy to offset the adverse publicity caused by the failures in the Pacific." Determined to pinpoint those he believed were directly responsible, Mitchell added: "All Aviation policies, schemes, and systems are dictated by the nonflying officers of the Army and Navy, who know practically nothing about it. The lives of the airmen are being used merely as pawns in their hands."
MITCHELL THROWS BOMB INTO RANKS OF WAR BUREAUS, Associated Press news release headlines

read on September 6, followed by Mitchell's complete statement. The following month Mitchell was to get his court-martial.

Meanwhile the search for the missing flying boat was stepped up as more ships arrived in the area and aircraft from the carrier U.S.S. *Langley* scoured the sea. Unfortunately all were too far south or west to sight the PN9-1, which sailed slowly west making about 50 miles per day. Its crew members were able to make slight variations to their course by deflecting the seaplane's rudder. "The sails worked quite well except when high winds and rough seas were experienced. Then we had to take them down to prevent damage to the plane," pilot Connell recalled later. Morale rose when they received a message transmitted blind to Commander Rodgers by the *Aroostook*. It read: "Cheer up John, we'll get you yet." However, they were not impressed when the *Langley* was heard reporting to search headquarters that "Twenty-one aviators on the *Langley* concur that the plane has sunk and the search should be discontinued."

On September 9, eight days after they force-landed, the airmen sighted Oahu on the southern horizon. Even though they had by then rigged keellike leeboards to the hull and had more directional control, there was no chance of tacking to the island. Some of the crew were alarmed when Rodgers changed to a course heading farther away from Oahu. However there was no option, and somewhere ahead over the horizon lay Kauai, the most northerly of the island group—their only chance of making landfall. The change of course was to prove a short-term blessing. Some of the crew were becoming severely dehydrated by lack of water. The problem was exacerbated by the prolonged motion sickness, induced by the wallowing seaplane, which caused them to vomit frequently. Shortly after changing course the airmen sailed into a torrential rainstorm, which probably saved the lives of the critically sick men. Rodgers recalled: "A rainstorm came right over us. Then we got quite a lot of water, a couple of gallons. We were fixed up fine, although the fabric we caught it in had been painted in aluminum paint, and that chipped off and mixed with the water, and it didn't taste very good."

The following day the airmen finally sighted Kauai through a break in a line of rain squalls. Flight engineer and second pilot C.P.O. Kiles Pope recalled the moment when it became obvious that they would not be blown past the island: "It loomed up as if we were right on top of it. Everybody was so happy we almost forgot we were so weak and started moving around again. We complimented the commander on his good navigation, telling him we owed our lives to him. All he did was smile."

By dusk they were about 20 miles from the shore. Concerned about making landfall at night through the reefs and swell, they dropped the sails, rigged a sea anchor, and spent another night at sea. The following day, as they prepared to sail to the island, they were spotted by the submarine R-4 that had been searching the area for nine days. "What plane is that?" the submarine semaphored as it closed on the seaplane. "PN9 No. 1 from San Francisco," Radio Operator O. G. Stantz proudly flashed back.

Rodgers and his crew insisted on remaining with their aircraft. Shortly after identifying the aircraft, the submarine radioed the good news to Pearl Harbor: "Plane PN9-1 located by R-4, fifteen miles north-east of Nawiliwili. Personnel safe. Am towing same to Nawiliwili." Three hours later the seaplane rode quietly at anchor in the harbor. Rodgers and his men had completed their journey to Hawaii.

FIVE MISSING HAWAII FLIERS ARE FOUND ALIVE, headlined the *New York Times*. THANK GOD! SAYS WILBUR, announced a lesser headline. Secretary Wilbur of the Navy Department had every reason to be relieved. On the same front page he and Army Col. Dwight Davis, acting secretary for war, were reported in disagreement over the forthcoming Mitchell court-martial. Davis was calling for a separate, impartial investigation of Mitchell's allegations. On the other hand a defensive Secretary Wilbur, clearly sensitive about the Navy's embarrassing disasters, did not welcome such close scrutiny. He was reported as saying: "Frankly, I think the general subject has been under investigation sufficiently. I have on my

On September 11, 1925, its epic voyage over, the PN9-1 is anchored in Nawiliwili harbor. The fabric missing from its lower wings was used as makeshift sails. (NASM)

desk a 600-page index of the testimony already taken before the committee of the Congress charged with such an investigation." The news of the missing fliers' rescue took a little of the pressure off Secretary Wilbur.

In Havre de Grace, Maryland, Commander Rodgers's family told reporters: "We had always been optimistic," but added that John's father, being a retired rear admiral, "was the least optimistic, knowing better than the others the conditions faced by the aviators."

Colonel Mitchell's court-martial began on October 28, 1925. He was charged with making statements that were insubordinate and prejudicial to good order and discipline. Seven weeks

later he was found guilty and suspended without pay for five years. There are reports that one member of the court, Gen. Douglas MacArthur, had voted for his acquittal. Refusing to be silenced, Mitchell resigned from the Army to continue his crusade for a separate air force. Eventually his strident calls were barely heard in the clamor of the Great Depression. In 1936 they were silenced completely when he died in obscurity.

Unintentionally the transpacific drama and the loss of the *Shenandoah* achieved the results that Moffett had hoped might come from a successful flight to Hawaii. Combined with Mitchell's vitriolic attack, the disasters caused President

Coolidge to appoint Dwight W. Morrow to head a board to look into the whole matter of military aviation. The board did not go along with Mitchell's visionary call for a third, independent service—that would not happen until after World War II. However, it raised the status of military aviation and recommended that undersecretaries for aeronautics be appointed to both the Army and Navy departments. Equally important, the Morrow board also laid the groundwork for government support of the ailing commercial aviation industry.

In terms of Pacific conquest, the Navy flight had demonstrated little, except that such an undertaking was still beyond the state of the art in 1925. Rodgers and his men had failed—gloriously. But they had been set up to fail by a Navy so desperate to publicly prove its aviation worth that it was prepared to take risks that would today be considered criminal. It had sent ten men in inadequately tested, insufficiently fueled, and problem-riddled machines on the most dangerous overwater flight yet attempted.

Top right: The exhausted but elated crew of the PN9-1 shortly after coming ashore at Kauai. From left: Stantz, Bowlin, Rodgers, Connell, and Pope. The bandage on Rodgers's left hand covers a broken finger suffered during the final tow into the harbor. (NASM)

Middle right: Ten days after sailing to Kauai, the PN9-1 was flying again. Its crew members wave triumphantly shortly after the flying boat took off from Pearl Harbor. It was later transported back to San Diego. (NASM)

Bottom right: Following the Hawaiian flight, Commander Rodgers was made Admiral Moffett's assistant in the Bureau of Aeronautics. He was tragically killed in August 1926 following this crash at the Naval Aircraft Factory in a Vought VE-9 biplane. Admiral Moffett died seven years later in the crash of the airship *Akron.* (NASM)

Lieutenants Lester J. Maitland (seated) and Albert F. Hegenberger convinced Generals Mitchell and Patrick that the Fokker C-2 *Bird of Paradise* was capable of reaching Hawaii safely. (NASM)

50

4

Hawaii
The Army Shows the Way

Authority is requested to attempt a flight from California to the Hawaiian Islands." The deceptively simple sentence opened a four-page proposal that arrived on Maj. Gen. Mason Patrick's desk in mid-March 1927. It was signed: "Albert F. Hegenberger, 1st Lieutenant, Air Corps." Less than two years had elapsed since the Navy's ill-conceived bid. With Mitchell's departure, the Army and Navy were no longer openly warring. However, there was fierce interservice rivalry between military aircrews, and some Army fliers were intent on demonstrating to their Navy counterparts how transoceanic flying should be conducted.

Lieutenant Hegenberger was not only a pilot but also had trained as a specialist navigator. His dual qualifications had made him the ideal choice as chief of the Army Air Corps' Instrument and Navigation Unit at McCook Field, near Dayton, Ohio. Since 1919, when their Navy rivals had crossed the Atlantic, the unit had been studying the problems of transoceanic flying. Indeed the

program for such a flight had been conceived in February 1920. Hegenberger's unit had spent eight years testing all types of navigation instruments and every known technique. It had also ramrodded the development and testing of aircraft flight instruments and pioneered America's early "blind" flying tests.

Unit members had made hundreds of flights, many in cloud and at night, and the 2,400-mile flight from California to Hawaii had been simulated on a number of occasions. As early as 1923 the unit had been certain that it could navigate from the mainland to Hawaii without any visual references—such as the line of marker ships used by the Navy in 1925—along the route. Astronavigation, using a modified ship's sextant to observe the sun, moon, and stars, was the technique used to fix their position. By taking sextant sightings to measure the angle between the horizon and the chosen body, a navigator could work out a position line.

However, to accurately fix the aircraft's position required several intersecting position lines. Thus astronavigation was more suited to night flying, when the navigator could obtain multiple position lines from the stars and planets; by day, only a single position line was available from the sun. With its crews trained in astronavigation and night flying, the unit's only problem had been the lack of a reliable aircraft with adequate range. That final obstacle had been overcome in 1926 when the Army purchased two Fokker C-2s, military versions of Anthony Fokker's superb F.VIIa, powered by three 220-hp Wright Whirlwind engines.

The proposed flight to Hawaii was no ill-considered publicity stunt. Army aviation was by now well established. Following Billy Mitchell's court-martial and the subsequent recommendations of the Morrow board, the Army air wing had been raised to Corps status in July 1926 and given a five-year expansion program. No longer did its commanders need to demand the sort of blind risks taken by the Navy with its 1925 transpacific catastrophe. Newspapers still made headline news of military aircraft crashes, a fact demonstrated a few months earlier following the tragic death of Comdr. John Rodgers, captain of the Navy's luckless PN9-1 flying boat. He had spun into the ground while landing at the Naval Aircraft Factory where he was to inspect a new military flying boat.

General Patrick was acutely aware that military aviation had much to lose should the venture fail and accordingly demanded a careful study of Hegenberger's proposal. It showed that the flight was to be conducted by an aircraft with the demonstrated range and reliability, equipped with flight and navigation instruments equal to the task, and flown by a crew that had spent years training and preparing. Furthermore, the fliers would be assisted by a revolutionary new aid to "blind" navigation recently developed by the Army Signal Corps, a directional radio beam. Using special beacons set up at San Francisco and Hawaii, the beam would indicate the correct course for hundreds of miles at each end of the route. Clearly the flight was not perceived primarily as a test of men and their machine, but rather as a stunning demonstration of the advances in long-range navigation—the culmination of eight years' work by Army aviation's unheralded back-room boys.

General Patrick finally approved the undertaking but insisted that there was to be no preflight publicity. Recalling the problems facing the Navy in 1925, when judgment was clouded by a highly publicized starting date, the general preferred not to have such pressures placed on the Army's Hawaiian flight.

Because Hegenberger needed to concentrate on the navigation during the flight, Lt. Lester J. Maitland was assigned as his pilot. For some time Maitland had also been petitioning General Patrick to make a flight to Hawaii. Based in Hawaii in 1918, he had been one of three Army fliers who had made a pioneering interisland flight. In 1922 he had flown an ailing Curtiss Racer into second place in the Pulitzer Trophy Race and the following year set a world speed record over a 1,000-kilometer course at Dayton, Ohio. More important perhaps, in terms of the Hawaii proposal, he had served as an aide to both Mason Patrick and Billy Mitchell.

Hegenberger was given overall command of the flight and the responsibility of preparing the Fokker. Besides the installation of an array of extra navigation equipment, radios, and flight instruments, the Fokker required extensive modification of the fuel system. In addition to his primary role as navigator and radio operator, Hegenberger was also to fulfill the task of copilot. Consequently, two auxiliary cabin tanks, with all the necessary plumbing, had to be installed so as to allow a passageway between the cockpit and the navigator's area at the rear of the fuselage.

By late May 1927, as the world went wild over Charles Lindbergh, a team of Army engineers worked in secrecy modifying the Fokker at Wright Field near Dayton, Ohio. When the work was completed the Fokker was given strenuous flight tests. On June 15 the team set out for California. Besides Maitland and Hegenberger, the crew included three engineers from their support team. Each had a specific task. One was to complete astronomical charts and check the naviga-

At McCook Field the Fokker C-2 *Bird of Paradise* is reequipped with long-range fuel tanks for the flight to Hawaii. One can be seen already installed in the fuselage. (NASM)

In 1922 Lieutenant Maitland (left) flew an ailing Curtiss Racer into second place in the Pulitzer Trophy Race. He also served as an aide to Gen. Billy Mitchell (right). (NASM)

tional equipment, another was to check the airplane and engines, and the third was to accurately determine the Fokker's fuel consumption in its final transpacific configuration, the most critical task.

When they landed en route at Kelly Field, Texas, the men were surprised to find a large crowd including photographers and reporters waiting for them. The Army had finally let the cat out of the bag. A cautious press release issued by the War Department stated: "Final authorization [for the Hawaii flight] will not be issued until tests have shown satisfactory results. These tests are to be concluded in California, towards which the two pilots are now headed aboard the plane tentatively selected to make the journey." The same press release also stated that the flight had nothing whatsoever to do with "any prize or any other offer made by private individuals for a successful flight across the Pacific."

Three weeks earlier, in the glow of Lindbergh's unprecedented publicity, Hawaii pineapple magnate James Dole had announced $35,000 in prize money to stimulate a flight from the mainland to Hawaii. There were also rumors that a New York businessman named William Fox was about to dangle a $100,000 prize for a transpacific flight.

Following the Fokker's 2,815-mile long-range test and delivery flight, an additional 70-gallon fuel tank was installed in San Diego. It brought the plane's total fuel capacity to 1,120 gallons, which gave it a safety margin of about eight hours for the Hawaii flight. Arriving June 25 at Oakland's new municipal airport on Bay Farm Island, Maitland and Hegenberger met an ebullient airmail pilot named Ernest Smith who was planning to make the same flight in a single-engine Travel Air monoplane.

Although originally interested in the Dole prize, Smith had decided not to wait until its August starting date and, instead, to fly for the glory of being first. He had dreams of being the "Lindbergh" of the Pacific—an idea that naturally appealed to his San Francisco businessmen backers. Thus Smith saw the Army team as competitors out to steal his thunder. If successful, he

The Fokker's interior showing the radio equipment (left) and the long-range fuel tanks (center) with visual quantity gauges stretching from top to bottom. The pilot's cockpit can be seen above and behind the tanks. (NASM)

The Fokker's rear door opened to show a technician sitting at the aircraft's British Aperiodic Compass. (NASM)

Drift lines painted on the Fokker's upper fuselage and horizontal stabilizers. Used in conjunction with landmarks, smoke bombs, or flares (at night), they enabled navigator Hegenberger to calculate the aircraft's drift. (NASM)

Mechanics make final adjustments as Maitland ground-tests the Fokker's Whirlwind engines. (NASM)

Maitland and Hegenberger pictured with their wives and Hegenberger's children shortly before taking off from McCook Field to fly to California. (NASM)

planned to make the return flight in sufficient time to take part in the Dole challenge. There was also word that the "Crash King of Hollywood," Dick Grace, was taking time from doing stunts for the cameras to attempt a flight from Hawaii to the mainland. His Cruzair monoplane had arrived by sea in Honolulu, where Grace was awaiting delivery of a new propeller. Grabbing at straws, the press began churning out stories of crews "racing" to be first.

Realizing that the Army fliers were only a day or two away from starting, Smith and his navigator, Charles Carter, now worked at a frenzied pace to get away. For Smith it was vital to be first. The Army team, however, still moved at its pre-arranged pace.

On the morning of June 28, the Army Fokker was rolled out of its hangar. On hand to watch the takeoff, General Patrick shook hands with Maitland and Hegenberger, ordering them formally to: "Go ahead." For the flight to Hawaii the aircraft had been christened *Bird of Paradise*—a delightfully exotic and uncharacteristic name for a military aircraft. Following engine run-ups, the airmen taxied to the 7,200-foot runway, waving to Smith and Carter, who were making final preparations. Smith is reputed to have yelled back that he would soon overtake their "flying boxcar"—not an unreasonable assumption as his aircraft was the faster.

As the Army's meticulous calculations had predicted, the *Bird of Paradise* had no trouble getting off. At the 4,600-foot mark, indicating 93 mph, Maitland lifted the big transport easily from the runway. Accompanied by an escort of other Army planes, it had reached 2,000 feet by the time it passed the Golden Gate and headed off along the Great Circle route to Maui.

Two hours later Smith and Carter were also airborne in their Travel Air *City of Oakland*. However, about five minutes into the flight a part of the navigator's windshield ripped off and Carter insisted they returned to Oakland. As their groundcrew made hasty repairs Carter, possibly realizing the dangers of the flight for the first time, refused to take off again, stating that it was now too late to catch the Army machine. Without

a navigator, the bitterly disappointed Smith had no option but to call off the flight.

Meanwhile the Army flight was proceeding exactly as planned. Shortly after takeoff Hegenberger checked the drift using a vane-sight set in the floor and sighting on almost stationary spume from breaking waves. He also had a second method of checking the Fokker's drift that involved dropping smoke bombs on the sea and measuring by drift lines painted on the airplane's horizontal stabilizers. Later checking his results by an astronomical position line, he confirmed that they had been accurate to within one degree. About a half-hour out he tuned into the special radio beacon erected near San Francisco by the Army Signal Corps. Its coded signals came through loudly, also indicating that he had assessed the drift correctly and the *Bird of Paradise* was flying along the beam's preset Great Circle course to Maui.

After an hour the radio failed. Hegenberger's postflight report illustrates the problems common in aircraft radios before the use of transistors. "I went back and changed one VT-5 tube of the BC-137 receiver, the filament of which appeared to be a little dull. This had no effect on reception. Two of the batteries were then changed and the reception came in again O.K. The reception continued less than half an hour and cut out again abruptly," he reported. Hegenberger was unable to make the beam receiver radio operate for the remainder of the flight.

The airmen had planned to hold course by their Pioneer induction compass—a recently developed instrument that was electrically operated and more accurate and stable than the old-style magnetic compass. However, it also failed early in the flight, forcing Maitland and Hegenberger to rely on the Fokker's two brand-new backup B-5 magnetic compasses.

For the first six hours they encountered strong crosswinds. Five hundred miles out they picked up the trade winds that the Navy had so desperately needed two years earlier. Pushed along by the tail wind, their speed over the water increased to 108 mph. Most of this time they navigated by dead reckoning, forced by a carpet of low cloud to

At Oakland's new airfield the *Bird of Paradise* and the *City of Oakland* prepare to race to Hawaii. The contest ended when the civilian crew was forced to turn back. (NASM)

Hawaii-bound, Maitland and Hegenberger take off from Oakland Airport in the *Bird of Paradise* on June 28, 1927. (NASM)

fly only 300 feet above the Pacific. When Hegenberger was finally able to take some observations on the sun, his figures suggested a dramatic heading change of 17 degrees was required to regain track. Since an error of only one-sixth that amount would make them miss the Hawaiian island it was understandable that Maitland was a little worried. Nevertheless he changed heading and hoped.

Deafened by the roar of the three engines the men resorted to passing notes to communicate important information. Hastily scrawled messages on an *Oakland Tribune* Want Ad form (now in the Smithsonian archives) recall the communications between the two men over the next two hours. Obviously worried at the magnitude of the heading change and concerned that they seemed to have strayed well off the shipping lines, Maitland wrote asking his navigator if they were due to sight any ships. Confidently Hegenberger wrote back: "[In] 30 to 50 mins. will be in the longitude of the *Sonoma*, and a little later will be on line with S.S. *President Pierce* and *Makiki*." Maitland then passed the paper back with a note asking if Hegenberger had tried contacting the *Sonoma* by radio. In reply the navigator scrawled: "I will transmit, but I cannot receive. Something haywire outside the receiver." He later advised his pilot that they should pass the *Sonoma* in 25 miles. They actually had covered 20 miles when they spotted the liner dead ahead. *Sonoma* passengers saw a relieved Maitland waving as the aircraft flew low alongside.

As night fell Maitland climbed the Fokker to 10,200 feet to clear the cloud tops and allow Hegenberger to check their position by the stars. However, the navigator discovered that most of his astronomical tables were of no use and was able to check only their latitude by taking sextant readings on Polaris. They carried on by dead reckoning. As the Fokker approached the midway point the two men decided it was time for some food. But after searching the aircraft they were unable to find the in-flight rations that were to have been stowed on board for them. At midnight they had just settled down to contemplate a hun-

gry flight when an engine started to miss. Hegenberger recounted:

The center engine began to cough and spit, and vibrate as it slowed down to idling speed. With the load we had, two engines could not hold us at 10,000 feet. Everything became total blackness as we settled down [lost height], and the stars disappeared from view. For the next hour and forty minutes the airplane was held on its course and controlled solely by instruments.

As they involuntarily descended through the cloud bank, the two men used their flashlights to check the engine instruments, which were located on the wing engine pods. Their flickering beams showed that they were covered in rime ice, or "frost" as airmen then called it. Hegenberger later recalled: "It dawned upon us that it was frost, forming on the carburetor's intake that had taken our engine out of service." Engineers from the Wright Aeronautical Company had recalled the icing problems encountered by the 1919 transatlantic fliers when they had warned the Army team to ensure the Fokker was equipped with carburetor heaters. Hegenberger commented on their poor judgment later, explaining: "We certainly never expected to encounter frost in the tropics and because we got a little more power for takeoff without the heater, we left it behind. We shall know better next time."

The aircraft had descended to less than 4,000 feet when the ice in the carburetor finally melted and the nose engine came back to life. From then on they stayed below the freezing level, climbing slowly back to 7,000 feet where they found breaks in the clouds. Shortly before dawn they spotted a rotating light just off the nose. Hegenberger identified it as Kilauea Lighthouse on the island of Kauai. Soon afterward the shoreline appeared in the predawn half-light. They were only 75 miles from their destination. With extensive low cloud cover and mountain peaks below them, the pair wisely decided to wait for daybreak before de-

The *Bird of Paradise* flies low along the San Francisco waterfront as it heads for the Golden Gate years before its famed bridge was constructed. (NASM)

Following a near-faultless flight, Maitland and Hegenberger approach for a landing at Hawaii's Wheeler Field. (NASM)

scending and crossing the channel to Oahu. As they circled Kauai they were unaware that below them another aircraft stood in the darkness on Barking Sands waiting for an improvement in the weather before setting off for California. After circling for an hour, Maitland and Hegenberger watched a brilliant sunrise before landing at Wheeler Field in pouring rain at 6:29 A.M. Honolulu time. Thousands had turned out to greet the airmen.

THEY'RE THERE! ARMY PLANE LANDS. . . . THEY DID IT. . . . PAIR DO 2,407 MILES IN 25 HOURS. 50 MIN RECORD WATER hop, next-morning American headlines trumpeted the Army's achievement. While the newspapers played up the risks and marveled that the Army fliers had gotten there at all, the airmen tried hard to play down the risk and emphasize that their success was merely a matter of routine planning and professional flying.

"Contrary to popular opinion, the significance of the Hawaiian flight was not the personal hazard involved but the triumph of careful preparation of the plane and equipment and avigation [aerial navigation] equipment," Hegenberger modestly, and accurately, told reporters. Maitland added: "When we landed we had enough gas left for an additional 800 miles of flying."

Stunt flier Dick Grace did little to build on the Army's success two days later when he blew a tire attempting to take off from Barking Sands in his Cruzair. Things got even worse on July 4 when, accompanied by his pet dog, he finally managed to become airborne but was unable to climb higher than 50 feet until he burned off fuel. Less than an hour out, struggling for height, he flew into rain and turbulence and lost control of the aircraft. Clearly suffering from center-of-gravity problems, the aircraft's nose was pitching up and down, one moment in a dive, the next in a stall. Somehow he managed to struggle back to Kauai, where he crash-landed on the beach. The survivor of twenty-four deliberate movie crashes, Grace lived again. However he was not wearing a seat belt and was catapulted out of the cockpit. Landing in soft sand, he escaped with only broken hands. His pet dog also survived, but the aircraft was a write-off.

Back in Oakland, Ernie Smith was still determined to be the first civilian to make the flight—particularly following Grace's failure. However he was not to have the Army fliers' fuel margin when he finally followed in their slipstream. His new navigator was master mariner Emory Bronte, who had insisted on many changes before agreeing to take the departed Walker's place. "I had looked the plane over and was shocked to find it didn't even have a radio and very little else in the way of navigation equipment," he recounted years after, explaining how he not only arranged for proper charts, a sextant, three compasses, and a radio but also insisted on having the engine modified to decrease its fuel consumption—a precaution that probably saved their lives.

The crew of the Travel Air *City of Oakland*, (left) navigator Emory Bronte and (right) pilot Ernest Smith, with their manager, William Royle. (NASM)

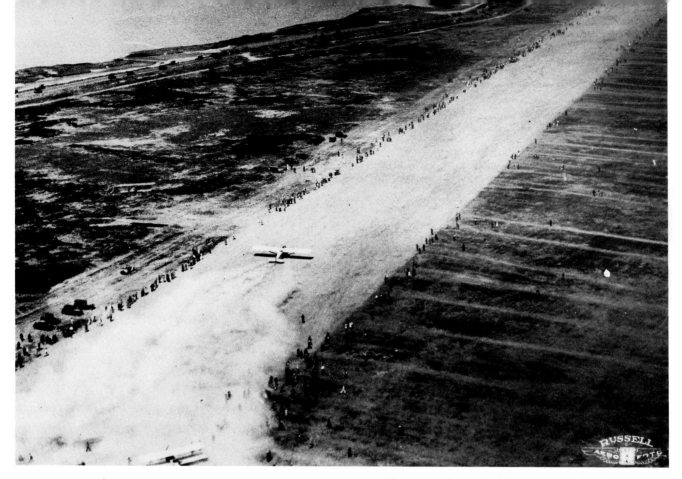

Showing more courage than common sense, well-wishers line the takeoff run. The *City of Oakland* throws up plumes of dust as Smith accelerates slowly down the new dirt runway. (NASM)

Smith and Bronte in their Travel Air, now christened *City of Oakland*, were ready to depart on the morning of July 14. On hand to wish them good luck and pass on advice were Hegenberger and Maitland, who had just returned from Hawaii by ship. After the long delay Smith was clearly nervous and was reported in tears as he bade friends good-bye. With the aircraft loaded down by 370 gallons of fuel, it took the efforts of exasperated spectators pushing on the wing struts to get the monoplane moving. It was gathering speed when a wheel caught in a rut and sent the machine careening into a ground loop. Fortunately there was no damage and shortly after, the pushing was repeated and the *City of Oakland* climbed safely out over San Francisco Bay.

Bronte quickly tuned in the radio and picked up the Army's beam to Maui. They were on course. However, like the Army fliers, the two civilians were also plagued with radio problems—

Ernie Smith climbs slowly over San Francisco Bay. Navigator Bronte peers above the hatch constructed in the fuselage to allow him to navigate by the sun and stars. (NASM)

their receiver soon failed. Like Hegenberger's, Bronte's navigation was superb and he kept the little monoplane close to course across the east Pacific. At regular intervals he broadcast position and "all's well" reports that were picked up by ships and ground stations throughout the flight. The fliers were closing on their destination when two ships picked up an SOS followed by a probable ditching position. The plane's engine had momentarily stopped when a gas tank unexpectedly ran dry. The emergency ended when they changed tanks and Smith hand-pumped fuel back to the starving engine. However, the pair now realized that they were running critically low on fuel, and throttling back, Smith leaned the mixture for maximum endurance. To their complete surprise the engine kept running for another three hours.

Crossing the Hawaiian coastline, Smith kept faith with his major backer by having Bronte transmit: "Everything going fine. I feel as safe as the Bank of Italy." His optimism was a little premature, for shortly afterward, over the island of Molokai and about 50 miles from Honolulu, the engine stopped. With no open ground below and a towering mountain abeam, Smith force-landed into a clump of trees next to the shoreline. The *City of Oakland* was a total loss, but Smith and Bronte walked away with only a few scratches from the trees. Despite their inglorious landing, the pair had completed the first civilian crossing and were welcomed in Hawaii as heroes.

It had not been a totally satisfactory ending in the eyes of the public and the aviation industry. Nevertheless, when viewed in conjunction with the Army's Hawaiian flight, Smith and Bronte's performance seemed to hold promise for the future of Pacific aviation. Certainly when looking at the total achievements of American pilots and aircraft for the first half of 1927, the picture was rosy. Besides Lindbergh, two other crews had successfully crossed the Atlantic. Now two aircraft had made even longer transoceanic flights to Hawaii, overcoming not only the distance but

also the problems of bull's-eye navigation to a tiny island target.

From a military point of view the most important result to come from the Army's Hawaiian flight were the prophetic recommendations made by Hegenberger in his official report. Highlighting the fact that he and Maitland had been forced to fly on instruments for much of the flight, he stated that insufficient attention had been paid by the Air Corps to training pilots and navigators for long-distance, all-weather operations. Among his many recommendations Hegenberger called for the establishment of an Air Corps School of Navigation and also that a course of training in the maintenance of instruments be added to the curriculum of the Air Corps Mechanics School— thus ensuring that pilots could rely on the accuracy of their blind-flying instruments. The visionary report was a blueprint for American military aviation to commence moving forward from a fair-weather service to one capable of operating anywhere in any weather.

Buoyed by the success of the *Bird of Paradise* and also of a stunning 20,500-mile South American flight by a formation of Army fliers, the military soon was talking publicly about its air services providing "new vistas of communication between America and its overseas possessions." The *Chicago Tribune* editorialized: "Aviation needed a dramatic challenge to the popular and business mind, and now the challenge has been furnished in a series of remarkable flights."

Aviation, it seemed, had finally emerged from its postwar doldrums. For those battling to find backing for commercial ventures, the future looked brighter. To a hitherto nervous public, air travel was taking shape as a possible alternative to ocean liners. In Honolulu people saw themselves as emerging from their mid-Pacific isolation.

The euphoria was to be short-lived. For in Oakland preparations were already underway for an air race that was to rock transoceanic aviation back on its heels.

The wreckage of the *City of Oakland* following Smith's forced landing on the island of Molokai. The two airmen walked away virtually unscathed. (NASM)

As the first civilians to make the United States–Hawaii flight, Bronte and Smith were welcomed as heroes despite their forced landing. (NASM)

Hollywood stunt pilot Art Goebel and his Travel Air *Woolaroc*. The highly successful monoplane was powered by the Wright Whirlwind engine, its reliability proven in Lindbergh's transatlantic Ryan *Spirit of St. Louis*. (NASM)

5

The Disastrous Dole Transpacific Race

At 10:24 P.M. on May 21, 1927, when Charles Lindbergh landed at Paris's Le Bourget airport, its military commander Major Weiss was the first to greet the conqueror of the Atlantic. The following day Weiss wrote eloquently in his diary: "Your exploit is eternal, Lindbergh, but the fever of that night of waiting is not. Who will ever give it us back? . . . The victor, the air athlete, the scaler of the ocean . . ." Half a world away, in the offices of Honolulu's *Star Bulletin,* two equally enthralled newspapermen began planning to recapture that frenzied fever.

To a world still mesmerized by Lindbergh's achievement, anything now seemed possible. One of the most remarkable results of his flight was the unprecedented worldwide media attention given to the unknown young flier. This was a catalyst to the fertile minds of the two Honolulu newspapermen. (At the time nothing was publicly known of the Army's plan to fly the Fokker *Bird of Paradise* to Hawaii.) The two journalists compared Lindbergh's Atlantic crossing with the distance between the United States mainland and Hawaii and came up with the idea of a transpacific challenge to focus attention on Hawaii. Tragically, their brainchild was to bring about a disastrous air race that almost negated the gains of Lindbergh's flight.

On May 23, 1927, two days after Lindbergh's triumphant landing in Paris, a strangely worded cable was tapped out from the offices of the *Star Bulletin.* Addressed to James D. Dole, a Hawaiian businessman visiting San Francisco, it read:

In view of Lindbergh's Atlantic flight the Pacific remains one great area for conquest aviation. This moment ripe for someone offer suitable prize non-stop flight Hawaii. From angle advertising islands and yourself we believe an exceptional opportunity your offer twenty-five thousand dollar prize for this achievement.

Particularly in view your national pineapple advertising featuring your name we believe you now to do this. Prize should be known Dole Prize. This will put your name in every newspaper in the world besides great credit Territory pineapple industry. We are prepared to cooperate every possible way. Await anxiously favorable reply on which we would like first announcement. Appreciate early reply by wire. Not publishing anything until hearing from you. Riley Allen. Joe Farrington. Star Bulletin.

Though never before seriously interested in aviation, Hawaiian pineapple magnate James Dole had also been fired by Lindbergh's flight and by the public and press reaction it generated. Never one to miss a good business opportunity, he acted quickly. Two days later, as the world continued to heap praise on Lindbergh, a special edition of the *Star Bulletin* announced:

James D. Dole, believing that Charles A. Lindbergh's extraordinary feat in crossing the Atlantic is the forerunner of eventual transpacific air transportation, offers $25,000 for the first flier and $10,000 to the second flier to cross from the North American continent to Honolulu in a nonstop flight within one year after the beginning August 12, 1927.

Though shorter than Lindbergh's flight, Dole's challenge involved an extra 440 miles of open sea, making it the longest overwater flight to date. Whereas New York hotelier Raymond Orteig had dangled a $25,000 carrot for Lindbergh's Atlantic crossing, James Dole decided to go one better and offer an extra $10,000 for the runner-up. The fact that Dole had so readily agreed to sponsor it said much for the instantaneous reaction to Lindbergh's achievement. Prior to his flight, all but a handful of America's hard-nosed businessmen had steered clear of investing in aviation. In 1927 airplanes were considered a dangerous form of transportation. But with Lindbergh now having demonstrated that aviation technology was rapidly maturing, some were already visualizing the dawn of transoceanic air services.

Besides a flood of advertising and movie contracts, Lindbergh received several more imaginative proposals. Philadelphia merchant Ellis A. Gimbel offered the sum of $100,000 to any company that would employ Lindbergh to operate a Philadelphia-Paris air service, while industrialist Harry F. Guggenheim offered to sponsor Lindbergh to tour the nation promoting commercial aviation.

In Lindbergh, Dole saw the opportunity not only to promote his pineapples but also to provide his beloved Hawaiian Islands with a better postal service. The Boston-born businessman had moved to Hawaii following a holiday in 1900 when he graduated from Harvard. His cousin Sanford B. Dole was the territory's first governor. James had eventually formed the Hawaiian Pineapple Company to develop the growing and marketing of the succulent fruit. In the early 1920s, like other business colleagues, he had watched the development of airmail services on the mainland and dreamed of them extending to Hawaii. However, few dared publicly to suggest such a service, particularly after the Navy's seaplane debacle in 1925.

The interisland flights started by Charlie Stoffer and his biplane "Charley's Crate" had come to an end in 1924 when he sailed for the mainland and a job as a Hollywood stunt pilot. In 1926 there had been an abortive attempt to form an interisland airline. Since then, Hawaii's only commercial service was being operated by a recently arrived pilot named Martin Jensen. Flying a five-place Ryan, the Honolulu-based joy flight pilot also made occasional charters carrying businessmen, newspapers, and urgent mail between the major islands.

Travel and mail services to the American mainland were still inhibited by the long sea voyage. Such was the problem that faced James Dole with pineapple plantations on the islands and his market on the mainland. In a second *Star Bulletin* press release on May 26, Dole explained:

The flight of Captain Lindbergh is an evidence of the startling progress being made in aeronautics. It seemed obvious that a flight from the mainland [to Hawaii] should be the next order to have the future of aviation brought nearer to the present. Consider the help given Honolulu's progress by the cable, the radio, the automobile, and the truck. What would we be without them today? The continued progress in aviation may mean within a few years mail delivered in Honolulu 20 hours from the mainland. It may mean that in the case of emergency the businessman or visitor can make the journey in a day.

Sounding a word of caution Dole also stated:

No precautions can be too great to satisfy all who are sincerely interested in the permanent development of aviation. It is natural for all of us in Hawaii as well as followers of aviation the world over to hope that this contest be doubly successful. First that it may cost no brave man either life or limb and second that the continent and Hawaii may be linked by air.

Believing that Lindbergh was the focal point to maximize race publicity and the flier most likely to succeed, Dole concluded: "I should be glad to see Captain Lindbergh the man first to make this flight successfully, and be able to greet him at the airport in Honolulu."

Dole's hopes were to be dashed. Lindbergh failed to respond and instead would come a brave but gaudy band of ill-prepared fliers attempting to match the Atlantic hero on an even more daring transoceanic flight. Lindbergh had made it look almost easy as, with the world press riding at his shoulder, he had casually conquered the Atlantic. Possibly he had made it look too easy for the ten impressionable fliers who would soon die for Dole's glittering prize.

The challenge was officially named the North American–Honolulu, Hawaii, Trans-Pacific Flight. This would later be shortened to the Pacific Air Race and in the press, thanks to Dole's public relations efforts, would be more commonly called the Dole Race or Dole Derby. Once the news hit the mainland newspapers there was no shortage of entrants. In 1927 America's commer-

cial pilots led hand-to-mouth existences and the prize money (about half a million dollars in today's value) represented a fortune. Scores responded—stunt fliers, World War I aces, barnstormers, and hopeful young "Waldo Peppers"— swashbuckling optimists high on courage and low on suitable experience.

Understandably, those seriously involved with America's struggling aviation businesses feared the Dole Race might bring a giant step backward in their efforts to promote air travel. No airline of any real consequence had yet appeared in America, whereas most European nations already had at least one major airline. Juan Trippe was still trying to form Pan American Airways and the other major carriers would not appear until the 1930s. Though Boeing was capable of producing excellent passenger aircraft, and in fact operated a small regional air service, the American public still traveled by train or, increasingly, by automobile. Few Americans were interested in the high cost and discomfort of flying. Nor did frequent newspaper reports of plane crashes help public confidence—seven Atlantic hopefuls had died in the two months prior to Lindbergh's flight!

To the average American, flight was still barnstormers, wing walkers, Hollywood stunts, suicidal mail pilots, and $5 joy flights in tumbledown biplanes. Many of Dole's entrants fitted those images. If aircraft were ever to be considered as people carriers rather than merely mail carriers, American aviation needed a period to consolidate; for the public to forget the tragic headlines and absorb Lindbergh's success and its promise for the future. Instead the struggling industry seemed destined to get a death-or-glory race.

From the beginning, Dole vainly attempted to ensure that his challenge should not turn into a game of aerial Russian roulette. In an effort to fulfill his wish that it "cost no brave man either life or limb," he enlisted the National Aeronautical Association to help organize the race. The N.A.A. was the American branch of the Federation Aeronautique Internationale—the recognized world governing body for all aviation competition.

It soon became clear that most entrants were

planning to leave at the first possible moment of the twelve-month period of James Dole's challenge. Realizing that the event now had all the makings of a race, the committee changed the rules and drew lots for allocated pilots' starting positions. As contestants would have to fly through the night, the start was set for noon on August 12, 1927—the day of the full moon. Fortuitously, it was also the twenty-ninth anniversary of Hawaii's annexation as a U.S. territory.

The rush to get away first also precluded the entry of the more professional contenders, who would have needed more time to obtain purpose-designed aircraft with adequate range and equipment. Instead most entrants were seat-of-the-pants fliers, lacking even the basics of the instrument-flying skills Lindbergh had gained as an airmail pilot. Nor did their aircraft compare with his specially built Ryan monoplane. Except for a few hastily thrown together backyard specials, competitors planned to use overtanked standard aircraft not designed to safely lift the massive fuel loads the flight required.

Overwater navigation posed another problem for pilots who still found their way by pinpointing landmarks, and whereas Lindbergh had the whole of Europe to make landfall, their island target would require bull's-eye accuracy. Just a couple of degree's compass error would be enough for the fliers to miss by 100 miles, and the unpredictable winds could blow them even farther off course. As one entrant, stunt pilot Art Goebel, succinctly put it: "There are but two goals. The Hawaiian Islands or the bottom of the Pacific Ocean." With such long odds only fifteen daredevils eventually paid the $100 entry fee. Most of them clearly lacked adequate flying experience.

The N.A.A.'s race committee included Maj. Clarence M. Young, head of the Enforcement Division of the government's year-old Aeronautics Branch of the Department of Commerce. Flexing the bureau's infant muscles, the committee introduced rules regarding crews and aircraft performance. With the benefit of hindsight after the event it was obvious that they were grossly inadequate. However, to the cavalier fliers of the day

they seemed exceedingly restrictive. Young appointed Lt. Ben Wyatt U.S.N., a pilot who specialized in aerial navigation, to weed out inexperienced crews and arrange for bureau inspectors to check the aircraft. Young also decreed that each plane must carry an experienced navigator who had passed a written examination and a flight test given by Lieutenant Wyatt. Furthermore, all competing aircraft would be required to demonstrate that they could carry sufficient fuel for the flight plus a 15 percent safety margin.

Six weeks before the race the civilian fliers were upstaged when the Army Fokker *Bird of Paradise* flew from Oakland to Hawaii. Two weeks later Smith and Bronte made their flight. However, as neither crew qualified for the prize, Dole decided his race should go ahead. With the glory gone it now became a gamble for cold, hard cash!

By early in August, ten of the entrants waited at Oakland's brand-new Bay Farm Island airfield to be checked by race officials. They were besieged by journalists who dissected the event daily in America's newspapers. The fliers' life stories, their hopes (and fears), aircraft and equipment details, the route, weather predictions, and navigation techniques filled page upon page. The race had become America's favorite topic. In offices and speak-easies, barber shops and hotel lobbies, everyone was talking Dole Derby. When short on hard news, reporters fed the insatiable public with girl-meets-flier stories. Socialites chatted with pilots. Wives, daughters, and the "girls they'll leave behind" were splashed across the pages. Model agencies had a field day providing the press photographers with pretty girls. "O-o-oh LIEU-tenant Goddard, what pretty black stripes you've got painted on your airplane. Why don't you paint some curly ones too," said model Merle Hanna, posing for the camera in front of Norman Goddard's monoplane *El Encanto* (The Enchantment). "I beg your pardon, young lady, but those lines are not decorations, they are a drift indicator," the former Royal Flying Corps pilot answered. "But I don't get your DRIFT, Lieutenant," cooed Miss Hanna. Such were the offerings of one West Coast paper.

Norman Goddard's Whirlwind-powered Goddard Special *El Encanto*. The Englishman survived a serious crash on takeoff. (NASM)

Martin Jensen's exotically colored Breese *Aloha*. Finished in sunshine yellow with a scarlet lei around its nose, the plane was emblazoned with the Great Seal of Hawaii. (NASM)

Not to be outdone, a rival newspaper found its girl-meets-flier nonsense when, complete with leis, hula dancers, and guitars, the Hawaiian contingent celebrated the naming of its lone entry. It reported:

> Substituting saltwater taken from the beach at Waikiki for champagne, Miss Ruby Smith, Oakland bathing beauty, yesterday christened Martin Jensen's monoplane *The Aloha*. While a Hawaiian stringed band played native airs, the girl stood on the wings, sprinkling the water on Jensen, Captain Paul Schulter, the navigator, and the plane.

However, the real female newsbreak was a "mad-on-flying school ma'm": WILL BRAVE DEATH IN HAWAIIAN AIR RACE, Oakland's *Post Enquirer* headlined, stating that Mildred Doran, a twenty-two-year-old schoolteacher from Flint, Michigan, was "radio operator and consulting navigator" in the Buhl Airsedan *Miss Doran*. Her father worked for the aircraft's owner, William Malloska, millionaire head of Lincoln Petroleum Products and operator of Flint's airport.

The air-crazy Mildred Doran flew daily as a passenger in one of the passenger aircraft Malloska operated. She had conceived the idea of becoming the first woman to fly the Pacific early in 1927 and Malloska, undoubtedly sensing the promotional value, had placed an order for the Buhl on the day Lindbergh flew the Atlantic. When the Dole prize was announced it had seemed a perfect opportunity and they entered the biplane, naming it after the dark-haired young woman who one reporter described as "the prettiest little pigeon on wings." When asked by a reporter of the San Francisco *Bulletin* about the dangers of the flight, she explained naively: "No, truly, truly I'm not in the least bit worried or anxious. This flight is the dream of my life! And as for taking chances—well, life is a chance, isn't it."

Mildred Doran at her window in the Buhl. Her participation in the race made headline news. Newspapers called her "a flower of American womanhood." (NASM)

Her pilot was John Augy Pedlar, a close friend who was employed by Malloska. An affable barnstormer and former wing walker whose lack of experience was matched by his lack of nerves, Pedlar epitomized the flying-circus image. He limped, chewed gum incessantly, and flew in gaudy knickerbockers and a straw hat. Alarmed by the pair's lack of navigational experience, Lieutenant Wyatt quickly intervened and appointed a naval navigator, Lt. Vilas Knope, to the *Miss Doran's* crew. Since the Buhl was not radio equipped, Mildred Doran's role was relegated to that of passenger, although her sponsor insisted she was the aircraft's "captain."

Randolph Hearst's *San Francisco Examiner* gave extensive coverage to its own entry and pre-race favorite, the prototype Lockheed Vega *Golden Eagle,* to be piloted by debonair New York stockbroker Jack Frost, an Army Air Service veteran who was looking for a way back into aviation. Another highly fancied contestant was Hollywood stunt pilot Arthur C. Goebel in the Travel Air monoplane *Woolaroc.* A second Travel Air, the *Oklahoma,* was piloted by Ben Griffin, an unusually quiet and conservative flier by 1927 standards.

Other contestants who had arrived at Oakland were former Lafayette Escadrille pilot Major Livingstone Irving in the Breese monoplane *Pabco Pacific Flyer,* World War I fighter ace Bill Erwin in his Swallow monoplane *Dallas Spirit,* and Charles Pankhurst in the Air King biplane *Miss Peoria.* The Air King was entered by its manufacturer, the National Airways System, owned by S. F. Tannus who hoped to promote his grandly titled but little-known organization. Another biplane, the International *Miss Hollydale,* was flown by barnstormer and Hollywood stunt pilot Frank Clark.

On August 10 the start was postponed when the race committee decided no aircraft or crew was ready to leave. Mechanics were still working feverishly on last-minute modifications. Organizers were still trying to recruit extra navigators capable of passing Wyatt's relatively simple test.

On the same day, the Dole drama began to unfold when an aircraft crashed minutes after taking off from San Diego to join the race. Its naval crew members, Lieutenants George Covell and Richard Waggener, were incinerated when their boxy Tremaine Special monoplane flew into a cliff. There had been reports that the Tremaine was tricky to fly, a problem exacerbated by the fact that the crew was located behind a massive fuel tank and, like Lindbergh in the *Spirit of St. Louis,* had no forward vision. Despite all James Dole's careful planning the race had already claimed its first victims.

On August 12, at Vail Field near Los Angeles another last-minute entry, the Bryant monoplane *Angel of Los Angeles,* took off on its first test

70

John Augy Pedlar, for once minus his straw hat, poses at the controls of the Buhl Airsedan *Miss Doran*. (NASM)

Bennett Griffin, pilot (left), and Al Henry, navigator, crew of the Travel Air *Oklahoma*. (NASM)

flight. It was a revolutionary design, well ahead of its time, in which pilot and navigator sat side by side in a short podlike fuselage that also housed two Bristol Lucifer sleeve-type radial engines. The Lucifers were mounted in tandem, one pushing and the other pulling—a design layout similar to that used by Cessna more than thirty years later. Only two days earlier the pilot, British war ace Arthur Rogers, and architect and part-time designer, Lee Bryant, had given up hope their machine would be completed in time, but were given a reprieve when the start of the race had been postponed. Rogers climbed steadily after lifting off from Vail Field. Just past the airfield boundary the Bryant appeared to stall, dropped a wing, and spun out of control. At the last moment Rogers parachuted from his twin-engined special but was too low to survive.

The following day the Fisk International triplane *Pride of Los Angeles* left Los Angeles for Oakland. A strange-looking machine advertised as a twenty-two-seat airliner, the Fisk had been flying in the Los Angeles area for some time. It had been purchased for the race as a publicity stunt by cowboy movie star Hoot Gibson. Then followed a mad scramble to have it reengined and the passenger area crammed with fuel tanks in time for the start. There were reports that Gibson had trouble finding experienced crewmen prepared to risk their lives in the aerial white elephant and had approached Charles Kingsford-Smith who was in America to prepare for a transpacific attempt. However, behind the Australian's carefree façade lurked a careful and meticulous pilot, and he retorted, "I doubt if the damn thing will ever get off the ground." At Oakland Kingsford-Smith talked with preparing competitors and was appalled at the overloads some were planning to carry and the general lack of planning and navigational experience.

The *Pride of Los Angeles* was being flown by a former military pilot turned lawyer, Jim Giffin, on the delivery flight to Oakland. He was one of two pilots among a crew of three nominated for the race. The crew sat side by side in an open cockpit just forward of the tail and had terrible forward visibility. This may have had something to do with pilot Giffin's decision to overshoot moments before touching down at Oakland. Believing he was balked by another aircraft, Giffin opened the throttles to go around. The right engine responded but the left engine backfired, then stopped as the lumbering triplane staggered low across the mud flats of San Francisco Bay. The Fisk clipped the water and came apart in a sheet of spray. Miraculously all three crewmen survived unharmed.

The prerace toll stood at three dead and three aircraft destroyed as three more contestants pulled out. San Francisco's Robert Fowler was unable to find a suitable airplane and Captain Fred Giles, of Brisbane, Australia, failed to arrive in his Hess Bluebird biplane *Detroit Messenger*. Finally on August 15, the day before the start, Frank Clark and his navigator, Charlie Babb, took off in *Miss Hollydale* and headed out across the Golden Gate. Many thought that the Hollywood flier had jumped the gun on a glory-seeking dash for Hawaii. However, despite his daredevil reputation, Clark had wisely decided that his International biplane was not suitable for the race and had returned to Los Angeles.

THEY'RE OFF TODAY, the *San Francisco Examiner* headlined on August 16. The front page had a special banner depicting aircraft streaming from Oakland to Honolulu. A photomontage of the pilots was captioned: "The crack pilots who will try to bat the Hawaiian home run." Diagrams showed the positions of merchant ships and seven Navy destroyers along the route, and illustrated the new-fangled radio beam that had helped guide the Army's *Bird of Paradise* and would assist those racers who had the foresight and the money to install radio receivers.

During the night huge rollers had compacted Oakland's sparsely grassed runway and water wagons had laid the dust. No one really knew how much of the mile-long strip the pilots would need to become airborne, as trial flights had been attempted only with the planes' special fuel tanks half filled. However, some measure of safety might be provided by the extra 2,000 feet of roughly leveled "overrun" at the far end of the airfield.

Miss Hollydale's navigator, Charles Babb, poses with Lt. Gov. Buron Fitts of California (in flying gear). The biplane was later withdrawn by pilot Frank Clark who, despite his reputation for daring film stunts, considered the plane unsuitable. (NASM)

The Tremaine *Hummingbird*, which crashed, killing Covell and Waggener. The pilot's only view was from windows beneath the wing braces, which provided no worthwhile forward vision. (NASM)

Hollywood star Hoot Gibson gained publicity for his Fisk International triplane when a glamour girl was used to help display to the press its special long-range tanks. (NASM)

The ungainly Fisk International triplane *Pride of Los Angeles* prepares to set out for the race start at Oakland. The caustic handwritten comment (Believe me or not. "Mother" it flies. but not much [sic]), almost certainly by pilot James Giffin, says it all. (NASM)

Engines were given a final test run before tanks were topped to brimming. Fuel loads varied between 350 and 480 gallons, giving all race aircraft massive overloads and limiting their cruising speeds to well below 100 mph for most of the race. Like Lindbergh, all the contestants had chosen 200-hp Wright Whirlwind J-5 engines. The superb new nine-cylinder, air-cooled radial was light, economical, and reliable (by 1927 standards). It was reputed to run for at least 40 hours without requiring repairs—a paltry performance today but a superb technical achievement at the time. Undoubtedly it was the best choice for the flight to Hawaii.

Less than an hour before the start the Air King *Miss Peoria* was disqualified following tests that indicated it would run out of fuel 200 miles short of Hawaii. Owner S. F. Tannus was furious and loudly abused the committee, the Department of Commerce aviation representatives, and the other contestants. However, *Miss Peoria*'s crewmen, Charles Pankhurst and Ralph Lowes, were relieved. They had encountered a succession of problems crossing the country from Illinois in the hastily modified airplane.

Only eight starters now remained and their crews watched anxiously as ambulances, fire engines, and crash trucks were parked at intervals along the length of the field. Some looked drawn and nervous. Art Goebel, pilot of the *Woolaroc*, was reported as being close to tears. Police and marines manned rope barricades holding back a crowd estimated at 50,000. Cameramen and reporters recorded the last hectic moments: final weather briefings . . . last-minute compass checks . . . the good-bye embraces . . . each pilot solemnly receiving a Bible . . . crews squeezing into their tank-cluttered cabins . . . local airplanes wheeling overhead waiting to escort their favorites to the coast.

Bulletin reporter Robert Willson's race-start assignment was to follow the "flying schoolma'am." As her crew was making final preparation to her red, white, and blue painted biplane, Mildred Doran waited in a small tent surrounded by a mountain of good-luck bouquets. In the days leading up to the race her presence had already

The *Pride of Los Angeles* overshoots the Oakland Airport. Moments later it crashed into San Francisco Bay. (NASM)

Below: The *San Francisco Examiner* carried a special front-page transpacific banner on race day. (NASM)

Bottom: Montage of contestants taken from another page of the newspaper.

San Francisco Examiner
Monarch of the Dailies

THEY'RE OFF TODAY!

9 DOLE FLYERS READY TO HOP

6 A.M. EDITION S. F. BOULEVARD BONDS URGED

THE CRACK 'NINE' OF PILOTS THAT WILL TRY TO BAT THE HAWAIIAN HOME RUN

EIGHT NAVIGATORS OF THE FLIGHT, WHO WILL KEEP THE SHIPS ON THE COURSE

The scene at the start. In the foreground is the *San Francisco Examiner*'s Vega *Golden Eagle*. Other contestants are lined up against the far fence. Only sparse patches of grass cover the new runway. (NASM)

Left: The Buhl Airsedan *Miss Doran* displayed the emblem of its owner, the Lincoln Petroleum Company. (NASM)

Bottom: The *Miss Doran* has its compasses swung at Oakland. In the background the Vega *Golden Eagle* awaits its turn. (NASM)

given the *Miss Doran* more publicity than all the other competitors combined. Now she was also the center of media attention at the start. Willson wrote:

> The comely little schoolteacher, attired in an olive drab costume, golf stocking, and a helmet, stepped into the plane named for her, smiling and waving at the crowd. J. "Augy" Pedlar, wearing his weather-beaten straw hat, and Lieut. Vilas Knope, the navigator, looked grim as though they seem to realize the responsibility their pretty passenger placed on their shoulders.

Goddard's *El Encanto* featured a huge underbelly fuel tank positioned around the monoplane's center of gravity to minimize balance problems. (NASM)

The wing of Goddard's *El Encanto* points skyward like a towering tombstone. Right of center is a primitive directional radio aerial. (NASM)

A few minutes before noon, Maj. Ed Howard took his position at the starting point and committee men checked the telephone circuits strung along the fringes of the takeoff run. On Howard's command the Travel Air *Oklahoma* was pushed up to the starting line, its tail almost touching the fence of the airport boundary. Exactly on the dot of twelve, the starter's flag dropped, and Ben Griffin had first spin in the deadly roulette. Men pushed to help his *Oklahoma* accelerate, falling away as it picked up speed. With only half the strip used, the monoplane was airborne—it had survived the first round.

Norman Goddard was next in *El Encanto*. He was not so lucky as Griffin. Despite having emblazoned the letters *HBH* on its tail, which he swore stood for "Hell Bent for Honolulu," the Englishman's lurching monoplane lifted only a few feet before dragging a wingtip and ground-looping in an explosion of dust. The tail came up, the aircraft rolled on its side, and the left wing and tail plane were demolished. The only thing "enchanted" about *El Encanto* was the lives of its crew, for miraculously there was no explosion, and they scrambled from the wreck uninjured. Surveying the remains the pair began a heated argument about who had been in control and caused the accident. Navigator Lt. Ken Hawkins later said: "I would rather have crashed in mid-ocean than have had this happen."

At 12:09 Livingston Irving's *Pabco Pacific Flyer* started its run. Following Goddard's accident the boisterous crowd had become quiet. The former Lafayette Escadrille pilot was Oakland's sole entry. Seven times his Breese monoplane skipped off the ground, each time flopping back in a cloud of dust. After the last bounce, Irving closed the throttle and ended his run just yards from where the overrun dropped into San Francisco Bay. His tail skid was broken. "Damn plane just wouldn't fly. Tow her back, guys, and we'll give her another go," Irving yelled to his ground crew.

During the twenty minutes it took to tow the *Pabco Pacific Flyer* clear of the airstrip, Jack Frost and navigator Gordon Scott waited patiently at the starting line with the *Golden Eagle*. Throughout the morning's proceedings Frost and Scott were noted as being the most relaxed and confident of the race crews. This may well have been due to their knowledge that Lockheed's superb Vega had performed brilliantly during a number of long trial flights. Furthermore, in its quest to produce its own race-winning headlines the Hearst organization had spared no expense with its entry. Its Vega was not only lavishly equipped with the latest instruments and equipment but in case of emergency could dump its heavy fuel load and jettison its landing gear to increase range, or safely ditch in the ocean. The fuselage also contained carbon dioxide-charged bags designed to keep the wood-skinned monoplane afloat for at least thirty days. When finally given the command to take off, Frost and the *Golden Eagle* made it look easy and had reached 200 feet by the airfield boundary. Minutes later he was waggling his wings to employees gathered on the roof of downtown offices of the *San Francisco Examiner*.

As Pedlar's *Miss Doran* was pushed to the line those nearby could see the pilot adjusting the tilt of his straw hat and furiously chewing on his gum. Its namesake, curls peeping out beneath her helmet, waved from the window of her cabin.

The Buhl was the most overloaded of the Dole racers; besides 400 gallons of fuel it also carried the weight of a superfluous passenger and her specially paneled cabin adapted to provide the young woman with a private dressing room! However, the 350 square feet of lifting surface provided by the Buhl's biplane wings were equal to the task. The crowd was ecstatic when the *Miss Doran*, though using most of the takeoff run, lifted safely "carrying a flower of American womanhood toward Hawaii."

As the *Aloha* took off past the crowds there was no doubt about its Hawaiian links. Sporting the most exotic paint job of the race, it was finished in sunshine yellow, had a scarlet lei painted around its nose, and carried the Great Seal of Hawaii on its sides. Pilot Martin Jensen climbed just enough to clear the roofs of San Francisco as he chased *Miss Doran* out across the Golden Gate.

The crowd began to relax as yet another airplane took off safely. This time it was Art Goebel and his navigator/radio operator, Lt. Bill Davis, in the Travel Air *Woolaroc*. They were followed by "Lone Star Bill" Erwin in his race-built Swallow *Dallas Spirit*. Among the cheering crowd was his twenty-year-old wife, Connie, who had originally been nominated to navigate on the flight before the committee decided she was too young and inexperienced. In her place Erwin now carried naval veteran Alvin Eichwaldt.

The crowd hung on as Livingston Irving's mechanics worked on the *Pabco Pacific Flyer*. The tail skid was repaired, and finding no fault in the engine, the crewmen were preparing to top up the tanks when their attention was diverted by the sound of an approaching aircraft. The drama was not over. Three aircraft were returning to the field: *Miss Doran* and *Oklahoma* with engine problems and *Dallas Spirit* with its fuselage fabric peeling away. Police rushed to clear the landing area as Griffin arrived over the field with smoke streaming from his engine. Despite his fuel overload Griffin landed safely. Mechanics soon confirmed his worst fears that he had "cooked the engine" and was out of the race. Griffin had previously been warned by a Wright Aero-

Ground crew works feverishly on Irving's Breese following its first abortive take-off. The second disastrous attempt proved the problem was sheer fuel overload. (NASM)

Friends say their farewells to Mildred Doran before closing the rear door. Her aircraft was painted a patriotic red, white, and blue. (NASM)

Jensen's Breese *Aloha* was the sixth plane to start but only the second to make a successful departure. (NASM)

Goebel had no difficulties getting the *Woolaroc* off the ground well before the end of the runway. (NASM)

nautical Company field engineer that the fuel he was using was likely to cause his Wright Whirlwind to overheat.

Pedlar arrived overhead with his engine missing badly. Dumping fuel, he landed safely. Erwin in the *Dallas Spirit* was unable to dump fuel, and his control problems were exacerbated by the drag from long streamers of fabric that flapped around the Swallow's tail. Making a long flat powered approach he executed a superb landing. An inspection showed that the slipstream had lifted the fabric around the navigator's drift sight hatch and had peeled it back from the side and bottom of the fuselage. Hearing it would take at least half a day to repair the damage, the disappointed Erwin withdrew from the race.

Meanwhile the *Pabco Pacific Flyer* had been repaired and the crowd held its breath as Irving made his second attempt to take off. After several bounces Irving showed his inexperience by desperately hauling the Breese off the ground. In

response the overloaded machine mushed into the air, clawing for height on the verge of the stall. After staggering to about 50 feet it flopped to the ground and disappeared in the now all-too-familiar cloud of dust. The crowd roared when the crew emerged unhurt and Irving's long-suffering wife, Madelaine, and their five-year-old daughter rushed to the crash site to embrace the frustrated flier.

The strain was telling on Mildred Doran, who was in tears and understandably was having second thoughts. Some of the crowd called out to her not to go. Pedlar seemed too busy supervising mechanics changing the Buhl's spark plugs to take much notice as navigator Knope tried to talk her into staying behind. However, it seems that after being the driving force behind the whole project, she feared humiliation more than the vast Pacific. Journalist Louise Landis later reported in the San Francisco *Bulletin*: "She started the second time knowing full well there

On its second takeoff *Miss Doran* climbs slowly over the sands of San Francisco Bay. Minutes later it vanished forever out over the Pacific. (NASM)

was real danger ahead. In fact I know she was scared to death when she entered the little cabin of that plane on the last trip. But no one was going to call her a quitter. She wouldn't stay behind."

When word came that the airplane was ready for another try, the white-faced schoolteacher walked quietly back to her cabin. Minutes later her aircraft was a speck out over the bay. Almost two hours behind the leaders, *Miss Doran* was the last to leave.

Next morning's headlines were predictable: DISASTER HAUNTS THE DOLE FLYERS . . . ONLY FOUR AWAY OUT OF 15 ENTRIES. . . . One paper reported a "publicity-mad promoter leaving a trail of carnage." Throughout the night newspaper switchboards had been jammed with anxious callers asking, "What's the latest news?" There had been little to report as only the *Woolaroc* was equipped with a two-way radio. Ships along the route reported vague "sightings" and a series of radio

The mangled remains of Irving's *Pabco Pacific Flyer* following its second abortive takeoff attempt. (NASM)

81

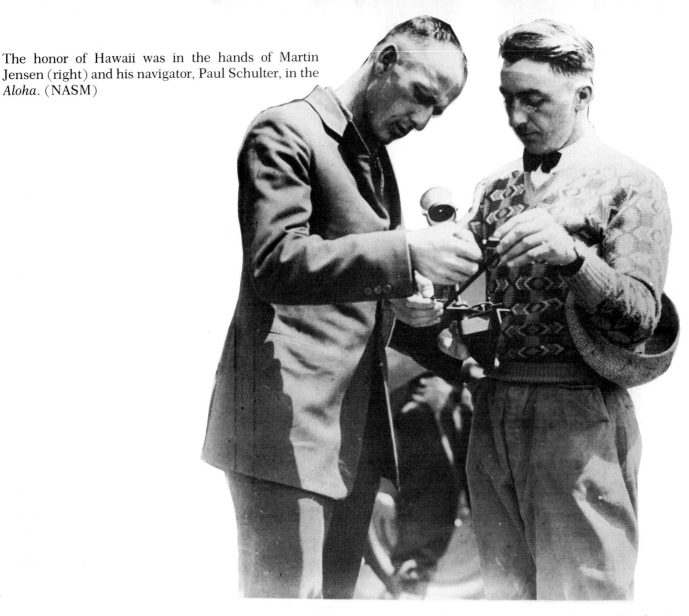

The honor of Hawaii was in the hands of Martin Jensen (right) and his navigator, Paul Schulter, in the *Aloha*. (NASM)

messages from the *Woolaroc*. Goebel had climbed above the solid layer of low cloud to 6,000 feet where navigator Davis had a sky full of stars for his celestial navigation. Terse Morse-keyed reports marked their progress: "300 miles out" . . . "517 miles out" . . . "750 miles out" . . . "1,485 miles out."

The *Aloha* had last been seen scuttling low over the Farallon Islands, 30 miles off San Francisco. The Hawaiian pilot had planned to stay low all the way, partly not to waste precious fuel climbing his headily laden airplane, but more importantly for the sake of accurate navigation. His crew mate, Paul Schulter, was a merchant seaman and had no flying experience. He was accustomed to reading a sextant from the deck of a ship and using the actual horizon while taking

bearings on the sun, moon, and stars. To do so while flying high required a number of intricate corrections to be made and Schulter was not confident of his ability to get accurate readings under such circumstances. Though it meant the added hazard of low flying over water, the pair had considered it the lesser of two evils, for without accurate navigation they would never find the islands. As the *Aloha* carried no radio, reception range was not a factor.

The Farallon Islands gave the race crews their only opportunity to visually fix their position on the long overwater crossing. Like the others, Schulter had pinpointed their exact position, checked the time, and rapidly calculated their drift and groundspeed since passing over the Golden Gate twenty-three minutes earlier. From his position behind the cabin fuel tank, he had to pass messages to Jensen along a string pulley line. He pegged a note on the line and sent it forward through the narrow gap through which he could just glimpse the pilot. Jensen pulled it down, scanned the instructions, and altered heading. Now there was nothing but open water to Hawaii, and any further changes would be based on astronavigation or indications of drift from the sea's surface.

Besides navigating, Schulter had the job of operating the hand pump of the *Aloha*'s auxiliary fuel system. Short of funds, Jensen had initially planned to top up the aircraft's fuel system in flight from a stack of five-gallon fuel cans. However, when forced by the committee to equip the *Breese* with a proper long-range tank, he had installed a last-minute, minimum-cost system that included no fuel gauges. The only way to ensure that the aircraft's main tank was not running dry was for Schulter to frequently top it up until fuel was seen to overflow through a vent hole. This not only wasted precious fuel but was also a serious fire hazard, compounded by Schulter's insistence on chain-smoking. All afternoon, as Schulter smoked and pumped, Jensen clung to that heading. An unbroken layer of low clouds prevented Schulter from "shooting" the sun. The clouds still persisted at twilight—the best time to take a star shot with the horizon still clearly visible—and by 8 P.M. the pair was enveloped in darkness.

Somewhere close by, the *Woolaroc* cruised about 4,000 feet above the *Aloha*. Art Goebel could afford the luxury of flying above cloud since Davis was an experienced aerial navigator and had the added advantage of also being a qualified pilot. Unlike Schulter, Davis did not worry about being denied a sight of the earth's horizon while using his sextant. Furthermore, the *Woolaroc*'s radio allowed him to tune in on the San Francisco and Maui radio beams. For the first four hours of flight Goebel had steered 250 degrees, the first of eight headings Davis had precomputed to follow the Great Circle course to Hawaii. Their aircraft was equipped with three magnetic compasses besides an electrically driven Earth Inductor Com-

pass, which was not subject to the oscillations and errors of ordinary compasses. Davis also had a Pioneer Drift Sight and a supply of smoke bombs with which he could determine how much the wind was affecting the aircraft's track.

An hour out Davis had tuned in the radio and had heard the steady "on course" signal in his earphones. As darkness fell the reassuring hum of the San Francisco beacon faded. They climbed to 6,000 feet where Davis resorted to taking regular sextant shots on Polaris through the open hatch alongside his position near the rear door. Every four hours he passed Goebel a new Great Circle heading on the "string telephone." Through the night Davis transmitted position reports and passed messages via the ships along the route. One addressed to his mother in Atlanta, Georgia, stating "All's well," reached the Davis home an hour and a half later. Starting from the *Woolaroc*'s Morse key, the signal went by ship's radio, shore radio, telegraph, and finally telephone to the far side of the continent.

Shortly after sunrise the clouds began to break and Davis was able to drop smoke bombs to check their drift. The predicted northeast wind had swung to the south, and he sent a message forward telling Goebel to alter heading to port. A note came back suggesting Davis had made a mistake, but the navigator insisted that there had been a big change in the wind, adding that it had boosted the *Woolaroc*'s groundspeed to 100 mph. Goebel altered course and Davis radioed their position "latitude 24.35 north, longitude 150.43 west." As this put them only 450 miles from Honolulu, Davis tuned in the Maui beacon. They should soon be in range and the navigator prayed it would confirm his calculations. Their position report was picked up by the S.S. *City of Los Angeles* and relayed to Hawaii. Two hours later, as they came in range, Hawaii's Wahaiwa radio station picked up another message from Davis estimating they would arrive at Honolulu's Wheeler Field in two and a half hours.

The information was passed to the thousands who were already waiting at the airfield. Most Honoluluans had been given the day off to attend the celebrations and within an hour the crowd had swelled to thirty-thousand. A 2-mile traffic jam trailed back along the road to Honolulu. Stunting Army planes, dancing girls, and bands kept the impatient crowd entertained. As James Dole and Hawaiian Governor Wallace G. Farrington joined the throng waiting at the airfield, Dole told waiting reporters: "Hawaii is on the lips of the world today and in the minds of countless millions of people."

Hawaii had gone aviation mad. Besides a stream of stories about the race preparations, newspapers had been filled with aviation advertisements, and Honolulu stores were offering free toy airplanes to their customers. The elegant new Royal Hawaiian Hotel had been chosen as race headquarters and was preparing to host all the arriving fliers. Besides a lavish reception, a luau-style dinner dance was planned for the following night.

About an hour out of Honolulu, the *Woolaroc*'s radio signals ceased and there was growing concern until Davis came back on air after discovering and repairing a broken connection. Shortly afterward he finally picked up the Maui radio beam. They were on course and about 75 miles from the finish. The *Woolaroc* passed Diamond Head shortly before one o'clock local time. The delirious crowd watched as an exuberant Davis began firing off all the aircraft's distress flares and smoke bombs. Waiting Army planes moved in to escort the *Woolaroc* to Wheeler Field. The two airmen had not realized that they were in the lead until a grinning Army pilot held up one finger to signify they were the first to arrive. The race was theirs.

At 12:24 P.M. local time the *Woolaroc* touched down. The Travel Air had taken 26 hours, 17 minutes, and 33 seconds from Oakland. It is said that Davis's first words on jumping from the aircraft were: "How are the rest of the boys?" and that he appeared distressed when told there had been no word of the other starters. One of the first to reach them was a despairing Marguerite Jensen who rushed up pleading for news of her husband. As Goebel said he had not sighted the *Aloha*, she listened, pale and close to tears, before

The race-winning Travel Air 5,000 *Woolaroc*. The Travel Air Company was formed by Walter Beech, Clyde Cessna, and Lloyd Stearman, each of whom in later years formed a highly successful aircraft company. (NASM)

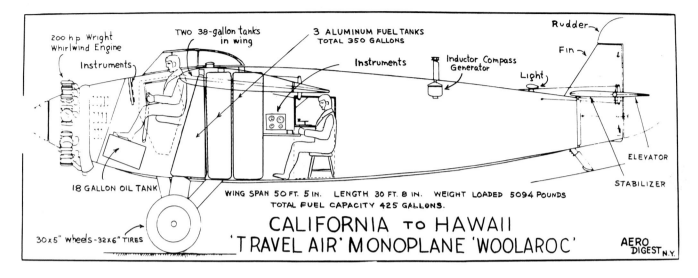

This cutaway drawing of the *Woolaroc* was published in *Aero Digest* magazine. (NASM)

briefly collapsing alongside the airplane.

The crowd surged forward as the airmen were garlanded in leis. James Dole wrung their hands then asked anxiously if they had seen anything of the other competitors. The two fliers shook their heads. The celebrations continued but Davis and Goebel were distracted. Like everyone else, they had one eye on the horizon. The exhausted airmen were eventually driven to the Royal Hawaiian Hotel to rest.

While the crowd waited anxiously for signs of other aircraft, Jensen and Schulter in the *Aloha* were north of the islands and short of fuel. Since nightfall the previous day they had been living a nightmare. Realizing the dangers of flying at night with no moon or stars to illuminate the ocean, Jensen had decided to climb above the clouds. He also hoped that Schulter could "shoot" the stars and fix their position. "I was able to climb to about 4,000 feet. It was still a dense fog [cloud]. Here I experienced vertigo when I was unable to get above it," Jensen recalled years later, telling how he completely lost control. One moment they were climbing with wings level, then a few seconds later the aircraft was spiraling to the left. In those days pilots called it "the grave-

yard spiral"—a dreaded maneuver in which the harder one tried to pull out, the tighter the turn and the faster the rate of descent became. Jensen's years of stunting at airshows across America finally paid off when he somehow managed to convert the spiral into a spin. He had done it so often for the crowds that he could come out of a spin with his eyes closed. Just using "the seat of his pants," he knew exactly when to push the stick forward, kick on the opposite rudder, centralize, and climb out of the ensuing dive.

Three times they entered a graveyard spiral. Following the third episode when the altimeter showed they had recovered just a few hundred feet from the water, Jensen decided to remain low again. Somehow they survived the night with Jensen concentrating on the quivering needles of the altimeter and his crude turn and bank indicator. Jensen recalled a miraculous encounter with the Pacific when the *Aloha* skipped on a wave top like a giant stone.

The altimeter registered 100 feet above sea level, which I had held for some hours. Perhaps the density in mid-Pacific was different and caused an error, for no doubt I must have

been actually no more than 5 or 10 feet above the water. I hit the top of a wave and the spray ripped a long slit in the stabilizer fabric. The fact that I never once during the flight took my hands off the throttle or stick saved us. I had instant control and climbed immediately to 500 feet.

At dawn Jensen was still at 500 feet and continuing to steer 248 degrees—the heading he had been given over the Farallons. When their estimated flight time expired without a trace of land, Schulter sent a note forward to Jensen suggesting they circle until noon. He was not confident of getting an accurate reading until the sun was highest. The frustrated pilot had no options left. Now concerned purely with survival, Jensen throttled back to conserve fuel. At noon—two and a half hours later—Schulter's sextant showed they were circling 190 miles north of Honolulu.

"Martin Jensen, where the hell have you been?" were his wife's first words when the exhausted fliers eventually reached Wheeler Field. From left: Schulter, Marguerite Jensen, and Martin Jensen. (NASM)

Clearly they had been thrown way off course by the wind change that Davis in the *Woolaroc* had detected. They had emptied the auxiliary tank and, with no gauges, had no idea how much fuel remained in the wing tanks.

Two hours later some of the crowd was leaving when the *Aloha* landed with just 4 gallons (twenty minutes) of fuel remaining. "Martin Jensen, where the hell have you been?" wailed his distraught wife, clutching the exhausted air-man. "Peg, I never saw so much damn water in my life," Jensen is said to have answered. Apologizing to Dole for not winning, Jensen explained that they would have won had he been able to afford a radio to home in on the Maui navigation beam. In fact, had Jensen not had to circle for two and a half hours waiting for Schulter to shoot the sun, they could have beaten the *Woolaroc* by a half-hour.

An hour later, it became clear that the *Golden*

Eagle and the *Miss Doran* were down in the Pacific. By then their fuel would have been exhausted. Next morning a massive sea search was mounted. Army, Navy, and civilian planes took off from the islands. Martin Jensen dragged his weary body back into the *Aloha* and searched for five hours. From San Diego the aircraft carrier *Langley* took her twenty-eight aircraft far out to sea to scour the mainland end of the route. The *Langley* was skippered by Capt. John Towers, who had commanded the NC-3 flying boat on its abortive attempt to cross the Atlantic Ocean in 1919.

Reports of flares seen burning high up on the slopes of Mount Mauna Loa led to an extensive search of the volcanic peaks of Hawaii Island. The brother of *Golden Eagle* navigator Gordon Scott spent much of the following year searching the island. He was frequently assisted by Martin Jensen, who by then was flying the *Aloha* on passenger flights for Lewis Hawaiian Tours. Although no trace was found, there are many who still believe that the *Golden Eagle* crashed near the peak and that wreckage will one day be discovered in a rocky crevice.

The official search was called off after ten days, but not before an Army search plane crashed into the sea killing its two crewmen. They were not the only searchers to lose their lives. The Dole affair was to suffer a final tragedy.

On August 18 "Lone Star" Bill Erwin announced that he and his navigator, Alvin Eichwaldt, intended to search along the route in the repaired *Dallas Spirit*. Following his forced withdrawal from the race, pilot Erwin had been criticized by his Texan backers for pulling out, and they urged him to try again. Furthermore Erwin had initially been keen to use the Dole race as part of a flight between Dallas and Hong Kong. Dallas businessman William E. Easterwood had offered $25,000 for such a flight. It seems that besides searching for the lost fliers, Erwin still had plans of continuing on from Hawaii in an effort to claim the Easterwood prize. With criticism already being leveled at the running of the Dole affair, officials of its organizing committee

were among the many who tried to dissuade Erwin. He refused to listen and announced to the press that he would "zigzag over and if necessary zigzag back."

Erwin equipped the Swallow with a radio acquired from the wrecked *Pabco Pacific Flyer* and set out from Oakland at 2:15 P.M. on August 19. For some hours all went well. The men were obviously still in high spirits at 5:45 P.M. when they radioed: "Just saw a rumrunner to the south and had a hell of a time keeping Ike in. Signed Bill." But six hours out, soon after nightfall, things started to go wrong. After several garbled messages, navigator Eichwaldt radioed: "SOS—we are in a tail spin. We came out of it OK but we're sure scared. It was a close call. I thought it was all over but came out of it. The light on the instrument board [panel] went out and it was so dark that Bill couldn't see the wings." It seems that Erwin had succumbed to the problems of vertigo that had plagued Martin Jensen. Moreover the Texan's troubles were exacerbated by the loss of his instrument lighting.

Ten minutes later a second pitiful signal was picked up. It started: "We are in anr [another?] . . . SOS—" The transmission ended abruptly as the aircraft presumably spun into the sea. Like Jensen's experience, Erwin's loss of control at night suggested the probable fate of the other lost fliers. Radio operators on the mainland later reported that over the last few minutes of flight the *Dallas Spirit's* transmissions rose and fell in pitch. This, they explained, was caused by the wind-driven generator slowing down then speeding up as the aircraft first lost then rapidly increased speed as Erwin battled to maintain control. As Eichwaldt's final message came over the air, the transmission pitch whined higher and higher until at 9:04 P.M. it ended in a last pitiful wail when the *Dallas Spirit* crashed into the sea.

Following the loss of the *Dallas Spirit* the *San Francisco Examiner* wrote on its front page: " 'Lone Star' Bill Erwin and his daring mate Alvin 'Ike' Eichwaldt today stand with that heroic quintet of Dole Racers in the shadowy wings of the Pacific's great amphitheater while a worldwide audience thus far clamors in vain to recall them to the stage."

Soon, however, the newspapers were reporting mounting criticism and public revulsion at the loss of life: DOLE'S RACE TO DEATH . . . AVIATION ASININITY . . . WAS IT WORTH THE PRICE—10 LIVES . . . headlines and articles slammed the race organizers. "Such an orgy of reckless sacrifice must never be permitted again in this country," the Philadelphia *Enquirer* asserted. Much of the criticism was unfairly leveled at the unfortunate James Dole, suggesting he personally had "enticed inexperienced and ill-prepared pilots to their death in homemade crates." It ignored the fact that the race committee had set the standards and run the race, not to mention the cavalier approach of many of the so-called professional pilots themselves.

Standard Oil aviation executive G. O. Norville echoed the feelings of many of the aviation community in a letter to National Aeronautical Association president Porter Adams. He suggested that planners had been blinded by Lindbergh's success and ignored basic safety matters. Seeking more positive regulation in the future, Norville wrote: "The progress of aviation has been retarded to such an extent that it will take at least two years of conscientious effort to place it again in the position it held on August 1, 1927."

In defense of James Dole the *Honolulu Advertiser* in its editorial of August 28, 1927, intoned:

> The lessons taught by the tragedies attending the Dole flight will have a moral effect on those who would now follow the others across the Pacific. Preparation, navigation, radio connection, a 100 percent expedition will be the result. Successful accomplishment of a new undertaking brings to light unheard of difficulties, and a way is pointed to solving the problems. Tragedy in pioneering breeds caution, and too much caution in hazardous undertakings is never possible.

By the end of the year, when the immediate furor had died a little, the Aeronautical Chamber of Commerce of America summed it all up in its prestigious *Aircraft Year Book,* which stated:

> The event was marked by unnecessary crashes and loss of life, due in part to a scramble to win prize money, in some instances without proper preparations and without regard for the fitness of equipment. When it is recalled with what care Lindbergh, Chamberlin, Byrd, Maitland, and a succession of transoceanic fliers went about their preparations, and to what constant testing their flying equipment was subjected, a statement made by Martin Jensen, winner of second place in the race, throws an interesting light on the rush and hurry attending the start of this hazardous undertaking. Jensen wrote: "Five days before the start of the race not even the fuselage was on my plane, but in those five days I worked night and day, making preparation, always against great odds." The storm of criticism against ill-considered ocean flights, under conditions of insufficient preparation, and possibly inadequate equipment, will have a steadying effect, it is believed, in all future attempts in this field.

By the beginning of 1928 that "steadying effect" was already being felt by at least one flier whose eyes were still firmly fixed on the conquest of the Pacific. Australian flier Charles Kingsford-Smith, busy preparing his trimotor Fokker *Southern Cross* for a flight from Oakland to Australia, was having problems finding backers to help cover his mounting debts. His project seemed doomed when, appalled at the loss of life in the Dole race, Smith's major Australian backer—the government of New South Wales—ordered him to sell the Fokker and return the money to the public coffers.

Charles Kingsford-Smith had first planned to fly from England to Australia in this Blackburn Kangaroo, which crash-landed in Crete. When forced out of the Blackburn's crew, he decided instead to obtain backing for a transpacific flight from the United States to Australia. (R. V. Rendle)

6

First Across

The Flight of the *Southern Cross*

On the morning of July 4, 1927, Charles Kingsford-Smith boarded the liner S.S. *Tahiti* in Sydney, Australia, bound for San Francisco to attempt the first transpacific flight. It was not the first time Kingsford-Smith had crossed the Pacific on the *Tahiti*. Seven years earlier he sailed home from California on the liner following a fruitless attempt to interest Americans in a transpacific flight. Then his determination to fly the Pacific had been sparked by the humiliation he had suffered when Australia's powerful and irascible prime minister, William Hughes, had insisted he was too inexperienced to fly in the 1919 England-Australia race. Now wiser, more experienced, and with enough money to buy an airplane, he was "going to make that bloody Hughes take notice."

Just five days earlier, accompanied by his friend and business partner Charles Ulm, he had completed a record-breaking 7,500-mile flight around Australia in a single-engine Bristol Tourer biplane. Their aim had been to attract backers for a flight across the Pacific. They made the ideal team: Ulm the serious, astute businessman and "Smithy" the superb pilot whose pranks and wide grin earned him almost as much publicity as his flying accomplishments. The day after they arrived back in Sydney the New South Wales state government announced it would guarantee £3,500 ($17,500) toward the transpacific flight.

On the voyage Kingsford-Smith and Ulm had been accompanied by another partner, Keith Anderson. In 1923 Anderson and Kingsford-Smith had been pilots with a struggling West Australian air service and later had started an outback trucking company. When that failed the pair had formed their own tiny air service and had been joined by Ulm early in 1927.

Following the end of World War I Kingsford-Smith, "Smithy" to his "mates," had teamed up with two other Australian Flying Corps pilots to

91

It was the ultimate Australian bush flight—an epic circumnavigation of the continent—that brought Charles Kingsford-Smith (left) and Charles Ulm to the public attention in 1927 as they searched for backers for a transpacific flight. Here the jubilant pair pose beside their battered Bristol Tourer following the flight. (TGJ)

crew a Blackburn Kangaroo bomber entered in the 1919 England-Australia Air Race. A £10,000 ($50,000) prize had been offered by the Australian government which saw the race as a means of promoting Australia and its aviation future. However, despite a personal meeting with Prime Minister Billy Hughes, Kingsford-Smith's crew had not been allowed to compete unless they employed an expert navigator or undertook further training themselves. Explaining to the British press that he and his race advisers considered the Kingsford-Smith team too inexperienced, Hughes said: "We feel we are responsible for the safety of these young fellows, and could not allow them to start on a voyage halfway around the world without any knowledge of navigation." Bert Hinkler, who later became famous as the "Aus-

tralian Lindbergh," was also forced out of the race.

In what seems to have been a fit of pique, the bitterly disappointed Kingsford-Smith resigned from the Kangaroo's team. While his teammates looked for a navigator, the twenty-two-year-old airman decided instead to visit a brother in Oakland, California. Bidding farewell to teammate Val Rendle, he promised, "I don't know when, or exactly how yet, but I'm going to make that bloody Hughes sit up and take notice of me . . . and I'm going to fly to Australia." The whole sad affair had received wide coverage in the Australian newspapers, which added further to Kingsford-Smith's belief that he had lost face. Soon after reaching California he wrote to his mother stating:

I am once again full of optimism after the last few black weeks I've had with this darn Australian flight falling through. . . . However, dears, there's lots of fight left in me, and I have every intention of coming home to you by air, but from this country. You know there is another prize offered for the job [transpacific] amounting to $50,000 and I think I can get people over here sufficiently interested to back me. . . . Of course I am keeping it right out of the newspapers. No second fiasco for me, thanks.

There is evidence that, secretly, Kingsford-Smith doubted the validity of the $50,000 offer. It had been made by Hollywood film producer Thomas H. Ince, a close friend of newspaper baron Randolph Hearst. Kingsford-Smith suspected that Ince would make sure he never had to pay the money, probably by following the example of Hearst who, in 1910, had placed impossible conditions on his prize for the first flight across America. The Australian wrote home suggesting that Ince's offer was a cheap publicity stunt. He also took the precaution of assuring prospective backers that including movie, magazine, and advertising rights, the flight would net almost double Ince's doubtful $50,000 prize. He estimated the flight would cost $22,000, the major item being $16,500 for a converted war-surplus Vickers Vimy bomber. The twin-engine Vimy was similar to the machines that had flown the Atlantic in 1919 and won Hughes' England-Australia challenge. It was clear that his disqualification from that race still preyed on the young airman's mind and that he felt honor-bound to prove himself to the Australian public. He wrote: "If I could only manage to do this job I would be able to justify myself in the eyes of the Australian people with a vengeance."

The young Australian approached the Los Angeles Chamber of Commerce but its members were not interested in his sponsorship proposal even though it offered them 50 percent of the profits—which he estimated would amount to $92,500. Nor could America's Manufacturers Aircraft Association assist. However, when Vickers cabled Kingsford-Smith stating bluntly, "Cannot supply Vickers machine," the AMAA did write to its members seeking suggestions for a suitable aircraft.

In response Kingsford-Smith was approached in November 1920 by Donald W. Douglas, then virtually unknown. The young designer offered to build a suitable aircraft. Another suggestion was that he purchase a government-surplus U.S. Navy F-5L flying boat for $12,400. "Buy it from the Navy" the letterhead extorted. The problem was Kingsford-Smith didn't have the money. San Francisco's prestigious Yolo Fliers' Club also had shown an interest in his proposal. However, its businessmen members eventually decided to support an American consortium involving war ace Eddie Rickenbacker.

With his meager savings gone, Kingsford-Smith found work as a stunt pilot for Universal Studios and a barnstormer with the Moffett-Starkey Aero Circus. He was still searching desperately for backers when a fellow stunt pilot, Omar Locklear, was killed during a film stunt. With the cameras rolling, the "Daredevil of the Skies" had dived vertically into an oil field, starting a huge fire. The nationwide publicity surrounding the fireball death of Hollywood's best-known stunt pilot virtually ended any hope he had of finding backers around Los Angeles. "Omar's death, which had been front-paged in the newspapers, did nothing to help people have confidence in planes," Kingsford-Smith said. When the air circus manager ran off without paying his pilots, the flat-broke Australian finally gave up. Swallowing his pride, he worked painting signs until he had enough cash for the cheapest berth on the S.S. *Tahiti*. He sailed for Australia in December 1920.

Seven years later, when Kingsford-Smith arrived back in San Francisco, America was on the happiness spree of the roaring twenties. In night clubs and dance halls the new craze was the slow fox trot danced, of course, to Tin Pan Alley's new offering, "Lindy—Youth with the Heart of Gold." Talking pictures were all the rage and at a thousand cinemas Americans clamored to hear Al Jolson in *The Jazz Singer* and cheer at Movietone

93

newsclips featuring Lindbergh as he triumphantly toured the country and Maitland and Hegenberger, who four weeks earlier had made their pioneering flight to Hawaii. Aviation had become a part of everyday life and the newspapers were filled with news of the upcoming Dole Pacific Air Race.

With aviation on everyone's lips it seemed inconceivable that the Australian trio would have problems raising the additional funds needed to pay for navigation equipment, radios, fuel, and living expenses. The day following their arrival they were knocking on doors looking for Californian sponsors. News of Kingsford-Smith's plans quickly brought two sponsors to his hotel. However, rather than bankroll his transpacific flight, both wanted the airman to take part in the Dole challenge. Reports indicate that one was an oil company executive and the other was Hollywood movie cowboy Hoot Gibson. Reporting to his business partners after one meeting, the disillusioned Australian said: "The heap of junk they offered me wouldn't stand a chance. And after all we don't want to be losers, do we?"

Some of Kingsford-Smith's public comments about "madmen" and "unsuitable" aircraft, though accurate, drew critical response. One would-be sponsor suggested that "the little Australian has a good line of patter but he hasn't got what it takes." This opinion was circulated widely and the Australians found that many possible backers remained behind closed doors. Kingsford-Smith was to learn that it did little for his cause to publicly criticize the Dole event. To make matters worse, when the race ended and the horror of its seemingly needless death toll had sunk in, it was impossible to find anyone prepared to back another flight over the Pacific. Not even the fact that the Australians had been able to purchase a trimotor Fokker similar to the Army's *Bird of Paradise* seemed to help.

Kingsford-Smith had bought the Fokker F.VII3m *Detroiter* from fellow countryman Hubert Wilkins, who had used it during his 1926 Wilkins-Detroit Arctic Expedition. Finding it unsuitable for a planned transpolar flight, the famed polar explorer was negotiating to purchase a

Kingsford-Smith purchased his Fokker from a fellow Australian, explorer Hubert Wilkins (right), who had previously used it on the *Detroit News*–Wilkins Polar Expedition. (Queensland Newspapers)

Lockheed Vega—having inspected the ill-fated prototype, *Golden Eagle,* at Oakland where it was being prepared for the Dole race. Ulm and Kingsford-Smith were introduced to Wilkins in San Francisco. It was an ironic meeting, for eight years earlier, when Kingsford-Smith had pulled out of the 1919 England-Australia race, Wilkins had taken his place. Although not a pilot, Wilkins was acknowledged as an expert navigator following the part he had played as a member of a polar expedition mounted in 1913 by Vilhjalmur Stefansson.

Kingsford-Smith paid $15,000 for the *Detroiter* minus its three engines. The problem of securing three new Wright Whirlwind J-5 engines was solved by another chance meeting in San Francisco. Visiting Australian retail magnate Sidney Myer heard of the three fliers' dilemma and immediately wrote a check for $7,500 to cover their

At San Francisco's Mills Field the *Southern Cross*, temporarily renamed *Spirit of California*, is prepared to challenge the world endurance record. Kingsford-Smith and copilot Lt. George Pond, U.S.N., climb aboard. (NASM)

cost. Nevertheless, over the following months the trio went $10,000 into debt equipping their Fokker, which was now renamed the *Southern Cross*. When funds promised from Australia failed to materialize, the project seemed doomed and Anderson returned home promising to come back if the flight became possible.

Worse was to come when a new government was elected in New South Wales and the incoming premier told the Australian newspapers he wanted nothing to do with "cheap stunts." Shortly thereafter, Kingsford-Smith received a cable from the premier "directing" him and his crew to abandon the flight and return home. Infuriated at such official arrogance, Kingsford-Smith tore up the government ultimatum declaring: "Who gave this man the right to order free Australian citizens around? He can go to hell.

We're not snotty-nosed schoolboys."

In Australia, where the Dole disaster had been given wide publicity, many newspapers ran stories echoing the outspoken premier. "It's a stunt that could easily backfire, and these foolhardy young men could end up being eaten by sharks somewhere in the ocean," one editorialized.

Meanwhile, deeply in debt and with no backers in sight, it seemed that Kingsford-Smith and Ulm had no alternative but to sell the Fokker and cut their losses. They were looking for a buyer when they were approached by the Fargool Oil Company. It offered to underwrite the transpacific flight if they could first break the world endurance record of 52 hours and 22 minutes held by Germany's single-engine Junkers W 33. The two fliers accepted immediately. They spent a week stripping the *Southern Cross* of every ounce of unnecessary equipment. To improve their chances, Ulm dropped out in favor of Lt. George Pond, a highly experienced Fokker pilot.

Preparations for the endurance flight also provided an opportunity for the team to conduct load tests on the Fokker for the Pacific crossing. They made five preliminary test flights, each time increasing the fuel load. "We carried loads ranging from 50 percent up to 95 percent before actually taking off with a full load," Kingsford-Smith wrote later. They established a maximum weight for takeoff of 15,807 pounds—almost two and a half times the Fokker's empty weight. Besides confirming the fuel load they could carry for the endurance attempt, it also proved they could lift the 1,300 gallons of fuel required on the critical 3,200-mile leg from Hawaii to Fiji.

On their first endurance record attempt Kingsford-Smith and Pond failed by almost three hours. However, the manager of Fargool Oil decided they had come close enough to warrant supplying the fuel for a second attempt. A week later the two men tried again. Somehow crammed with a few extra gallons of fuel and right on its 15,807-pound limit, the Southern Cross took nearly the full length of the Oakland airfield to take off. The wheels just missed clipping the barbed-wire perimeter fence. Leaning out the mixture controls until the engines were consuming the minimum safe fuel flow, the fliers eked almost another hour out of the Southern Cross. But it was still not enough. After 50 hours and 7 minutes they landed, totally exhausted and with the tanks dry. Following their second failure, Fargool withdrew their support. In a postflight interview Charles Pond told newsmen that he had just spent more than two days in a plane with the only man capable of flying the Pacific. "We all know his name is Charley Kingsford-Smith," he added admiringly.

A few weeks later Kingsford-Smith and Ulm were in Los Angeles where they hoped to sell the Southern Cross to the Vacuum Oil Company. While there the despondent Australians visited banker Andrew Chaffey, who had shown some interest but had been unable to help them. Professionally he regarded their plans as "absolutely

crazy," but he admired their courage. Knowing they were broke, Chaffey thrust a $100 bill into Kingsford-Smith's hand, saying "pay me back when you're famous and rich." Then he suggested they join him for lunch with a friend. "He'll like you. He's a bit crazy too," the benevolent banker joked.

Chaffey's lunch companion turned out to be Capt. G. Allan Hancock, a millionaire shipbuilder. Sensing that the down-and-out Australians needed a little relaxation, he invited them to join him the next morning on a ten-day cruise on his yacht Oaxcia. He suggested that there were some helpful people among his other guests, and that at worst, the cruise would give them time to consider their future. Exhausted by the events of the preceding months, the two Australians accepted. It was to be the turning point of their lives. Four days into the voyage, Allan Hancock called them to his cabin and made an extraordinary offer. He would buy the Southern Cross for the $16,000 they needed to get out of debt. He would loan them the airplane for the transpacific flight, arrange for a film about them when the attempt was over, and lend them the money needed for the flight against profits from the film.

After the callous treatment they had received from their Australian backer, Hancock's munificence seemed almost out of a Hollywood movie. So too did the scene when they docked a week later and found the Southern Cross had been impounded by their creditors. A check from Hancock quickly solved that problem.

While Ulm concentrated on planning the flight, Kingsford-Smith took the Southern Cross to the Douglas factory in Santa Monica for final modifications. He then flew it to Oakland where the last instruments and radios were fitted for the flight. Like Maitland and Hegenberger, they carried the latest navigation equipment, leaving nothing to chance. Besides the navigator's master aperiodic compass and a Pioneer earth inductor compass, the aircraft was equipped with two steering compasses. It also had two drift meters, sextants, long- and short-wave radios, and the latest blind-flying instruments. Two Americans were chosen to make up the crew: Capt. Harry

Newsreel cameras record Kingsford-Smith and Pond on takeoff. Their endurance flights were made in a fruitless attempt to secure a San Francisco backer. (NASM)

Lyon of Maine, a highly-qualified merchant marine navigator, and James Warner of Kansas City, Kansas, an experienced radio operator.

Kingsford-Smith now began to show the meticulous professional that lurked behind his happy-go-lucky public image. He spent hours aloft refining the accuracy of his blind flying by using only the Fokker's quivering turn-and-bank and rate-of-climb indicators—normally he would also have the altimeter, airspeed indicator, and compass to help. The four men made long practice flights to get used to operating together as a crew. On one Allan Hancock occupied the copilot's seat while Ulm and Andrew Chaffey sat down in the back to observe how Warner and Lyon reacted to "air conditions." Discovering that the noise level in the Fokker was too high for them to communicate, even using an electric intercom, they developed an orderly system of note passing. To increase their physical stamina, Ulm and Kingsford-Smith worked out a "training course" that involved alternating between driving a car, doing exercises, flying the plane, more exercises, more driving, and so on. The training period was gradually extended until the pair were able to stay active for forty hours.

In the role of navigator, Harry Lyon was critical to the success of the flight. Having never before navigated in flight, Lyon worked out his own unique method of training. In his unpublished memoirs he explained: "I had never even seen a bubble sextant, let alone used one. I began to practice taking sights with this instrument, and had a man along with a [marine] sextant. At the same time as I took altitudes with my bubble artificial horizon, he took altitudes using the normal horizon for a matter of comparison." The two men slowly progressed until Lyon was taking sights standing up in a car speeding along the coast road south of San Francisco. His assistant confirmed them from a series of preset points along the car's route. The dry-humored navigator recalled:

We got in quite a bit of practice at this but after the third arrest [for speeding] it became too expensive. After taking the sights I used to lean over, using the dashboard light to see by, and try and see how fast I could work them out with the car still bumping along. In fact I made myself as uncomfortable as possible and it was good practice for the flight. I found that working in the fuselage of the *Southern Cross* was far easier than the front seat of a Cadillac.

97

The *Southern Cross* flies low over Fred Giles's Hess Bluebird biplane *Wanda* at San Francisco's Mills Field. Giles, also from Australia, had withdrawn from the Dole Race and was planning to fly the Pacific alone in the single-engine biplane. Fortunately his wild scheme was never realized. (NASM)

Lyon also recalled his initial airborne training, carried out in the open cockpit of a two-seat Swallow biplane. "The [pilot] controls were in the after seat and so when I took a sight, Smithy had to put the bus in some awful banks so I would get the object clear of the top wing. We had a lot of practice at this."

The team's final consideration was to provide for the "remote possibility" that they might have to ditch. They came up with a unique solution utilizing one of the Fokker's immensely strong plywood-covered wings. Confident that a detached wing would float indefinitely, Ulm explained:

We fitted a dump valve that would drop the bulk of our gasoline load in 50 seconds. We carried steel saws that would enable us to cut off the outboard motor and steel fuselage and turn the wing into a raft. In the wing we placed emergency rations, a still to condense water, and a watertight radio transmitter. Four gas balloons were carried to lift the aerial of this transmitter. Thus we were equipped and safeguarded as far as it was humanly possible.

On May 31, 1928, after ten months in the United States, they were finally ready for the great adventure. Even the anger of being robbed

The *Southern Cross* prepares to depart for Australia from Oakland Airport. (NASM)

in their hotel room two nights earlier had subsided as hundreds of well-wishers crammed around the *Southern Cross*. The last of the 1,200 gallons of fuel was pumped into the tanks and moments before the fliers climbed on board someone handed Kingsford-Smith a small silken Australian flag. Next a woman broke through the police cordon and ran over to him. In tears she revealed she was the mother of Alvin Eichwaldt, who had perished in the *Dallas Spirit* searching for the missing Dole racers. Slipping a silver ring on one of his fingers, she begged him to wear it for good luck, explaining that her son had made it from a franc piece during the war. After quickly embracing Kingsford-Smith she returned to the crowd, leaving the Australian, for

once, momentarily at a loss for words. Swiftly recovering his normal cheery aplomb he reassured friends and a crowd of reporters, "Nothing has been left to chance. We are fully prepared, and if we fail, have not the slightest regret." Shouting "Cheerio," he climbed aboard the *Southern Cross* and prepared to attempt the longest ocean flight ever undertaken.

Poised at the end of the sand and gravel runway, Kingsford-Smith revved the engines to full power and the heavily laden aircraft accelerated slowly. After the aircraft rolled only a few hundred feet, the center motor died and Kingsford-Smith quickly cut the other engines. Anxious spectators clustered around as the two pilots

99

American friends bid the crew of the *Southern Cross* farewell shortly before takeoff from Oakland Airport. Navigator Harry Lyon is second from left. Radio operator James Warner stands with hands folded. Charles Ulm (right) and Kingsford-Smith both wear leather helmets and boots for warmth in the Fokker's open cockpit. (NASM)

looked for the problem. Leaning out of his window, navigator Lyon plucked a cigarette from a reporter and joked, "This may be my last drag." It was soon found that copilot Ulm had inadvertently allowed the fuel mixture control to slip, thus starving the engine. "It's a good omen. You've all heard the saying 'a poor start is a good ending,'" said the irrepressible Lyon.

Minutes later they were airborne and heading out over San Francisco. Ahead of them lay the world's greatest ocean, which they planned to cross in three stages. The first leg was 2,400 miles to Honolulu. The second, from Honolulu to Suva in the Fiji Islands, was a staggering 3,200 miles. The final run home was the 1,900-mile hop to Brisbane, Australia. It was not only the shortest but also the "easy one" for navigator Lyon—who suggested that even an "amateur" could not miss an island as large as Australia.

Later, for *National Geographic* magazine, Kingsford-Smith and Ulm poetically described their departure from the American mainland as they climbed slowly to 2,000 feet:

In 12 minutes the skyscrapers of San Francisco, looking white and spectral, were swallowed up in the gray-brown pall that enshrouded the Golden Gate. Our last picture of them was as they stood, baseless and serene, like a magic city hanging in the clouds. We were to see more magic cities rising and crumbling to nothingness in the amazing cloud banks that we encountered farther out. We

climbed at 92 miles an hour, and chuckling over our favorable start on the long air trail, we stuck a small silken Australian flag between two gasoline gauges in our cockpit. In the hours that followed, it was so beaten by the wind that only the stick remained.

The first six hours of flight were uneventful. Warner was able to confirm that they were on course by listening to the U.S. Army's radio beam until the signal faded 700 miles out. Kingsford-Smith flew while Ulm kept the ship's log. "We're as happy as hell. Everything is going as smooth as silk," he wrote, although Lyon might have used different words. He found the Fokker's vibration enough to "shake your teeth loose." To relieve their boredom the crew passed humorous notes around some spiced with colorful adjectives.

Eight hours out the boredom suddenly vanished in the pilot's cockpit as Kingsford-Smith detected an apparent increase in fuel consumption. The primitive glass-tube fuel gauges indicated that the wing tanks were running low. Not until three hours later, after deliberately running them dry, then topping up from the huge auxiliary tanks, was he satisfied that the problem was merely inaccurate gauges. Through the night they struck occasional rain showers which soaked the unprotected pilots and gave a bumpy ride to Warner and Lyon in the Fokker's passenger cabin. Occasionally Lyon threw out flares to check the drift. At one stage they passed over a

At Oakland Airport, ready to start on the transpacific flight, the *Southern Cross* is towed out to the runway by the airport's new "Caterpillar" tractor. (NASM)

ship and Kingsford-Smith signaled with the Fokker's searchlight—a 6,000-foot beam fitted with a Morse key. The vessel answered by flashing its mast lights. About 800 miles from Honolulu Warner was able to communicate with the Matson liner S.S. *Maliko,* which was equipped with a radio compass, and passed a series of check bearings.

Shortly after daybreak Ulm passed a note back to Lyon stating that a small island was in sight to the left of the nose. To the navigator this was alarming as it indicated that the aircraft was well off course. He wrote:

> The sensation of having missed my landfall was sickening. A check back on my last sights showed me to be on my course but I knew there were no rocks in that vicinity, so we changed course and headed for the rocks. As we neared them they suddenly came up out of the water and drifted away—clouds. The reaction of the crew was peculiar: the other three took it as a great disappointment. I was elated. So we changed back to our original course.

Kingsford-Smith watches a mechanic hand-crank the electrical energizer to start the Fokker's Wright Whirlwind engines. (NASM)

101

Radio operator James Warner at his position in the cabin. The Fokker carried the very latest in radio equipment. (Queensland Newspapers)

During the remainder of the flight the crew of the *Southern Cross* was to encounter many similar marine mirages caused by rain showers, clouds, and their shadows. They constituted a real trap for unwary fliers desperately scanning the horizon for island pinpoints. One wonders if early fliers lost in the Pacific may have wandered way off course chasing "islands" that vanished.

Shortly after the aircraft returned to its original course, Lyon's superb navigation was confirmed when Warner picked up the Hawaiian radio beacon. They were within a couple of miles of his plotted position. Their first sight of land was the peak of Mauna Kea poking above the clouds. Beneath it lay the island of Hawaii.

As they descended toward the island of Oahu a formation of Army escort aircraft took off from Wheeler Field. It was lead by the Fokker *Bird of Paradise,* which had pioneered the route. At the controls was Capt. Lowell Smith, leader of the U.S. Army World Flight. Shortly after noon the *Southern Cross* landed at Wheeler Field. The flight from Oakland had taken 27 hours and 25 minutes.

They were greeted by Governor Farrington and an excited crowd of fifteen thousand. Among the first to congratulate them were Dole Derby winners (and survivors) Art Goebel and Martin Jensen and Hawaiian air pioneer Charlie Stoffer.

"The thing we really craved most was a cigarette," recalled Lyon, adding, "We carried none on the flight and were really afraid to smoke in the air. We were all more or less deaf and people were wondering why we were yelling at each other while apparently holding an ordinary conversation."

While the men slept that night at the Royal Hawaiian Hotel, Lowell Smith and a team of Army mechanics generously made a thorough inspection of the *Southern Cross*. Late the following day the Fokker was ferried to Kauai as it required the expanse of Barking Sands for the maximum-load takeoff for Fiji. Workmen had cleared trees from the edge of the beach to provide a 4,500-foot takeoff strip. Gone was the safety of Oakland's long runway, but at least the sand strip was longer than Wheeler Field. Kingsford-Smith had calculated that in the cool of the morning Barking Sands' runway should be sufficient for the Fokker's heaviest-ever takeoff. For the leg to Suva they would carry 1,300 gallons of fuel—100 more than their Oakland load. It gave them a no-wind safety margin of about 600 miles (six hours' cruising).

Arriving at Honolulu's Wheeler Field, the crew of the *Southern Cross* is given a traditional Hawaiian welcome. From left: Warner, Kingsford-Smith, Lyon, and Ulm. (NASM)

At 5:22 A.M. on June 3, they took off with 1,000 feet of the hard, wet sand runway to spare. It took 6 minutes to climb to 300 feet where they soon encountered turbulence. Ulm watched tensely as Kingsford-Smith struggled to minimize its effect. Both men were well aware that turbulence posed the greatest danger during the early overloaded stages of the flight. Until they had burned off fuel the buffeting could easily cause a structural failure. Once they had passed clear of the islands the turbulence stopped and both men relaxed.

Their navigation on departure was assisted by the obliging men of the Army Signal Corps who had rotated the Maui beam and aligned it with their track. However, its welcoming guidance was short-lived, for soon after intercepting the beam about 100 miles out, the aircraft's radio failed. As the Hawaiian Islands vanished astern, the *Southern Cross* was being pushed along by a strong tail wind. "It was very helpful and, in fact, assured us of reaching Suva," Lyon wrote, explaining their emergency plan of action should they strike unusual head winds:

Our plan was to fly until abreast of the Phoenix group of islands which were only 200 miles off the course, then check the fuel and see if we could make it. If we were sure we could not do so, we had planned to make a forced landing on Enderbury Island at daylight but to send out an SOS before doing so.

An hour later they ran into a succession of storms that were to batter them for the rest of the flight. Kingsford-Smith recalled:

The dark curtains closed in on us, beset us from every side, and merged into a great belt of swishing water. We were flying at 600 feet, and overloaded as we were, this rain blown by choppy gusts was a specially unwelcome turn in the weather. Visibility shrank, the rain became thicker, and at 11:50 we were flying blind and climbing to get out of the deluge. In the heavy water-laden air and the waves of heat from the engines we began to perspire. As we took our coats off we swept past a cloud bank that was just dissolving into a rainstorm that looked even more wicked than those through which we had just passed.

After several hours they broke into the clear and Ulm took over while the exhausted and soaked Kingsford-Smith slept at the controls. Through the afternoon and into the night the succession of storms continued. Staying low to conserve fuel and maintain visual contact with the sea, they were averaging 106 mph. But by 7:45 P.M. they were cruising at 8,000 feet. This greatly increased their fuel consumption but they had been forced high to avoid severe turbulence, and to locate cloud breaks so that Lyon could fix their position by the stars. Since nightfall Kingsford-Smith's blind-flying training had paid dividends as he concentrated on his instruments to maintain heading and altitude. At one stage they circled for an hour as Kingsford-Smith fought for height to cross above a particularly violent storm cloud. Around midnight they briefly topped the clouds at 10,000 feet and Lyon glimpsed the glittering constellation of the Southern Cross. Taking a fix, he was able to advise his companions that they had passed the equator and were in the Southern Hemisphere. Their celebrations were cut short by another towering tropical storm. Ulm wrote in his log: "The storm seems all around us now. Smithy is at the controls. Thank God he is the flier he is. . . . Rain bloody rain all around and that ripsnorter of a wind!"

Shortly before daybreak they were confronted by a line of severe electrical storms and had to descend to 400 feet. The wind swung around onto the nose and they became worried that they might not reach Suva. Warner had managed to repair the radios and Ulm instructed him to transmit their position regularly. The storms intensified as bolts of lightning illuminated the sea and severe turbulence shook the Fokker. Maintaining control required the combined efforts of both pilots and in the cabin Warner and Lyon had to abandon their jobs and hold on for dear life. In the predawn half-light Kingsford-Smith ordered Warner to reel in the trailing antenna so that he could take the aircraft down to the wave tops, not only to conserve fuel but also to keep visual contact with the sea. Even then, they flew blind for short periods as the Fokker passed through patches of particularly heavy rain.

At about 7 A.M. they broke out into relatively clear skies and Lyon was able to do a new calculation which indicated they were about 700 miles from Suva. Their respite was brief as shortly thereafter they entered another area of storms, which cut the Fokker's ground speed back even further. They had been airborne nearly 30 hours and were physically and mentally exhausted. Kingsford-Smith appeared depressed and an equally gloomy Ulm wrote in the log: "Very doubtful whether we can make Suva or not." Sensing the despondency up front, Lyon passed forward a note saying that he and Warner had just held a special meeting and had voted to nominate "Smithy for President of the United States" for the way he had battled through the night. Moments later they got another boost. The weather cleared sufficiently for Lyon to get a sighting proving they were still on course for Suva and had just enough fuel to get there.

In midafternoon they had just broken out into sunlight when the Fiji Islands appeared on the horizon. At 3:50 P.M. local time Kingsford-Smith brought the *Southern Cross* in for a landing at Suva's Albert Park sports ground. As theirs was the first aircraft ever to come to the islands, there was no airfield in Fiji and the 1,300-foot-long park was the only suitable cleared ground. Even

Kingsford-Smith was forced to resort to performing an intentional ground loop to land the Fokker in Suva's tiny Albert Park. (NASM)

The *Southern Cross* pulled well above the high-water mark for its overnight stop on Fiji's Naselai Beach. (NASM)

though surrounding telegraph lines had been lowered and trees lopped, rising ground on the approach made it impossible for Kingsford-Smith to touch down until well into the field. With the boundary fence coming up fast, and the Fokker not equipped with brakes, a crash seemed inevitable. However, at the last possible moment Kingsford-Smith brought the aircraft to a halt by swinging it around in a deliberate ground loop. The bush-pilot maneuver was timed to perfection and left the Fokker undamaged. Stone deaf and dizzy from their 34½-hour ordeal the crew stum-

bled groggily to the ground unable to hear that Fiji's British governor was inviting them to a ceremonial lunch. "Yes, sir, isn't it," a confused Kingsford-Smith shouted in reply, before spotting an old friend among the crowd and yelling, "Hey, Mac. Give me a smoke—quickly."

Two days later fuel had been transported by sea to Naselai Beach on a nearby island—the only suitable takeoff run in the Fiji Islands. A check had shown that the Fokker had reached Suva with just 30 gallons (about forty-five minutes) of fuel left in the tanks, and a little extra was added for the flight to Naselai Beach. In the midafternoon of June 8 the *Southern Cross* made a trouble-free takeoff. For the flight to Brisbane, Kingsford-Smith wore a ceremonial whale's tooth—a good-luck gift from a Fijian chief. The charm seemed to have little effect, for soon after takeoff their vital earth inductor compass failed. Its failure, Lyon later admitted, was their own mistake as they had forgotten to oil it before leaving Fiji. But their compass problem was insignificant compared with the storm clouds that quickly appeared on the horizon. Kingsford-Smith described their encounter with the worst weather of the Pacific crossing:

> The visibility dwindled to a mile, then down to a few yards, then to nothing. Torrential rain began to drum and rattle on the windshield. I began to climb to get above it. Raking gusts jolted the plane so that we had to hold on to our seats. We were tearing through a black chaos of rain and cloud at 85 knots (98 mph) and our very speed increased the latent fury of the storm. We plunged on with no idea whatever of where we were. Any attempt at navigation was useless. We were circling, plunging, climbing, dodging the squalls as the poor old *Southern Cross* pitched and tossed wildly about. For four solid hours, from eight until midnight, we endured these terrible conditions.

For most of this time it again required the combined strength of Kingsford-Smith and Ulm to keep the Fokker under control. Although the weather improved after midnight, they struck more storms before daylight. But with much of their fuel load used, they were now able to climb above the worst of the weather. At daybreak they flew into clear weather. Having been unable to do any worthwhile navigation throughout the night, Lyon could only guess at their position. He suggested a due-west heading, knowing full well that they could not fail to make landfall with the whole of Australia only a few hours ahead. He must have been thankful that they had not encountered similar conditions approaching Suva, for

when the *Southern Cross* eventually crossed the Australian coast, they were 110 miles off course!

Crowds jammed Brisbane's Eagle Farm airport to greet their hometown hero. The four crewmen were carried shoulder high from the *Southern Cross* as police tried vainly to control the crowd. Everyone was determined to pat them on the back. Later as they drove into the city the streets were lined with cheering crowds. At the City Hall, desperately battling deafness, the four men spoke briefly of their ordeal and in particular of the final 21½ hours—the most difficult and slowest part of the flight. The following day they flew to Sydney where three hundred thousand people greeted them at Mascot Aerodrome. The men were bombarded with welcoming speeches by a bevy of distinguished politicians though, as Ulm wryly pointed out: "There were many wanting to shake our hand who had earlier called us idiots, and demanded we return by ship."

Interviewed by an American correspondent, Lyon and Warner were asked their impressions of their "Australian boss." "We wouldn't be standing here in Sydney now, being idolized, if it weren't for Smithy's skill as a flier. I like the guy. He knows what he wants and how to go about getting it," said Warner. Lyon, however, was a little more guarded with his praise, saying:

> He is a hellish stickler for perfection. While he has the ability to delegate tasks he also sees to it that each member of his crew keeps right on top of his particular job. I wouldn't want to fly with him too often. He's a tough boss. Although I like the man personally, and greatly admire his skill, he can be short tempered— even a bit hard to get along with. He's a real individualist.

The first true transpacific flight had taken eight and a half days, during which the crew of the *Southern Cross* had been airborne for 83 hours and 15 minutes. Kingsford-Smith was at the controls for 52 of those hours and Ulm for the remainder. Nearly half the 7,400 miles between Oakland and Brisbane had been flown in storms.

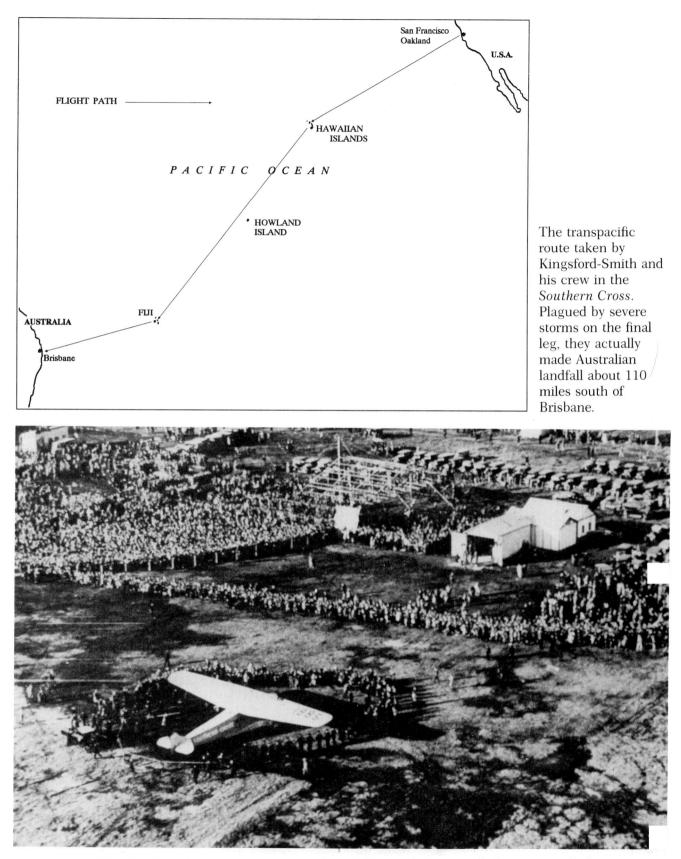

The transpacific route taken by Kingsford-Smith and his crew in the *Southern Cross*. Plagued by severe storms on the final leg, they actually made Australian landfall about 110 miles south of Brisbane.

FLIGHT PATH ⟶

San Francisco
Oakland

U.S.A.

HAWAIIAN ISLANDS

PACIFIC OCEAN

HOWLAND ISLAND

FIJI

AUSTRALIA

Brisbane

The *Southern Cross* arrives at Brisbane's Eagle Farm Airport following the first successful aerial crossing of the Pacific Ocean. (NASM)

107

Pith-helmeted Queensland
police help move the
Southern Cross following
its arrival at Brisbane's
Eagle Farm Airport.
(Queensland Newspapers)

The Pacific had been conquered, but clearly it could at best be considered an experimental victory. The time involved and the hazardous flying conditions were totally unsuitable for any thoughts of mounting a passenger service. Nor could consideration be given a transpacific airmail or freight service until aircraft were available that could carry a profitable payload as well as the required fuel. Like Lindbergh, Kingsford-Smith and Ulm had been attention getters, key figures among the band of pioneer fliers who were aviation's public relations team during those formative years. They captured the limelight by bridging oceans and displaying the airplane's intercontinental potential, and by firing the public imagination, they helped keep the dream alive until design caught up with promise.

Among a host of congratulatory cables from around the world the one that most moved Kingsford-Smith and Ulm came from their American benefactor, Allan Hancock. It read:

I am delivering to the California Bank of Los Angeles for transmission to the Commercial Banking Company of Sydney a bill of sale transferring to Kingsford-Smith and Ulm the *Southern Cross* together with release and dis-

charge of all your indebtedness [approximately $20,000] to me. I beg you accept this gift as a token of our mutual friendship, and as my tribute to you and the *Southern Cross* and also to commemorate the magnificent achievement of yourselves and your brave American companions in bringing our two countries closer together. Andrew Chaffey joins me in saying "Advance Australia!"

No longer in debt to Hancock, Kingsford-Smith and Ulm had no need to make the film that was to have repaid their American backer. Lyon and Warner headed back to the United States, and the two Australians, believing that their Pacific flight would attract investors at home, turned their attention to forming a new domestic airline. They also had plans for initiating an airmail service to New Zealand. Nevertheless, in the years that followed, Charles Ulm's ultimate goal was to establish an international airline across the Pacific.

In America another visionary shared Ulm's dream. Juan Trippe's infant Pan American Airways was already flying international passengers from Key West 90 miles across the Straits of Florida to Havana, Cuba. One of the pilots flying the

Kingsford-Smith and his crew are taken by motorcade to Brisbane's City Hall for an official reception. In the lower picture a film crew captures the airman as he addresses the crowd. (B. Hand)

Continuing its transpacific flight from Brisbane, the *Southern Cross* descends
low over Sydney for a landing at Mascot Aerodrome. (NASM)

run in Pan Am's new Fokker trimotors was a former Army Air Service instructor named Edwin C. Musick. He was just one of a band of brilliant young men Trippe was gathering around him. Experts like Charles Lindbergh, who had been offered a position as technical adviser, and a gangling former Radio Corporation of America engineer named Hugo Leuteritz, who was working on a new lightweight navigation system that would revolutionize transoceanic flying.

"We'll fly to Latin America. We'll fly the Atlantic and the Pacific," Trippe predicted as Pan Am spread across the Caribbean. Lindbergh, Leuteritz, and Musick were going to help the young airline builder achieve that goal. Like Kingsford-Smith and Ulm, all of them knew it was only a matter of time and the right airplane.

Safely landed at Mascot Aerodome. Although this photo doesn't show it, at Sydney a crowd of three hundred thousand, almost half the city's population, welcomed the *Southern Cross*. (NASM)

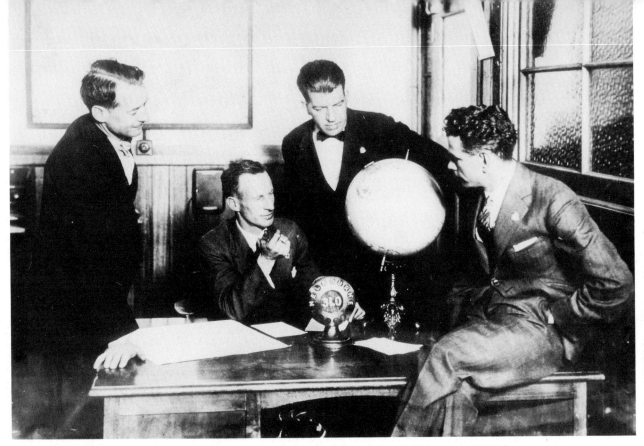

After continuing their triumphant aerial tour to Melbourne, the four airmen discussed their flight on national radio. From left: Warner, Kingsford-Smith, Lyon, and Ulm. (NASM)

In 1978, marking Australia's fiftieth anniversary celebration of his father's Pacific conquest, Charles Kingsford-Smith, Jr., of Colorado, copiloted a Cessna 340 on a transpacific delivery flight to Brisbane, Australia. The most poignant moment of the celebration came when Charles sat in the *Southern Cross*. (TGJ)

Ulm recalled that many on the official welcoming dais at Sydney Airport had earlier "called us idiots." The crew of the *Southern Cross* poses for photographs. From left: Kingsford-Smith, Ulm, Lyon, and Warner (below Lyon). (State Library of New South Wales)

Today the *Southern Cross* is housed in a special display building at Brisbane's Eagle Farm Airport. (TGJ)

A part of the enormous crowd that gathered in Christchurch, New Zealand, to greet the *Southern Cross* following its 1928 trans-Tasman conquest. (State Library of New South Wales)

7

Trans-Tasman Flights

The Tasman Sea at the southwest extremities of the Pacific Ocean separates Australia and New Zealand. Between 1,250 and 1,350 miles across, depending on the points of landfall, it is fed by the warm, swirling East Australian Current and is notorious for its violent and unpredictable storms. Early in 1928 the Tasman, like the Pacific, remained unconquered by air.

At the time New Zealand lay too far south to be considered as a transpacific steppingstone between Australia and the United States. However, the little British colony looked to the day when its own air services would wing over its long-established sea routes to Los Angeles and Panama. But for the present there was a more pressing need to inaugurate airmail and passenger services with Australia.

Australia and New Zealand, both members of the British Empire, shared close cultural and trade links that also extended back to mother England. Already a number of fliers had linked Australia with the "old country." In terms of future air services the most important had been the round trip from England to Australia and back made by Alan Cobham in 1926, surveying the route for Britain's expanding Imperial Airways. It was only a matter of time before someone attempted to extend that route, across the Tasman, to New Zealand.

The first bid was announced following Lindbergh's Atlantic crossing. Two Air Corps reserve officers, John Moncrieff and George Hood, decided to claim the honor for New Zealand. Hood, a World War I veteran with a wooden leg, had won his place by the toss of a coin with a third airman. Like Lindbergh, the airmen chose a high-winged Ryan monoplane for their attempt. Their machine was a B-4 Brougham—a five-seat passenger machine. The prototype B-1 had been under construction at the time Lindbergh placed his order for the *Spirit of St. Louis*, and the Brougham series eventually bore a striking resemblance to his specially designed transatlantic

New Zealand Air Corps reserve officers John Moncrieff (left) and George Hood shortly before their tragic trans-Tasman flight. (Whites Aviation)

machine. The New Zealander's Ryan was shipped by sea to Australia where it was assembled and christened *Aoeta-Roa* (Land of the Long White Cloud), the Maori name for New Zealand.

The venture was delayed when the prime minister of Australia banned the flight, pointing out that Commonwealth aviation regulations did not permit airplanes to fly more than 50 miles over the sea. Evidence suggests the real motive was his concern that the New Zealanders had insufficient experience and that the Ryan was inadequate for the flight. Only when the New Zealand premier intervened, pointing out that his aviation experts were satisfied, was permission finally given for the airmen to leave Australia.

They took off from Richmond, near Sydney, on January 10, 1928. Since neither man could operate a radio, they had equipped the *Aoeta-Roa* with an automatic transmitter. It sent out a series of "bleeps" every 15 minutes to let listening radio stations know they were still airborne. The automatic signals were heard regularly and two ships reported seeing the Ryan pass overhead. In New Zealand thousands gathered at Wellington's Trentham Racecourse to greet the heroes.

The *Aoeta-Roa* was estimated to be less than 200 miles out when the signals ceased. Even so,

no one was unduly alarmed because wireless transmitters of the day were notoriously unreliable. However, as the hours passed, concern grew for the airmen's safety. As always there were rumors. The plane had been seen crossing the coast; it had landed safely elsewhere; it was nearing Wellington. The crowd lingered until midnight keeping the vigil with the two airmen's wives. Finally, glancing at her watch, Moncrieff's wife said quietly, "Their petrol is out."

A massive sea and land search was mounted. While ships searched the Tasman in the area where it was thought the last radio signal would have been transmitted, ground parties scoured the coastal Rimutaka Ranges where some believed the airmen had crash-landed. A violent storm in the Tasman finally ended all hope that Moncrieff and Hood might be found alive. All New Zealand mourned their loss.

Nine months later, on September 10, 1928, the Tasman was finally crossed when Charles Kingsford Smith and Charles Ulm took off in the *Southern Cross* following in the slipstream of the lost New Zealand fliers. Fresh from their Pacific conquest, the Australians were promoting their plan for a trans-Tasman airmail service. Departing from Richmond Airport, near Sydney, they

Hood and Moncrieff purchased a Ryan Brougham. This heavily retouched picture shows them preparing for the Tasman flight. Sharing some common features with Charles Lindbergh's Ryan NYP, Broughams were sold as "sister ships" of the *Spirit of St. Louis*. (Whites Aviation)

flew through severe storms for much of the flight and for the first time in their careers encountered icing. Not only was the Fokker's airframe loaded with ice but at one stage the airspeed indicator registered zero as the pitot tube iced over. At night an electrical storm put the radios out of action as lightning danced around the aircraft. After 14 alarming hours, they dived down through a small break in the clouds, and sighted New Zealand.

Thirty thousand fans mobbed the Australians at Christchurch and the New Zealand government awarded them a grant of $4,000, worth about $50,000 today. Conditions were even worse on the return flight. Again flying through violent storms and buffeted by freezing head winds, it took 23½ hours. When the *Southern Cross* finally landed back at Richmond only ten minutes' fuel remained.

Although the Tasman had been conquered, the public still waited to see who would be first to make a solo crossing. Like Lindbergh's solo Atlantic flight—which had been preceded eight years earlier by Alcock and Brown in their multiengine Vickers Vimy—the public had a vicarious fascination with the idea of the lone pilot challenging the odds in a single-engine aircraft. Three years passed before a pilot took up the challenge, and unlike other Tasman flights, it took

place in secret. A twenty-one-year-old Australian, Guy Menzies, aware that he would not get approval from Australia's tough Department of Civil Aviation, pioneered "wrong-way" flying. A similar stunt brought world fame to America's Douglas Corrigan seven years later when, supposedly setting out on a nonstop flight from New York to California in a beat-up old monoplane, he "mistakenly" set the compass incorrectly and ended up in Ireland! However, unlike Corrigan, who never admitted to his transatlantic aspirations, the dapper son of a Sydney doctor later made no bones about the fact that he deliberately bamboozled the authorities.

Menzies was a part owner of the Avro Avian IVA *Southern Cross Junior*, which had previously been used by Charles Kingsford-Smith on an England-Australia record flight. Powered by a 120-hp de Havilland Gipsy engine and equipped with special fuel tanks, the little biplane had a range of 1,700 miles and a cruising speed of 94 mph. Even though three years had passed since the *Aotea-Roa* had vanished, the authorities were violently opposed to overwater flight by single-engine aircraft, particularly involving young, unknown pilots. To cover his plan, Menzies announced a westbound flight across Australia to test the maximum range of Avro. He did not confide his real destination even to his family.

Just after midnight on January 7, 1931, moments before taking off from Sydney's Mascot Aerodrome, Menzies beckoned his brother to the plane and handed him a bundle of letters addressed to family and friends. All were marked "Not to be opened until after takeoff" and contained the news of his real intentions. The reckless airman was out over the Tasman by the time the letters were opened. There was little anyone could do besides notify New Zealand that Menzies was on the way, and pray. Even though the flight was considered to be a dangerous prank, there was great excitement when the news reached New Zealand. But excitement soon turned to anxiety when he appeared to be overdue. Unknown to the authorities, the airman had made a fast crossing fanned by strong tail winds. However, on reaching the rugged coast he had been unable to locate a landing ground. For some time he flew north along the beach looking for an open area. Eventually, with fuel running low, he landed on what he thought was a smooth patch of ground on the banks of the Wanganui River. On touching down the wheels bogged in marshy ground and the *Southern Cross Junior* flipped over on its back. Menzies crawled out unhurt. He had taken 12¼ hours to cover the 1,200 miles and had less than a gallon of fuel remaining.

Following the flight, Australia's director of Civil Aviation received a postdated letter from Menzies. In it the audacious young flier stated that he took sole responsibility for the "unsanctioned flight," had known that the director would have prevented it, and fully understood that the department would be "compelled to take some action." Explaining his motivation, Menzies wrote: "It has been my lifelong ambition to fly a single-engine plane to New Zealand, and having this opportunity, I found it quite impossible to resist the, shall we say, temptation." With Menzies a national hero, and touched possibly by the cavalier young flier's letter, the director showed remarkable understanding, decreeing that "Prior to any congratulations on his remarkably courageous and highly expert effort, Menzies on his return to Australia will be officially admonished."

The excitement over Menzies's flight had hardly died down when a New Zealand pilot announced his intention to cross the Tasman in the other direction. Francis Chichester, long before he became famous as a round-the-world yachtsman, was planning a seaplane crossing via the minuscule Norfolk and Lord Howe islands. At the age of eighteen the British-born adventurer had emigrated to New Zealand with twenty dollars in his pocket. To establish himself in his adopted country he took any job: stoker, shepherd, lumberjack, coal miner, and prospector. He eventually became part owner of a tiny aviation business and decided to learn to fly.

Chichester trained in England and in 1930, two years after Australian Bert Hinkler's pioneering flight, became the second pilot to fly solo from England to Australia. Upon arriving in Sydney, Chichester and his de Havilland Gipsy Moth *Madame Elijah* sailed home to New Zealand—the little British biplane had insufficient range to cross the Tasman.

Back in New Zealand Chichester was plagued by an obsession to do something that no other pilot had yet achieved—to become the first flier to solo around the world. He decided to continue with his flight from England and carry on eastward, land-hugging across the Pacific via the Aleutian Islands and Alaska, then over Canada before crossing the Atlantic via Greenland, Iceland, and the Scottish isles. His first hurdle was to recross the Tasman and intercept a suitable air route via Australia, New Guinea, and the Philippines to Japan. His Moth lacked the range to span the Tasman so he decided to use a circuitous flight path via the tiny islands of Lord Howe and Norfolk. As neither of the craggy little islets was suitable for landing, he equipped *Madame Elijah* with floats.

Though ignored by most aviation historians, Chichester's flight was to have a great bearing on future aviation navigational techniques. He was faced with the problem of locating the microscopic islands after flying more than 500 miles over open sea. Norfolk Island is only 5 miles long and 3 miles across. Lord Howe Island is even

The "wrong-way" crossing of the Tasman by Guy Menzies (in white shirt) ended with his Avro Avian upside down in a New Zealand swamp. (Whites Aviation)

In 1928 Francis Chichester and his business partner, Geoffrey Goodwin, formed a small charter and joy flight company. Shown here is one of the company's four pilots in an Avro Avian. Chichester became fascinated by flying and in 1929 sailed to England where he gained a pilot license at the de Havilland School. (Whites Aviation)

smaller, less than half the size of Norfolk. With no navigator, no radio aids, and no features on the open sea to visually check his progress, he was faced with flying a precomputed heading that allowed for the forecast wind. However, wind reports were notoriously unreliable and pilots were lucky to hold an accurate heading to within 2 degrees. Thus Chichester estimated that an overall track error of 10 degrees was quite possible. That could mean missing Norfolk Island or Lord Howe by at least 80 miles—a potentially fatal margin.

He decided to teach himself marine navigation, using a sextant and reading the sun to fix his

Madame Elijah is lifted from the sea to the jetty at Norfolk Island's Cascade Bay. (Queensland Newspapers)

position. To overcome the seemingly impossible task of taking accurate sextant readings from a bumping aircraft, he spent days practicing in the back seat of an open car being driven along a beach. Despite becoming skilled at taking accurate readings, he found that the marine system did not work for aircraft. Refusing to give up, Chichester searched scores of books for a solution. He eventually came upon a clue to a new method of astronavigation in a British naval textbook published in 1840. From it he evolved a system of flying a curved path, based on the sun's position, to a point on the chart 80 nautical miles abeam his destination. Once at that phantom

point, having deliberately aimed well to one side of the island, he knew which way to turn down a precomputed "line of position" joining the sunshot, abeam point and the island. The procedure was dubbed "Chichester's theory of the deliberate error" and became a standard navigational technique used by early transoceanic airlines and by Allied maritime patrol aircraft during World War II.

Chichester took off from Auckland harbor at dawn on March 28, 1931. He had just twelve hours of daylight to reach Norfolk Island, 600 miles away, and this included a stop at the northern tip of New Zealand to top off his little fuel

Chichester's flight almost ended at Lord Howe Island when his aircraft overturned at its moorings during a severe storm. (Queensland Newspapers)

Chichester (on ladder) rebuilt the *Madame Elijah* with help from Lord Howe Islanders. (Queensland Newspapers)

Chichester and a Lord Howe Islander repairing the wings of the *Madame Elijah*. (Queensland Newspapers)

tank. The flight was a formidable task in an aircraft that cruised at 70 mph. Recalling a moment of panic when a miscalculation of time produced an apparent error of 100 miles, Chichester later wrote:

> I felt desperate at thinking of all the blunders of this kind I could make. However, I recovered; the work required extraordinary concentration. It had been easy enough in a car driven at 50 mph by someone else; in a seaplane it was at first difficult to concentrate enough while attending to the five instrument readings, maintaining a compass course, reducing the sun sight, and solving the spherical triangle involved. The 100-mph wind of the propeller slip-stream, which struck the top of my head just above the windshield, made concentrating difficult; so did the pulsating roar from the open exhausts.

Due to Chichester's superb navigation, Norfolk Island came in sight within minutes of his estimated time of arrival and he landed safely in Cascade Bay. Two days later, after repairing a leaking float, he headed for Lord Howe Island. Less than three hours out, the aircraft started to vibrate. As it became more severe Chichester noticed that the screws holding the compass had worked loose and the compass had rotated out of place. Using a small pocket compass he realigned the aircraft compass as best he could, crossed his fingers, and carried on. By the time he reached the turn-off point for Lord Howe the vibration was so severe that both altimeters and the airspeed indicator had stopped working. At his estimated arrival time, no land was in sight. Chichester was reaching for something to eat to ease the worry when the jagged peak of little Lord Howe emerged from a rain squall ahead. He landed safely, moored in the harbor, and went ashore to spend the night at the home of one of the island's handful of residents.

During the night Chichester was awakened by a violent Tasman storm and the next morning he found *Madame Elijah* upside down and partially submerged at her mooring. The only salvageable parts were the fuselage, the engine, and the floats. Over the next forty days, in an old boat shed under a Banyan tree, a minor miracle took place. Chichester had no training in engineering, yet, helped by unskilled but inventive islanders, he dismantled and cleaned out the engine, built new wings, then reconstructed and recovered the Moth's wood and fabric airframe.

On June 10, after taking each of his island helpers for a short flight in "their" plane, Chichester resumed his trans-Tasman crossing. During the six-hour flight to Australia, Chichester was bombarded by torrential rain, winds, and turbulence and flew blind for several hours. Even when he finally broke into the clear he experienced another fearful phenomenon when he was confronted by a UFO. He later described it as a huge white airship with gleaming lights marking its nose and tail. Chichester reported that it seemed to vanish, then reappear directly in front of his aircraft. As it drew closer the phantom airship seemed to shrink, then become transparent before vanishing completely. Alarmed and confused, Chichester could think of no explanation for the ethereal aircraft—in 1931 the world had not yet been bombarded with reports of flying saucers and other UFOs.

Chichester finally landed safely in Jervis Bay, south of Sydney, where he became the honored guest of the Royal Australian Navy aboard the aircraft carrier H.M.A.S. *Albatross*. When toasted for having completed the first east-west Tasman crossing, Chichester, with a twinkle in his eye, replied: "One day I am going to write a book on that flight called 'Lord how I found Lord Howe Island.' "

Six weeks later he took off again to continue his flight around the world. Following Australia's eastern coastline he eventually island-hopped around the rim of the Pacific to Japan. There the flight and Chichester's aviation pioneering came to a tragic end. Charles Lindbergh and his wife were arriving in Japan on a Pan American Airways survey flight from Alaska as Chichester prepared to fly the reverse of their route. Taking off at Katsuura, he had just become airborne when *Madame Elijah* collided with telegraph lines

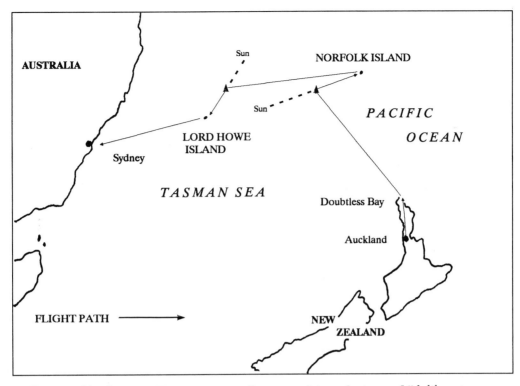

Francis Chichester's Tasman route illustrates his technique of "deliberate error." The triangles mark the points where he intercepted his predetermined lines of position.

stretching between hills flanking the harbor. His eyes injured, Chichester was blind as the stricken biplane fell several hundred feet into the sea wall. Chichester received terrible injuries but miraculously survived, and surgeons managed to save his sight.

In 1967 Chichester finally accomplished his dream of circumnavigating the world alone. In place of his beloved de Havilland *Madame Elijah,* Chichester sailed a yacht he wistfully named *Gipsy Moth* nonstop around the world—becoming the first ever to do so. Finally world famous, he was knighted by Queen Elizabeth II for his lifetime of adventures. Before his death in 1972 Sir Francis Chichester recalled: "I found flying more exciting than sailing, particularly that flight across the Tasman Sea. Evolving a new method of navigation and knowing if you failed you would finish up in the drink. That sort of challenge is what life is made of."

Despite Chichester's trans-Tasman flight, other New Zealanders were still determined to make a nonstop crossing from Australia. None was more patriotic, or more reckless, than Raymond Whitehead. On the spur of the moment, encouraged by an Australian-born friend, Rex Nicholl, Whitehead decided to attack Charles Kingsford-Smith's 10-hour trans-Tasman record. Their crazy plan had all the trappings of the foolhardy flights that were taking place over the Atlantic where, attempting to emulate Lindbergh, inexperienced pilots in dubious aircraft were setting out for fun, to win a bet, or just (in the case of several socialites) to be fashionable. Yet it is doubtful if even the most bizarre Atlantic fliers matched the stupidity of Whitehead and Nicholl.

Their aircraft, a de Havilland D.H.80A Puss Moth, had not been adapted for long-range flight, having neither extra fuel tanks nor an increased-

Francis Chichester and his de Havilland Gipsy Moth 60 *Madame Elijah*. (NASM)

capacity oil tank. Extra oil was vital as the Moth's 120-hp Gipsy engine was a notorious oil burner that required topping off even after a normal flight of only a couple of hours' duration. With this deplorable thirst for oil, the sump would be empty long before Whitehead and Nicholl reached New Zealand and the engine would seize. Clearly requiring a method of airborne reoiling, the airmen devised a system that was as crude as it was fraught with danger. They ran a length of hose from the main reservoir in the engine back into the cockpit. The hose was sealed off at the pilot's end with a wooden plug. To add oil the flier would remove the plug and replace it with a tin funnel into which spare oil could be poured as it was needed. The Puss Moth's normal fuel tank held only 42 gallons, and without major modifications, the only place to carry the required extra 100 gallons of fuel was in its narrow enclosed cockpit. To make space for the tanks,

Whitehead and Nicholl were forced to gut the little cabin and replace the pilot's seat with a small wooden board. They tied a small cushion onto the board with string to give some small degree of comfort.

As their preparations advanced it became obvious that flying the aircraft and topping off the engine was a two-man job. But with the extra tanks on board and the seats gone, it appeared impossible to fit a second man. The only space remaining where a body could possibly just squeeze in was on the floor between the pilot's legs! Nicholl and Whitehead tried it. By playing amateur contortionists, they managed it, but only just; so tight was the fit that they even had to remove their shoes. Satisfied that their machine was now adequate to the job, they applied the final touch, painting *Faith in New Zealand* on the engine cowling.

Their homespun modifications would have

124

Chichester takes off from Sydney Harbor on his planned transpacific flight via the Philippines, China, Japan, and Alaska. (Queensland Newspapers)

The mangled wreckage of Chichester's Gipsy Moth on the sea wall at Katsuura, Japan. The airman miraculously survived, but his terrible injuries ended his solo flying days. (Queensland Newspapers)

given an aircraft engineer nightmares, yet the two fliers could see nothing really wrong. Thus they stood in mute disbelief when astounded Department of Civil Aviation inspectors took one look at the bastardized aircraft and immediately withdrew its Certificate of Airworthiness, grounding it on the spot. The experts considered the whole project suicidal and had taken the only step available to them in an attempt to prevent a likely disaster. Their action did not have the desired effect. In fact it made the young men more determined than ever to make the flight, and they decided to defy the law and make a secret crossing. Possibly they thought back to Guy Menzies and how he got away with thumbing his nose at authority.

Late in the evening of November 21, 1934, Whitehead and Nicholl smuggled *Faith in New Zealand* to Gerringong Beach, on the coast south of Sydney. Their frenzied spur-of-the-moment preparations over the previous 48 hours had left no time for either man to sleep, let alone complete the tiresome chore of organizing proper flight and navigation plans. So, while waiting for the tide to go out, they prepared their flight plan for the crossing. On their map they drew a straight line across to Auckland on New Zealand's North Island. The first half of the line they labeled "Water," and the second half they labeled "More Water."

A small group of close friends, sworn to secrecy, waited with them on the beach. Shortly after midnight the tide was well out and bright moonlight illuminated the broad expanse of hard sand now exposed by the receding water. The fliers began their final preparations: fuel tanks were filled to brimming and the vital extra oil was stowed aboard. Somehow space was found for a flask of coffee, sandwiches, chewing gum, and caffeine tablets. The sand was at its hardest and it was time to go. The barefoot aviators did their sardine act and squeezed between the cabin tank and the aircraft's controls.

The engine burst into life, shattering the silence of the lonely beach. With Whitehead at the controls they pointed down the longest available takeoff run. A handful of flickering flares and a car's headlights augmented the moonlight as the Puss Moth started its long, trundling takeoff run. It lurched slowly across the sand seeming hardly to accelerate as its overweight, the sticky sand, and the lack of wind all combined to retard the de Havilland's progress. Finally the wheels broke ground and the aircraft staggered slowly into the air not a moment too soon. Within seconds they were over the water and the onlookers froze as one wheel clipped the crest of the surf. It seemed that a crash was inevitable as the nose yawed and the wing dipped but somehow Whitehead maintained control of the nearly stalled aircraft. Back on an even keel, *Faith in New Zealand* skimmed the waves, inch by inch gaining height. Once safely clear of the sea the aircraft gradually turned east and headed out across the Tasman.

Whitehead later admitted that during the early hours of the flight he had great difficulty in controlling the overloaded aircraft. Their cruising speed was well below normal and attempts to climb brought them dangerously close to stalling. They had to wait until the burn-off of the excess fuel lightened the aircraft before it began to handle normally. The pilot's control problems were severely aggravated by his cramped position— jammed on the tiny wooden bench with his companion squatting between his unnaturally wide stretched legs. Nicholl's plight was not much better. He had an equally difficult task as, from his squatting position, he had to continually transfer fuel from the cabin tanks with a hand pump and every hour pour a quart of oil into the thirsty engine's sump.

They were only a hundred miles out when trouble struck. The cabin quickly filled with choking fumes from the hot engine oil. Whitehead opened the aircraft's windows but the situation rapidly got worse and the men feared suffocation in the confined space. Nicholl desperately searched for the cause and not a moment too soon his flashlight beam disclosed the trouble: the wooden plug of their ill-conceived reoiling system was not sealing properly. Both men realized that if they could not rectify the problem they were in diabolical trouble. Several attempts to seal it were unsuccessful and they searched for a suitable replacement. Nicholl eventually manufactured a new stopper out of a flashlight battery wrapped with adhesive tape. It made an airtight fit and the fumes died away as the Puss Moth flew steadily toward the dawn-lit horizon.

Four hundred miles out Whitehead spotted a steamer. It broke the monotony of the empty sea but did little else to encourage them. They were unable to communicate with it or anyone else for that matter because their aircraft carried no radio. Whitehead had reckoned that there would be so few ships on the route that an SOS call would be of little use if they went down in the Tasman. Besides, they could not afford the extra weight.

At daylight both men were suffering from agonizing cramps and decided to change positions. By then the aircraft had burned off sufficient fuel to make handling less critical. Earlier they had not dared to make the changeover and risk losing control of the critically unstable aircraft. The reversal of positions seemed almost impossible. It had been one thing to practice it on the ground, but now in the unstable aircraft above the empty sea it was a frightening experience. First Whitehead stood with his head and shoulders doubled up under the cabin roof and his legs wide apart. Then Nicholl forced his way back, then up between his companion's legs, as Whitehead simultaneously folded down to assume the crouched position his companion had just occupied. It required the agility of Harry Houdini and, as one wit said, "You needed to be real close friends!"

As the day passed and no coast was sighted it was obvious that the anticipated tail winds had not developed. Whitehead and Nicholl's spirits fell as the time allowed to beat the record expired and they were still over the sea. Their only consolation was the Gipsy engine which, with its hourly feed of oil, had not missed a beat. Their navigation was as simple as it was unreliable. They merely held their planned heading and hoped that the wind wasn't on their beam and that their compass was accurate. They had not even bothered to carry out a proper compass swing before their flight. Thus the nonchalant pair were unaware that the compass was faulty and that the *Faith in New Zealand* had been heading off course from the moment it left the beach at Gerringong.

Late in the afternoon the men changed positions again in an attempt to relieve the agony of their cramped quarters. Both were now gravely concerned. Landfall was long overdue and the sun was low on the horizon behind them. Both knew that if they reached land after dark there was little chance of surviving an attempted landing in unknown country. No one knew they were coming, so they reasoned that no landing strips would be illuminated. Shortly after sunset they sighted seagulls and minutes later driftwood was clearly visible from their cruising height above the water. Land must be near. They peered desperately into the gathering gloom. Moments later they sighted a group of islands that Whitehead recognized with utter disbelief as the Three Kings group. They had made it, but they were impossibly off track. The Three Kings are 40 miles off the northern tip of New Zealand. They were nearly 250 miles off course and had missed the mainland altogether!

Quickly they turned south, and half an hour later landed at nightfall on the first suitable mainland beach. They flopped from the cockpit and it took some time before the airmen could unknot themselves and regain sufficient circulation to walk. Both were physically and mentally exhausted. Enveloped in darkness and with no lights in sight, they elected to spend the night alongside their aircraft.

Meanwhile news of the fliers' clandestine flight had leaked out. In New Zealand it spread like wildfire and crowds of people had flocked to possible landing sites. Anxious eyes scanned the western horizon and they waited in near silence hoping to catch the sound of an approaching aircraft engine. By dusk fears were growing for the fliers' safety, and as darkness fell flares were readied for a possible night landing. The crowds waited well into the night but as the hours passed with no sign of the Puss Moth it seemed obvious that the airmen had run out of fuel. Most believed that Whitehead and Nicholl had suffered a similar fate to Moncrieff and Hood and the *Aotea-Roa*.

The next morning aircraft from all over New Zealand began an air search covering the coastline of both islands. Ships in the area were alerted and ground parties prepared to search the bush. Meanwhile, blissfully ignorant of the national concern, Whitehead and Nicholl had spent a miserable and hungry night on the beach. Too cold to sleep, they had sat up by a small fire and at daylight decided to carry on to Auckland. The Puss Moss had sufficient fuel left for the flight and navigation was simple. Keep New Zealand on the left and they couldn't miss. Two hours later they arrived at Auckland's Mangere Airport, still unaware that they were the center of a massive search. Later pilots from Mangere returned to base tired and dejected after hours of fruitless searching. As they taxied in they stared in disbelief. Parked on their hangar line was the missing *Faith in New Zealand* and on the grass nearby, Whitehead and Nicholl, bathed and breakfasted, calmly dozed in the sun. The searchers were not impressed.

News of Whitehead and Nicholl's arrival met with very mixed reaction. To the public they were gallant young pioneers. But to the authorities and the aviation industry, they were a pair of irresponsible young fools. Their illegal flight had been little more than a public nuisance costing the authorities and the searchers a great deal of time, money, and effort. A journalist was soon on the scene and the *Auckland Star* carried a story headlined GAME YOUNG MEN. It read:

> The story told by Ray Whitehead and Rex Nicholl to an *Auckland Star* reporter and the description of the interior of the cabin of their machine add together in a tale of thoroughgoing gameness and enthusiasm to do a heavy job in a most cheerful manner. To the delight of a small crowd at Mangere the airmen demonstrated how they had changed over their seats in the air. Even with the aeroplane on the ground, the operation appeared extremely difficult, and the spectator wondered how they must have felt when performing it in the air over a lonely sea. Only by seeing this changeover accomplished, and the conditions which made it necessary, could one realize what a remarkable feat the whole flight was. "We found that making the change was rather easier than we thought it would be," said one of them.

"We will do the six months provided they give us nice, cozy cells," Nicholl answered when the reporter suggested that the pair might be in trouble with the authorities. An unrepentant Whitehead chimed in heatedly: "You are allowed to take a boat anywhere you like. It is our craft and if we wished to bring it across, I don't see why they should stop us. We were risking only our own lives."

The magnitude of their gamble was illustrated when Nicholl admitted to the reporter that, other than watching their compass heading, neither pilot had any real means of checking their position. "We had an occasional peep at the stars in the early part of the flight," the Australian said, before conceding they had no real knowledge of astronavigation. Remarking that the pair appeared to "live on excitement," the newspaper report concluded:

> Less than $10 spent on petrol and oil was the cost of the actual flight. Preparations, however, were more expensive, but in this work they had the aid of many of their friends. When the pilots took off from Gerringong, Mr. Nicholl's watch showed five minutes before two o'clock. On their landing at the beach it showed 4:35 P.M. (6:35 P.M. New Zealand time), so that the actual flying time was 14 hours 40 minutes.

The pair had failed to beat Kingsford-Smith's record by more than four hours, but Whitehead had become the first New Zealander to cross the Tasman Sea.

The New Zealand Aero Club was holding its annual general meeting on the day Whitehead and Nicholl reached Auckland. A motion was passed that the club should "discountenance the recognition of any flights made in contravention of the law," and it issued a strongly worded release to the Auckland press. The reactions of of-

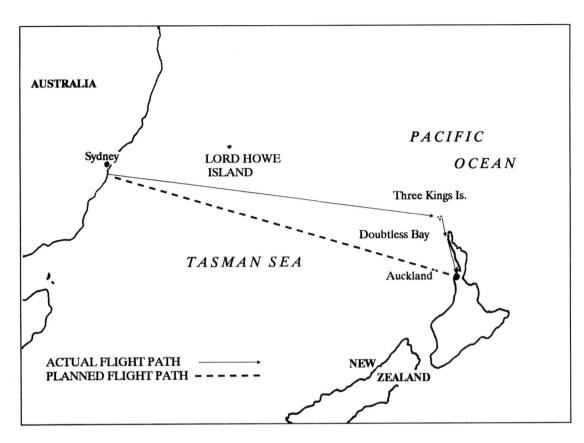

Just how close Whitehead and Nicholl came to missing New Zealand completely can be seen on the map. They were north of the Three Kings when they sighted the islands on the horizon.

ficials representing a number of the nation's aero clubs were reported. "We applaud their courage, but we don't applaud their foolhardiness," said one, suggesting that the flight could have given the general public an impression that pilots were "harebrained and light-headed" and that the authorities were not adequately controlling flying. Another angry aero club official told reporters: "I think we should not take any steps at all to recognize the flight. When I heard of the flight I was amazed and shocked that these two men should risk their lives and be so callous to all for the anxiety they caused."

From Australia came news that the controller of civil aviation had declared their actions to be foolhardy and against the interest of aviation. He stated that the Australian government was considering legal proceedings against the two pilots. The New Zealand authorities finally charged Whitehead and Nicholl with making a flight in New Zealand airspace in an aircraft not possessing a Certificate of Airworthiness. The sea cross-

ing was not mentioned as New Zealand held no jurisdiction over the Tasman Sea. Thus Whitehead and Nicholl escaped being charged with making an illegal international flight.

The adventurers had little choice but to plead guilty. They faced steep fines or a six-month jail sentence. On December 8, 1934, they appeared on the charges in the Auckland Police Court. Although they were convicted, the magistrate, possibly swayed by a secret admiration for their escapade, did not fix a penalty and freed the men. He warned, however, that others would not get off so lightly if they were foolish enough to try to emulate the fliers. Public enthusiasm had cooled off and seemed more in line with officially expressed opinions. But following the magistrate's unexpected leniency, the controversy flared again.

The cause of aviation was not helped when New Zealand's governor-general declared that all patriotic New Zealanders should feel admiration for the young men. He said: "Their revelation of

Whitehead (right) and Nicholl with the oil container and tin funnel they used for their makeshift in-flight reoiling system. (*New Zealand Herald*)

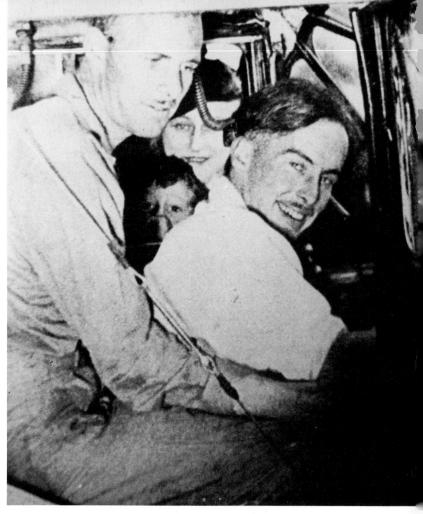

Whitehead squats between Nicholl's legs, demonstrating how the two men managed to squeeze into the tiny space that remained after the 100-gallon cabin tank was installed. (*New Zealand Herald*)

the possibilities of aviation in this part of the Empire should stimulate the imagination and zeal of many youthful New Zealanders to emulate their skill." The governor-general's grandiose statements were clearly those of a man totally unaware of the possible tragedy his suggestions could have caused. Nor were his opinions appreciated by aviation authorities desperately trying to discourage such irresponsible flights.

The irrepressible Whitehead and Nicholl remained as unconcerned as ever. Certificate of Airworthiness or not, they announced they were taking the Puss Moth on a barnstorming victory tour of the country. It was too much for the au-

thorities, who immediately withdrew their pilot licenses. Nicholl was eventually to join Qantas. His companion ended his flying career when he lost a leg in a crash in China. In the years following their flight, when experience had brought wisdom, the two men must have thought back to the moment they made landfall on their notorious adventure. They had been 10 degrees off course when they saw the Three Kings Islands at the northern tip of New Zealand. It would have been a sobering thought to realize that had they been just 1 more degree off course, they would have been 20 miles farther north and missed Three Kings also. Ahead lay the Pacific—and Peru.

In 1948, following in the slipstream of Francis Chichester, Qantas began airline services to Norfolk and Lord Howe islands. Here a converted Consolidated PB2B-2 (Catalina) unloads passengers at Lord Howe Island. (Qantas)

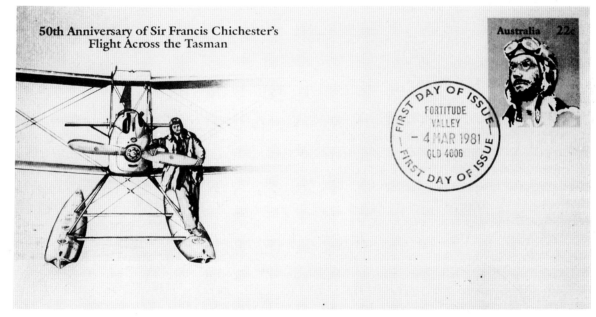

In 1981 Chichester's epic Tasman flight was honored by this special stamped envelope produced by Australia Post. (Australia Post)

In May 1928 Kawanishi completed the first of its two K-12 transpacific monoplanes. The pride shown by these company employees turned to despair when the
K-12 proved an embarrassing white elephant. (Robert C. Mikesh)

8

Eastward They Battled
Nonstop from Japan

Charles Lindbergh's immortal Ryan monoplane *Spirit of St. Louis* is undoubtedly the most cherished airplane of aviation's adventuring years. For the millions who visit the Smithsonian Institution's fabulous National Air and Space Museum each year, the Ryan NYP and the Wright brother's *Flyer* are the most popular attractions. Yet few of those who stand in the Milestones of Flight Gallery, mesmerized by the little silver airplane, are aware that Ryan built a second NYP. Its role in aviation history was to act as a catalyst for Japanese airmen to conquer the Pacific.

Lindbergh had hardly touched down in France before his stunning success had awakened Japanese interest in a transoceanic flight. Rather than an island-hop air race like James Dole's Derby, or emulating Charles Kingsford-Smith's staged transpacific flight, Japan's aviation industry decided to attempt an amazing nonstop flight to the United States.

While the world still bathed in the afterglow of Lindbergh's success, the Tokyo newspaper *Mainichi Shimbun* placed an order with Ryan for an exact replica of Lindbergh's long-range monoplane. Delivered to Japan in 1928, the NYP-2 (New York–Paris No. 2) was not purchased to attempt the flight. Lindbergh's aircraft had been designed strictly to fly the 3,600 miles between New York and Paris—plus a few hundred extra for safety. A flight from Japan to America's west coast required an additional 1,000-mile range. Although the Japanese buyers may at first have thought it possible to extend the Ryan's range, it seems more likely that its role was to act as a design guide for Japan to manufacture its own long-range monoplane.

Japan's transpacific intentions were announced in July 1927, when its Imperial Aeronautics Association mounted a project that it believed would surpass even Lindbergh's achievement. Worldwide it declared that a Japanese pilot flying in a Japanese-owned and manufactured aircraft would make the first nonstop flight across the Pacific. Wasting no time, the association selected the Kawanishi company to construct a suitable aircraft. Two of the transpacific machines were ordered, one as a back-up in case of an accident. As designer Eiji Sekiguchi commenced work, four Kawanishi pilots were selected for the project.

What little is known concerning the design and construction of the Kawanishi K-12 transpacific monoplanes is best explained by Robert C. Mikesh, a senior curator of aeronautics at Washington's National Air and Space Museum. A specialist in Japanese aviation, he wrote:

> What happened is still a mystery. Never confirmed, and perhaps apocryphal, the widespread belief is that the concept of the airplane design amounted to creating a machine larger than the *Spirit of St. Louis* in the same proportion by which the span of the Pacific exceeded the Atlantic. The concept in simplest terms was this: Greater size was to produce greater range. The Kawanishi firm's K-12 looked remarkably like an overfed Ryan NYP, Lindbergh's plane. It relied on a massive landing gear to support a huge boxy fuselage. That, in turn, was needed to accommodate the vast quantities of fuel required for the long flight. It had twice the wing area of the NYP. Its relatively pointed nose contained a 500 horse power BMW water-cooled engine, built under license by Kawasaki. The cockpit, unlike Lindbergh's, accommodated a second crew member. It looked as if it were defying the laws of physics. But the plane's appearance aside, everything seemed set for the big Pacific crossing.

While the aircraft were being built, crew training got underway. A Great Circle route was chosen across the North Pacific. Arching northeast from Japan it would give the pilots some protection by tracking close to the Aleutian Islands before swinging southeast to the American mainland. In case the crew was forced to ditch, it was decided that the K-12 would be more easily spotted if it was painted silver with red stripes on the wings. The four pilots were given intensive training in long-range flying and overwater navigation by the Japanese Naval Air Corps. In February 1928, one of the pilots, Yukichi Goto, was killed when his aircraft crashed into a cloud-shrouded mountain during a long-range training flight. As one Japanese writer suggested, it was "a bad omen."

In May 1928 the first K-12 was rolled out of the factory for flight testing. Officially called the *Nichi-Bei-Go* (Japan-US Model), it was christened the *Sakura* (Cherry Blossom). Fully loaded, the machine weighed in at a massive 11,300 pounds, more than twice the weight of Ryan's NYP. The finished aircraft was closely inspected by officials of Japan's Civil Aviation Bureau. Extensive testing showed that the K-12's gross weight when loaded with maximum fuel greatly exceeded the aircraft's safe design limit. Furthermore, its fuel capacity was found to be insufficient for the flight. Adding to Kawanishi's problems, flight tests determined that the lumbering monoplane failed to meet a performance requirement—it was unable to climb to a minimum altitude of 50 feet in a given period of time following a takeoff run of 2,790 feet.

Following lengthy arguments with the bureau, Kawanishi reluctantly agreed to modify the second K-12, including strengthening its airframe to accommodate a greater load of fuel. Unfortunately the whole design concept was flawed and the second K-12 was also eventually rejected when the Imperial Aeronautics Association's project committee determined that its maximum range was only 3,782 miles—more than 1,000 miles less than required for the flight. By this time Kingsford-Smith's *Southern Cross* had successfully crossed the Pacific—albeit in three stages. Finally accepting the fact that no amount of modification could ever prepare the K-12 to complete a nonstop Pacific crossing, the association formally suspended its transpacific project on July 7, 1928. Bob Mikesh wrote:

The Kawanishi K-12 transpacific hopeful inspired by Lindbergh's Ryan monoplane *Spirit of St. Louis*. (Robert C. Mikesh)

A ground crew inspects the K-12 outside its hangar at the Kawanishi factory. (Robert C. Mikesh)

The upshot was devastating. The Tokyo government would not qualify its own preferred aircraft for civil registration or give clearance for the transpacific flight. In the denouement, a red-faced Kawanishi found itself strapped with an expensive white elephant, providing an inglorious end to the firm's last private venture, nonmilitary aircraft. Its owner hung the aircraft over the assembly shop where for many years it gathered dust. Hung beneath the forlorn flying machine was a bitter and humorless message: "How Not to Design or Build a Special-Purpose Airplane."

As the Japanese debacle came to its sad conclusion a similar venture was being planned on the west coast of America in Tacoma, Washington. Lumber tycoon John Buffelen and the city's chamber of commerce had decided to put their town on the map and were backing a daring Canadian-born flier named Harold Bromley. If perseverance is rewarded by success, the twenty-nine-year-old ex-Royal Air Force pilot should have been the first to fly nonstop across the Pacific Ocean. Bromley was to attempt the flight four times.

Visiting Lockheed's new Burbank factory early

in 1929, Bromley had discovered the fuselage shell of an experimental monoplane. Designer Jack Northrop had started work on the long-range design in 1927 hoping it would interest Arctic explorer Hubert Wilkins for his planned trans-Polar flight. When Wilkins instead chose Lockheed's new Vega, work was stopped on the special monoplane. Bromley realized that the design had the potential to carry the fuel for a non-stop transpacific flight and placed an order for it to be completed. Called the Explorer, the single seat monoplane carried a fuel load of 902 gallons, and was the first low-wing airplane built by Lockheed. Several months later, Bromley carried out full-load tests on the long, concretelike bed of Muroc Dry Lake (near the site of today's Edwards Air Force Base). Satisfied with its performance, he flew the Explorer to Tacoma's Pierce County Airport where it was formally christened *City of Tacoma*.

On the morning of July 28, 1929, Bromley made his first transpacific attempt. His Lockheed sat on top of a long wooden ramp at the Pierce County Airport. The ramp's downhill run was to give an initial boost to help the *City of Tacoma* attain takeoff speed on the relatively short grass runway. After checking the 450-hp Pratt & Whitney Wasp engine, Bromley opened up to full power and rolled down the ramp onto the airfield. The Lockheed was gathering speed and had gone about 1,000 feet when the crowd of ten thousand saw it swerve toward rough ground. Seconds later the right landing gear collapsed and the wing shattered. As the aircraft came to stop with its tail perched in the air Bromley leapt from the cockpit. Miraculously there was no fire. Later, explaining that he had been blinded by fuel venting from a tank breather in front of his windshield, Bromley lamented, "Nobody is to blame but myself. I can do it if they'll give me another chance."

Tacoma's indulgent businessmen were to give him three more chances. The next came to an end two months later when Lockheed test pilot Herb Fahy survived a terrible crash in the second *City of Tacoma*. The brand new Explorer went out of control when tail flutter caused the rudder to fall off in flight. By May 1930 a third *City of Tacoma* was built and, with Bromley again at the controls, breezed through its initial flight testing. However, as Lockheed could no longer afford the special insurance policy required for Bromley to conduct the full-load test at Muroc, company pilot Ben Catlin flew the critical flight.

Positioning himself 1 mile down the lake bed at the planned point of liftoff, Bromley watched as Catlin commenced the test with the required 900 gallons of fuel on board. As the Lockheed pilot reached the 1-mile mark he was still having trouble getting airborne. Half a mile ahead a 12-foot-high railway embankment bisected the lake bed. Catlin forced the reluctant aircraft into the air and, flying on the verge of the stall, just cleared the railroad. It seems almost certain that the Explorer had been flying aided by the cushion of air known as "ground effect." The tiny increase in altitude needed to cross the embankment brought on a stall. Dropping a wing, the aircraft crashed in a ball of flame. As Bromley ran to the scene he was horrified to see Catlin, wreathed in flames, staggering out of the inferno. Before dying later, the luckless airman apologized "for wrecking the ship."

Incredible as it may seem, Bromley's Tacoma backers were still prepared to finance one last attempt. However, it was decided to look for another make of aircraft. Bromley eventually chose an elegant Emsco monoplane. Manufactured by the little-known E. M. Smith and Company, the 36-foot-span aircraft was powered by a 450-hp Wasp engine and had a maximum still-air range of 4,000 miles—about 500 miles short of the distance between Tacoma and Tokyo. Because the Emsco had room for a crewman, Bromley decided to carry a navigator. He chose a former ship's officer, twenty-seven-year-old Australian Harold Gatty, who was making a lean living teaching air navigation in Los Angeles. Unable to increase the Emsco's fuel load, the two men decided to reverse the route, confident they would pick up tail winds on a west-east flight. In view of the bad publicity that had been generated by the previous attempts, Bromley's backers insisted that no pre-

On August 26, 1929, while Bromley awaited delivery of the second *City of Tacoma*, the German airship *Graf Zeppelin* touched down in Los Angeles following a nonstop flight from Tokyo. Not eligible for the transpacific prize, the airship's 9-hour east-west Pacific crossing was part of a remarkable 21-day circumnavigation of the world. (NASM)

The elegant Emsco monoplane *City of Tacoma* was the fourth aircraft purchased for Bromley to fly the Pacific. The Emsco was equipped with a 450-hp Pratt & Whitney Wasp engine that gave it a still-air range of about 4,000 miles. Its relatively short range forced Bromley to fly from Japan hoping for westerly tail winds. (NASM)

Harold Bromley (right) also teamed up with Wiley Post's superb Australian navigator, Harold Gatty. (NASM)

flight publicity be given to the fourth *City of Tacoma* attempt. For that reason the actual flight received little attention in the United States.

After shipping the aircraft to Tokyo, Bromley and Gatty erected it and flew to a large naval aerodrome. When load tests proved that the runway was too short for a full-load takeoff they searched for a suitable beach. They finally located one at Sabishiro, about 200 miles north of Tokyo. At low tide the sands stretched for 1¼ miles. Even so, with a full 1,100-gallon fuel load, the Emsco still required a ramp to boost its takeoff performance. For three weeks local villagers helped build a sand hill which they compacted with a steam roller before laying a runway of planks leading down to the beach.

On September 15, 1930, the improvised airstrip was ready. The generous villagers, who refused to accept any payment for their labors, lined the beach. At the top of the ramp, anchored to a big pile by a thick rope, the Emsco strained as Bromley checked the engine. When he was satisfied that the Wasp was delivering full power, Bromley dropped his hand and a man with an axe severed the rope. Trundling slowly down the ramp, the Emsco slowly gathered speed. Even with the ramp's assistance the airplane did not become airborne until it reached the end of the sand, and for several hours it required climb power just to remain clear of the waves.

Four hours out, the *City of Tacoma* entered a low cloud bank that was to persist for most of the next twenty-one hours. Minutes after entering the exhaust system's collector ring fractured and exhaust fumes began to seep into the cockpit. Neither man was aware of the insidious situation even though Bromley found himself laughing uncontrollably and Gatty was having coughing spasms.

Unable to climb above the clouds, Gatty relied on dead reckoning navigation. Bromley's task of blind-flying was not helped when the Emsco's Sperry artificial horizon—one of the first fitted to a civil aircraft—"turned over on its back and died." Soon afterward the wind-driven fuel pump failed, which forced Gatty to spend most of his time operating the emergency hand pump to keep the engine's main fuel tank topped up. He later recalled, "The first hour was pure hell but after that I didn't feel anything." During a break in the clouds Gatty was able to fix their position by sextant and discovered they had covered only 1,250 miles. The anticipated tail wind had not developed and after some rapid calculations Gatty estimated that they were still 36 hours' flying time away from Tacoma. It was clear that they did not have enough fuel remaining and had no option but to return to Japan. Gatty recalled being worried that Bromley continued his fits of laughter despite the knowledge that he had again failed.

As they headed back toward Sabishiro the airmen used friction tape to repair leaks that had developed in the fuel lines. As the time approached to reach the coast Bromley noticed a hole in the clouds. Diving down through it, the aircraft broke into the clear directly above a steamer. "I don't know who was more scared— the people on the ship or me," Gatty recalled. Leveling off from the dive the fliers saw a red and white striped lighthouse directly ahead—the same lighthouse they had passed shortly after takeoff the previous day. After twenty-two hours of nearly continual blind flying, this was a testimony to the accuracy of Gatty's navigation and Bromley's piloting.

Although Sabishiro Beach was only 15 miles away Bromley elected to land on the first clear stretch of sand. Just before touchdown Gatty dumped their remaining fuel. The moment the Emsco stopped a clearly irrational Bromley grabbed a life raft and dashed toward the water. Gatty chased after him. A few yards from the water's edge Bromley fell down and was fast asleep by the time his navigator arrived. When he awoke, eight hours later, Bromley was quite lucid again, and told his companion that he had taken the life raft because he thought they had ditched in the sea. A doctor later diagnosed Bromley as suffering from carbon monoxide poisoning from the leaking exhaust system. Three days after they landed Gatty also collapsed from a delayed reaction to carbon monoxide poisoning.

When Bromley was advised that there was lit-

Flying across the Bering Sea, one-eyed Wiley Post and Australian navigator Harold Gatty crossed the northern extremities of the Pacific in June 1931. Two years later Post repeated the flight, this time flying alone in his Vega *Winnie Mae*. (NASM)

Opposite: The first Japanese pilot to attempt a nonstop Pacific crossing was the daring Seiji Yoshihara. In 1931 he set out alone in a tiny Junkers A-50 floatplane. (Robert C. Mikesh)

tle chance of getting further backing from the United States, the kindly villagers of Sabishiro volunteered to attempt to raise the money. Although amazed and touched by the generous offer, Bromley and Gatty elected to turn it down, and they returned to the United States leaving the *City of Tacoma* in Japan to be sold. Two years later Bromley made a long-distance flight in a diesel-powered Lockheed Vega and there was talk of his making yet another transpacific attempt, but he failed to find backers and never did conquer the Pacific. In 1931 Gatty crossed the northern fringe of the Pacific—hopping across the Bering Strait between Siberia and Alaska—as

he navigated Wiley Post's *Winnie Mae* on its epic flight around the world. Years later, recalling his flight with Bromley, Gatty said: "He never made the big time but he was a magnificent pilot."

In February 1931, attention was again focused on Japanese fliers when the Tokyo newspaper *Hochi Shimbun* announced it was sponsoring a nonstop flight to America. Its pilot was to be Seiji Yoshihara who had just made a sensational light airplane flight from Berlin to Tokyo. He had displayed both skill and perseverance by averaging more than 600 miles each day flying in a tiny Junkers A-50 Junior powered by an 85-hp Arm-

Yoshihara's Junkers A-50 floatplane was powered by an 85-hp Armstrong Siddeley Genet engine. Sponsored by the *Hochi Shimbun* newspaper it was christened *Hochi Nichi-Bei* (Hochi's Japan–United States). (Robert C. Mikesh)

strong Siddeley Genet engine. For the Pacific flight Yoshihara planned to use the same machine equipped with floats and named it *Hochi Nichi-Bei* (Hochi's Japan–US). Only the barest facts are recorded of the daring flight.

On May 14 Yoshihara took off from Haneda, near Tokyo, following a Great Circle route similar to that planned by Bromley and Gatty. He had covered around 1,000 miles and was flying in fog close to Russia's Kuril Islands when the Junkers developed engine trouble. The Japanese flier ditched at sea and was adrift for seven hours before being rescued by a passing Japanese ship. Still determined to complete the flight, the *Hochi Shimbun* newspaper acquired a second Junkers Junior, which was christened *No. 2 Hochi Nichi-*

Bei and shipped to Shinshuri Island in the Japanese-controlled Kurils. This was the closest suitable point to the site of Yoshihara's crash the previous month they could get. Before the flight could be recommenced, the aircraft was damaged during a test flight and Japan's Civil Aeronautics Bureau suspended the flight on the grounds that the aircraft was unsuitable.

Believing that a big financial incentive might attract a suitably equipped Japanese challenge, the Imperial Aeronautics Association again became involved. It offered a prize of 200,000 yen ($100,000) to the first person to fly the Great Circle route "from a point of departure in Japan south of the 45 degree north latitude." In simple terms this meant a nonstop flight from the main islands of Japan to any land south of Canada's Vancouver Island. Tokyo's *Asahi Shimbun* newspaper added a further 100,000 yen ($50,000) for a successful Japanese pilot—half that amount if a foreigner made the flight. To fully understand the immensity of the Japanese prize it must be understood that $150,000 in those days would equate to well over $2 million dollars today and such an amount was a king's ransom in those depression years. With such a huge financial catalyst it was not surprising that both Japanese and American contenders quickly appeared.

Despite the failure of its tiny Junkers Junior, the *Hochi Shimbun* had not given up and had purchased a Junkers W33 transport. It was similar to the W33 *Bremen* that had made the first west-east Atlantic crossing in 1928. Powered by a 300-hp Junkers-L 5 engine, the all-metal monoplane was noted for its rugged construction and load-carrying ability. The newspaper hired Mitsubishi to equip the aircraft for long-range operations and then searched for another W33 to commence crew training. Germany's Baron von Hunefeld, who had been on board the *Bremen* during the Atlantic flight, had donated a W33 to the Imperial Aeronautics Association and this was loaned to the newspaper to train its crew. Eiichiro Baba of the Japan Air Transport Research Institute was selected as the pilot and Comdr. Kiyoshi Homma and M. Sgt. Tomoyoshi Inoshita of the navy were appointed as navigator and radio operator, respectively. The three men conducted intensive training but by the time their W33 *No. 3 Hochi Nichi-Bei* was ready the advent of winter in the North Pacific forced the flight to be postponed until the following year.

While the Japanese had been preparing, several American crews had arrived in Japan. Seduced by the rich cash prizes, Thomas Ash made a hastily arranged first attempt on May 31, 1931. He purchased the Emsco *City of Tacoma* and renamed it *Pacific*, but was unable even to get it off the sands of Sabishiro Beach. The next American bid was made by Cecil Allen and Don Moyle who became the third owners of the ill-fated Emsco. This time rechristened the *Crasina Madge*, the plane successfully took off from Sabishiro

Beach on September 8. Allen and Moyle made it as far as the Aleutians where bad weather forced them to land. They took off again later only to be forced down again. This time their landing was on an uninhabited island and a week passed before they were rescued.

The next nonstop attempts were mounted from America. Besides the *Asahi Shimbun* prize, a group of Seattle businessmen had offered $28,000 for a flight between Japan and Seattle. As it appeared that both prizes could be won by a flight in either direction, Reginald Robbins, a Fort Worth, Texas, barnstormer and sportsman flier Harold S. Jones, a wealthy oil man, decided to make their attempt from Seattle. Their plan was revolutionary for its day. To complete the flight they planned to refuel their Lockheed Vega *Fort Worth* in-flight from a Ford Tri-Motor. Aerial refueling was still at an experimental stage, but Robbins had used the new technique two years earlier to set a 172-hour endurance record while circling over his hometown. To reduce the *Fort Worth's* fuel consumption on the Pacific flight Robbins had its 425-hp Wasp engine replaced by a 220-hp Wright Whirlwind.

Taking off from Seattle's Boeing Field on July 8, 1931, the pair arrived over Fairbanks, Alaska, where they met their flying gas station and took on 200 gallons. As they approached Nome, where they were scheduled to take on more fuel, the two aircraft were being buffeted by severe wind squalls. Robbins was unable to keep the Vega steady and get close enough to the tanker for Jones to grab the dancing hose. After many fruitless attempts the two exhausted Texans landed in Alaska. A month later their second transpacific attempt also failed. After successfully refueling over Fairbanks they lost contact with the tanker in cloud before being able to take on the vital second load. A few days after Robbins and Jones returned to Fort Worth another westbound attempt failed when a flier named Bob Wark was forced down at Vancouver, Canada, 100 miles from his starting point.

The approach of winter seemed to spell an end to 1931's transpacific drama when two more American pilots, Clyde "Upside Down" Pangborn

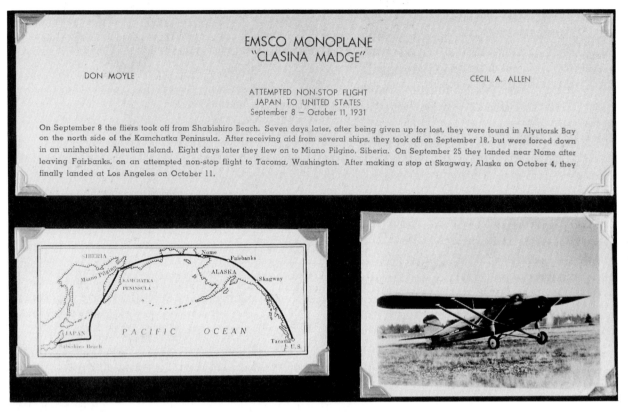

The Emsco was renamed *Crasina Madge* for its third transpacific attempt. This montage in the National Air and Space Museum recalls the flight. (NASM)

A letter carried aboard the *Crasina Madge*. Although it was not delivered nonstop as the cover promised, it did eventually make a delayed crossing as explained by a special frank on the envelope. (NASM)

Cecil Allen and Don Moyle with the *Crasina Madge*. They redesigned the Emsco's engine cowling and incorporated a supercharger as well as making a number of other modifications. (NASM)

Clyde Pangborn (nearest camera) and Hugh Herndon pose with their wives before departing from New York's Roosevelt Field on July 28, 1931. The pair were confident of breaking Wiley Post's around-the-world record. (NASM)

and Hugh Herndon, Jr., strutted onto center stage. They had left New York's Roosevelt Field on July 28, 1931, with high hopes of setting an around-the-world speed record and had ended up under house arrest in Tokyo's Imperial Hotel. Espionage and making an illegal flight were among the fifty-five charges brought against the American airmen. They were detained for almost two months after landing in Tokyo on August 8.

Daredevil Pangborn, stunt pilot and wing walker extraordinaire, was well known in American aviation circles. He was the chief pilot and part owner of the Gates Flying Circus. His playboy copilot Hugh Herndon was a wealthy Princeton dropout with a penchant for flying and the good life. Herndon's socialite mother, Alice Boardman, was a Standard Oil heiress. Anxious to see her son make a name, she had not turned a hair when he asked her for $100,000 to finance the world flight.

Pangborn and Herndon's hopes of cutting the world speed record set by Post and Gatty a month earlier had come to an end in Russia. While landing in a rainstorm at Khabarovsk, Siberia, their Bellanca Skyrocket *Miss Veedol* slid off the runway and became hopelessly bogged in mud. Already well behind Post's *Winnie Mae*, the two men finally acknowledged that they no longer had any chance of beating the record. While delayed at Khabarovsk waiting for the airfield to dry out, the pair decided to salvage something from the trip by competing for the *Asahi Shimbun* prize. As they carried no maps of Japan, Pangborn cabled the editor of the English-language *Japanese Times* asking for a track and distance from Khabarovsk to Tokyo and requesting that the American Embassy obtain landing permission from the Japanese Aviation Bureau.

The field had dried out before their cable was answered and they decided to take off before it was again swamped by a threatening storm. They were flying a rough heading for Japan when a radio message was relayed from the *Japanese Times* giving a track and distance and advising that landing approval was being sought. After landing to get directions at an airport being constructed at Haneda, near Tokyo, they finally reached Tachikawa Airport where they were met by angry officials demanding to see their landing papers. As Pangborn recounted:

> We were arraigned on three counts. That we had flown over fortified areas and that we had photographed these areas. True we didn't have a flight permit with us, but we assumed it would be routine for our embassy to arrange it. As for flying over fortified areas and taking pictures, we were just tourists taking what we thought were pretty landscape shots.

What Pangborn ignored was the fact that Japan and China were at war and, understandably, did not take kindly to foreign pilots arriving unannounced and photographing military restricted areas and warships.

The fliers were eventually tried in Tokyo's district court, found guilty, and sentenced to 205 days hard labor or fines of $1,050 apiece. When the fines were eventually paid, Pangborn and Herndon revealed their plan to attempt the Japan–United States flight. Because of the spate of recent failures, Japan's Civil Aviation Bureau had restricted future flights to "approved" aircraft only. After days of haggling, approval was reluctantly given for their Bellanca to attempt one overloaded takeoff from Japan.

On September 29 they flew *Miss Veedol* to Sabishiro Beach where they made final modifications for the flight. During their detention in Tokyo, Pangborn had been working on a clever plan to extend the Bellanca's range. The plan had been previously used in 1919 by Australian Harry Hawker in an attempt to cross the Atlantic. The scheme involved removing the bolts holding the Bellanca's landing gear to the fuselage and replacing them with a series of clips and springs attached to a cable. By pulling on the cable Pangborn would jettison the whole structure following takeoff. For the landing he attached steel skid strips to *Miss Veedol*'s potbelly. As he explained later:

> We determined that to make the transpacific flight we would have to take off with the heavi-

Still elegantly dressed in his camel's-hair coat and derby hat, Pangborn prepares
to start from New York as Herndon hand cranks the engine starter. (NASM)

est wing loading [fuel load] we had ever attempted with the Bellanca. Even then it was
marginal that we would have enough fuel to
take us the 4,500 miles to the U.S. west coast
even at the most economical cruising speed.
Studying the problem I calculated that we
could increase our speed approximately 15
miles per hour if we could rid ourselves of the
drag of the fixed landing gear. On a forty-hour
flight that would be the equivalent of adding
600 miles to our range, and that might make
the difference between success and failure.

While they worked on the aircraft the two
Americans were guests of the people of nearby

Misawa City. The mayor had publicly announced
that fliers of any nation seeking such an honor-
able goal should be hosted in friendship. However not all Japanese were so friendly, as the fliers
discovered when their painstakingly prepared
flight charts were stolen. They were certain that
the culprits were members of the radically patriotic Black Dragon Society who for weeks had
been violently speaking out against the Americans and their proposed flight. Obtaining and
preparing new charts delayed Pangborn and
Herndon a day, but they were finally ready to go
on October 2. Just before he climbed on board the
Bellanca, Pangborn was overwhelmed by a touching gesture made by a tiny Japanese boy who
rushed out from the crowd and presented them

Pangborn's early flying career included wing walking and stunts. Here, in 1920,
he falls while trying to transfer from a car to a low-flying plane. (NASM)

with a gift of five apples from his father's orchard. The American's hometown of Wenatchee, Washington, like Misawa City, was famous for its apples.

Miss Veedol used the takeoff ramp that had been built for the 1930 attempt by Bromley and Gatty. Even so the Bellanca seemed to be having trouble accelerating as it rolled down onto the wet beach. To save weight the airmen carried no radio, no survival equipment, not even a seat cushion, and they limited their food to hot tea and some fried chicken. Yet with 915 gallons of fuel and 45 gallons of oil on board the airplane was still 3,400 pounds above its designed gross operating weight. With its 425-hp Wasp engine screaming at full revs, the monoplane was only up to 60 mph with two-thirds of the beach gone. Pangborn had estimated he required 90 mph for liftoff. As *Miss Veedol* approached a pile of logs that marked the end of the makeshift runway Pangborn could be seen rocking the aircraft from wheel to wheel in an attempt to break the friction of the wet sand. He later recounted his thoughts

at that moment: "I was determined to get off, or pile into those logs. We had permission for only the one attempt and in no way was I going to spend any more time in Japan."

Pangborn and Herndon made it with less than 200 yards to spare. Flying straight ahead, wallowing near the stall, they slowly inched up above the waves. When they had a safe margin of height Pangborn turned slowly onto a course of 072 degrees true—heading up toward the Aleutians. Three hours out, on track and approaching the Kuril Islands, Pangborn was satisfied that everything was operating normally and jettisoned the landing gear. He was concerned to see that two of the gear's bracing rods had not dropped clear. Pangborn realized that they posed a real threat to a safe belly landing and thus that he would have to work them free sometime during the flight.

Devoid of 300 pounds of landing gear and its parasite drag, *Miss Veedol* climbed slowly to 14,000 feet where it picked up a good tail wind. As the sun went down the fliers began to encounter airframe icing in the clouds and increased

148

height to 17,000 feet. Clear of the clouds conditions were smooth, and Pangborn decided it was the ideal time to try to get rid of the two dangling struts. Handing over control to Herndon, he put his years of flying circus skills to good use. Struggling against the frigid 100-mph slipstream, the steel-nerved airman eased out of the cockpit and placed his feet on the broad strut that supported the Bellanca's wing. Holding on for dear life with one hand he used the other to remove one of the offending brace rods. Pangborn clambered back into the cockpit, warmed himself, then repeated the procedure on the other side.

Through the night it was bitterly cold. "The water in our canteens and even our hot tea froze," Pangborn recalled. His first real position check was a volcano in the Aleutians and the two men were delighted to see it loom directly below them. One of Herndon's few responsibilities was to keep the main wing tanks topped up from the huge auxiliary cabin tank. This required him to transfer fuel using a hand-operated wobble pump. Twice he forgot the task. The first time he was able to pump fuel fast enough to keep the spluttering Wasp engine running. However, on the second occasion the propeller stopped dead, and not equipped with an electric starter, Pangborn had no alternative but to dive the Bellanca in the hope of getting the propeller to windmill in the rarefied air. Yelling at Herndon to start pumping, Pangborn steepened the dive desperately trying to turn the propeller. They had lost 13,000 feet, and were only 1,500 feet above the ocean, when the engine finally turned over and burst into life again. Herndon's carelessness had come close to costing their lives.

During the flight the only word of Pangborn and Herndon's progress came from an island in the Aleutians where an amateur radio operator radioed the United States that he had heard an airplane passing over above the clouds. No one was quite sure of their final destination, although Pangborn's mother was adamant that her son would choose Wenatchee, Washington, as his landing site and was among thirty locals who maintained a vigil at the town's little airfield.

Pangborn and Herndon's *Miss Veedol* was specially built by Guiseppe Bellanca, designer of superb long-distance planes. It had a 735-gallon fuel tankage and provision to refuel the main tank in-flight from additional 5-gallon cans the airmen carried. (NASM)

Pangborn (closest to camera) was a part owner of the Gates Flying Circus. His copilot, Herndon, had secretly married during the last-minute flight preparations and later proved to be unprepared for his navigation duties. (NASM)

As Pangborn sighted the tip of the Queen Charlotte Islands, off the northwestern coast of Canada, he knew the worst of the navigation was over. He had been at the controls for more than thirty hours and, aware that the tricky job of belly landing lay not too far ahead, decided to catch a few hours sleep. Handing over the controls, he instructed Herndon to hold height and heading and wake him when he saw the lights of a big city. "That will be Vancouver, British Columbia," Pangborn yelled. Once again Herndon's inattention let them down. When Pangborn awoke some hours later his cavalier copilot had wandered off course and missed both Vancouver and Seattle. Ahead of them was Mount Rainier. Pangborn decided to carry on inland to Boise, Idaho, which would also give them a new world's nonstop distance record. Two hours later, however, when it became evident the

Boise area was covered in fog, he turned toward Spokane, Washington. When that destination was blocked by low clouds he decided to head for his hometown of Wenatchee.

At 7:14 A.M. on October 5, 1931, the big red monoplane swooped in over the hills and circled Wenatchee's little airfield, dumping fuel to reduce the chance of fire. Approaching slowly, Pangborn sent Herndon to the rear of the cabin hoping that his weight would help hold the tail down during the landing. At the last moment he cut off the fuel and ignition switches and, as the Bellanca flared close to stalling, lowered it gently onto the ground. For a moment it was obscured by a cloud of dust, then, decelerating rapidly, *Miss Veedol* slithered to stop, teetering for a moment, then falling on its left wing tip.

After being hugged by his mother and brother, Pangborn was stunned when he was greeted by a

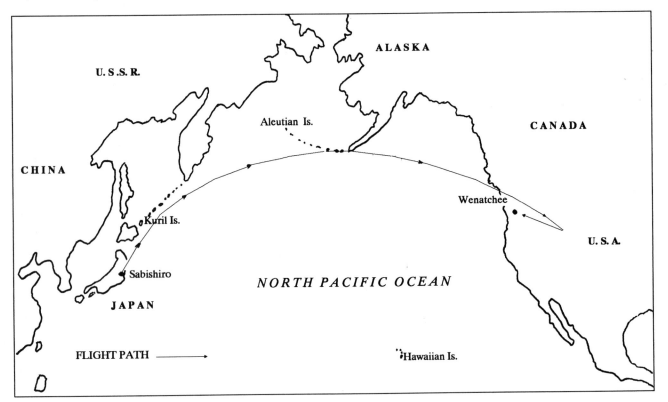

Miss Veedol's transpacific Great Circle route. Although on this type of flat map projection the flight path appears circuitous, it is actually a straight line across on the globe. Over the United States, Pangborn was close to Boise, Idaho, when bad weather forced him to divert to Wenatchee. A similar route was used by all the unsuccessful Japan–United States fliers.

representative of *Asahi Shimbun* who presented the fliers with their $25,000 check. By some quirk of fate, the newspaper's emissary had selected Wenatchee as their most likely landing point. Another among the little group that had waited through the night was Carl M. Cleveland, then a young reporter for the *Wenatchee Daily World.* He had commandeered the only telephone at the airfield on the off-chance that he might get a world scoop. He was not disappointed: PANGBORN-HERNDON SPAN PACIFIC . . . BOY ARE WE GLAD TO GET HERE, PANGBORN PUTS IT . . . IT'S LIKE A DREAM COME TRUE. Cleveland's hometown newspaper headlines were mirrored around the continent as he passed the story to his editor, who relayed it to the wire services and the world.

The *Asahi Shimbun* prize was the only money realized by the epic flight. As foreigners they were ineligible for the Imperial Aeronautic Association's prize, and Wenatchee was too far from Seattle for them to receive the prize offered by that city's businessmen. From Pangborn's point of view, worse was to follow. With relationships already strained with Herndon, their partnership was quickly dissolved. As backers for the original world flight, Herndon and his mother claimed the prize money and the cash from the sale of *Miss Veedol.* They gave Pangborn $2,500 for his efforts.

The split between Pangborn and Herndon became public a couple of months later when the Albany *Times Union* carried the headline: HERNDON INCOMPETENT SAYS PANGBORN. In the story that followed Pangborn disclosed that his copilot had known nothing of navigation because he had been courting a girl instead of studying prior to their flight. He disclosed that Herndon had been little more than a passenger in *Miss Veedol,* stating: "Out of the 200 hours we were in the air, Herndon flew at most ten of those hours."

Even though Pangborn gained little financially, the nonstop Pacific flight brought other more lasting rewards. He was honored with American aviation's most prestigious award, the Harmon Trophy, joining other greats such as Charles Lindbergh and Jimmy Doolittle. And from Japan came news that, forgiven for his ear-

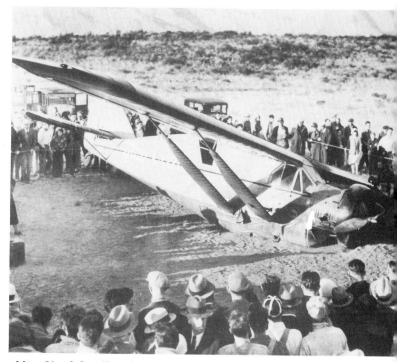

Miss Veedol suffered only minor damage during Pangborn's superb no-wheels landing at Wenatchee. A flying oil can caused a small cut over Herndon's eye. (NASM)

The triumphant airmen photographed moments after their Wenatchee crash landing. Herndon (left) still sports blood from the cut on his right eyebrow. (NASM)

The front page of the *Wenatchee Daily World* announces the first nonstop crossing of the Pacific Ocean. (NASM)

lier transgressions, Pangborn had been awarded the Imperial Aeronautical Society's White Medal of Merit. But the most lasting memento of *Miss Veedol*'s flight was a present that Pangborn arranged for the mayor of Wenatchee to send to his counterpart in Misawa City. To reciprocate the little Japanese boy's touching gift of five apples, five cuttings from Wenatchee's famed Richard Delicious apples were sent to Misawa City. There they were grafted onto local trees, and within a few years, cuttings and seedlings were distributed around the country. Today Richard Delicious apples are grown throughout Japan.

Even though Americans had captured the *Asahi Shimbun* prize, Japan was still determined that its pilots should make the Pacific crossing. In light of Pangborn and Herndon's success, the *Hochi Shimbun* newspaper was desperate for its team to safely complete the flight. To minimize the risk it was decided to provide two backup aircraft for their Junkers W33. The luckless Seiji Yoshihara was sent to England to ferry a Saro

Other than Pangborn being awarded the 1931 Harmon Trophy, there was little official recognition of the first nonstop Pacific flight. In 1981, after many years of pressure from Wenatchee, the U.S. Postal Service issued this Fiftieth Anniversary commemorative stamp. (NASM)

Cutty Sark flying boat back to Japan, and two army fliers were dispatched to the United States to bring back a Bellanca, similar to the victorious *Miss Veedol.* In March 1932 the *Hochi Shimbun's* carefully laid plans suffered the first setback. Their transpacific Bellanca, *Rising Sun,* crashed at New York's Floyd Bennett field during a flight test, killing its pilot, Capt. Yoshinori Nagoya. Six weeks later Yoshihara survived a crash of the Cutty Sark during a test flight in Oakland, but the plane was a total loss.

Reduced again to only one aircraft, the Japanese transpacific project finally got underway again on September 10, 1932, when the *No. 3 Hochi Nichi-Bei* departed from Haneda Airport for Sabishiro Beach. At 5:37 A.M. on September 24, after taking on board a full load of fuel, pilot Eiichiro Baba took off on the long-delayed flight to the United States. Navigator Homma set course on their Great Circle route and radio operator Inoshita checked his equipment. Five hours out, Inoshita reported their position as south of Iturup Island in the Kurils. They were on course and making good time. Operators in Japan waited for the next position report from the Junkers. It never came. Baba and his crew vanished. Despite a massive sea search, no trace was ever found of the missing plane.

In the five years since Lindbergh had inspired transpacific ventures, seven Japanese attempts had failed. All five of the unfortunate *Hochi Shimbun's* aircraft had crashed, costing the lives of four airmen. All that remained of the Imperial Aeronautics Society's Ryan-inspired *Nichi-Bei-Go* project was an abortion of an aircraft gathering dust beneath the roof of the Kawanishi assembly shop.

It is not in the Japanese nature to give up on a project once begun, and during the years that followed the 1932 disaster, there were still those who dreamed of making the flight. In the offices of the *Asahi Shimbun* plans were formulated for an even greater challenge—an incredible 8,100-mile flight from Tokyo to New York. However, as an order was placed for a suitable aircraft, the world was slipping toward war.

In 1932 the Japanese made a final bid to fly the Pacific. This Junkers W-33 *No. 3 Hochi Nichi-Bei* vanished after radio contact was lost six hours out from Sabishiro Beach. (Robert C. Mikesh)

The Japanese erected a monument at Sabishiro Beach marking the takeoff point of *Miss Veedol.* In 1981, celebrating the fiftieth anniversary of the flight, the monument was visited by Lt. Gen. Charles L. Donnely, Jr., commander of U.S. Forces, Japan (center), Col. Leland F. Small (left), and Col. Stephen L. Sutton, commander of the 6112th Air Base Wing stationed at nearby Misawa Air Base. (NASM)

The Airspeed Envoy *Stella Australis* in which Charles Ulm attempted his second crossing of the Pacific. (State Library of New South Wales)

9

The Loss of the *Stella Australis*

Somewhere in the depths of the Pacific lies the remains of a sleek British Airspeed Envoy. It is probably within a radius of 200 miles of Honolulu, but its exact position remains as great a mystery today as it was in December 1934 when it vanished on a flight between San Francisco and Sydney. At the controls of the silver and blue airliner *Stella Australis* was Charles Ulm, who was trying for a new transpacific record while surveying a route for his new airline.

Six years had passed since he and Kingsford-Smith had flown the Pacific together. In that time their fortunes had fluctuated as they tried to establish themselves in the airline business. In 1930 they had formed Australian National Airlines operating a fleet of five Avro X airliners, British-built versions of the highly successful Fokker F.VIIB. Their dream of running Australia's greatest airline had vanished a year later when one of their Avros, the *Southern Cloud*, disappeared in the Snowy Mountains between Syd-

ney and Melbourne and a second, the *Southern Sun,* crashed on a special mail flight to England.

Following the collapse of A.N.A. the two men had ended their business partnership and pursued separate aviation goals. As managing director, Ulm wound up the company's affairs and purchased their remaining Avro X, *Southern Moon*. He modified the airliner for long-distance flying and renamed it *Faith in Australia*. Flying his Avro, Ulm concentrated on making a name in his own right, rather than merely being regarded as Kingsford-Smith's copilot. However, with his more serious, businesslike manner, Ulm did not radiate the glamour of his gregarious former partner. Nevertheless in 1933 he set a new England-Australia record of 6 days, 17 hours. He next refocused his attention on trying to obtain long-term government airmail subsidies. Ulm realized that mail contracts were the vital first step toward establishing airline services to New Zealand and eventually across the Pacific.

In 1934 *Faith in Australia* completed three

Ulm's skills were demonstrated while flying the Avro XI airliner *Southern Sky* in 1930. Trapped by violent storms, he and copilot J. Sheppard force-landed in this two-acre mountain paddock. The wheels collapsed upon hitting dead trees, but none of the passengers were injured. (J. Moore)

Following their transpacific flight Ulm and Kingsford-Smith were granted honorary commissions in the Royal Australian Air Force. While in New Zealand Ulm passed his final flying tests and here proudly displays his New Zealand Air Force "wings." (Queensland Newspapers)

Ulm's Avro XI *Faith in Australia* in New Zealand following its first trans-Tasman flight. The Avro was a British-built version of the Fokker FVII. Here Ulm (in waistcoat) and copilot Scotty Allan (in white shirt) are greeted in Napier by the League of Frontiersmen. (State Library of New South Wales)

return trans-Tasman crossings. On one of these flights Ulm conducted the first official airmail services between Australia and New Zealand. On another he carried the first Tasman women "passengers"—his wife, Mary, and his secretary, Ellen Rogers. In July 1934 he also flew the first airmail between Australia and New Guinea.

Ulm had never wavered in his belief that improvement in aircraft design and the public's slowly changing perception of air travel would eventually bring about an air service across the Pacific Ocean. As early as 1931 Pan American Airways had surveyed a transpacific route and now, three years later, as Ulm turned his attention to the challenge of Pacific air transport, Pan Am was again considering possible routes.

Ulm did not have the resources to consider purchasing one of the new four-engine Sikorsky S-42 flying boats that were just coming into service with Pan Am. Instead he planned to commence operations by using an ingenious, albeit unwieldy, compromise service between Australia and Honolulu—staging through New Zealand, Fiji, and tiny Fanning Island (1,000 miles south of Hawaii). Once in Hawaii passengers would travel the 2,400-mile leg to San Francisco on one of the numerous fast ocean liners that plied regularly between Honolulu and the mainland. Later, when a suitable aircraft was available, Ulm intended to add San Francisco and Vancouver, Canada, to the route. For the initial service to Hawaii he calculated that separating the flight into four sectors would reduce the fuel load required. This would enable a profitable passenger and airmail load to be carried. At each refueling stop passengers and crew would rest overnight.

157

Faith in Australia carried the first two women to fly the Tasman. One was Ulm's secretary, Ellen Rogers, here alighting from the aircraft. The other was his wife. (State Library of New South Wales)

In February 1934, Ulm prepares to take off from New Zealand's Muriwai Beach carrying the first official airmail to Australia. (State Library of New South Wales)

Another reassuring factor would be the knowledge that there were other islands dotted close to the route should an emergency arise.

Unlike the Pan Am plans, which relied on flying boats, Ulm already had a new landplane airliner in mind for the Australia-Hawaii service. Donald Douglas had recently produced his all-metal DC-2. It was the talk of the world's airline fraternity following its record-breaking performance in the 1934 MacRobertson England to Australia Air Race. Douglas's revolutionary DC-2—the immediate forerunner of the immortal DC-3—was already in use on K.L.M.'s Far East routes. It also had been ordered by T.W.A. for its vital New York–Chicago service. Ulm calculated that the new generation of airliners had the range to handle his proposed Pacific island-hop.

With businesslike caution he decided to survey the whole route before he commenced the service—at the same time making it a publicity exercise by establishing a new transpacific record. Rather than purchase one of the new and expensive Douglas aircraft before he had proved the feasibility of his service, Ulm chose to use a smaller aircraft of similar performance for the trial run. If all went according to plan he would then raise the necessary capital.

The English Airspeed Company had recently produced the A.S.6 Envoy, a graceful, twin-engine six-passenger airliner. It was codesigned by Neville Norway, later famous as Neville Shute the author. A modified version built to compete in the MacRobertson race had been forced to withdraw because of mechanical problems. Nevertheless, from all reports, it was ideal for Ulm's needs. It had a cruising speed of 170 mph and there was sufficient room in the passenger compartment to fit extra fuel tanks, giving the Envoy a range of 3,100 miles.

Mortgaging his house and *Faith in Australia* to finance the flight, Ulm cabled an order to Airspeed. He instructed that his aircraft have the passenger seats removed and be modified to include a long-range cabin fuel tank, the latest blind-flying instruments, an automatic pilot, and radios. He also put a strict time limit on delivery. The company had an Envoy already in produc-

tion for a customer in India and to meet the deadline they allocated it to the Australian. Five weeks prior to the delivery date Ulm and his copilot, George M. Littlejohn, chief flying instructor of the New South Wales Aero Club, arrived at Airspeed's Portsmouth factory to supervise the final preparations. The manufacturer's chief designer and technical director, Hessell Tiltman, later recalled: "Ulm was a dynamo, energetic and impetuous and very popular at the factory. We found him most knowledgeable and very thorough."

The Australian's frankness frequently caused hilarity in the workshops. While inspecting the aircraft's interior for the first time, he saw that a special toilet had been installed as for a normal passenger model. "You can take that bloody thing out at once," he roared. When asked how he and his crew would manage on the long flight ahead he grinned and replied, "Simple, we'll just use the bloody windows!" Ulm knew weight and space were at a premium. Even those few pounds could make the difference.

One of Ulm's decisions caused serious concern. The position of the massive cabin fuel tank left only a tiny space between the pilots' seats and the front wall of the tank. Ulm insisted that the navigator's table be moved to the rear of the cabin where there was more room. Though the navigator would be more comfortable, he would also be isolated from the pilots by the cabin tank and Ulm would be unable to personally check the courses or computations. This may have been a fatal mistake. We will never know. However, when Ulm and Kingsford-Smith had flown the *Southern Cross*, navigator Harry Lyon had been similarly positioned. He had passed messages to the pilots over the top of the tank on a long stick and Ulm had no reason to believe the same system would not be satisfactory in the Envoy.

Airspeed worked day and night to get the aircraft finished. The last items of equipment to be fitted were an automatic pilot and a 30-second fuel-jettison valve. If an engine failed, the fuel-jettison system would allow the crew to quickly dump the huge overload of fuel and remain airborne on one engine. Christened *Stella Australis*, the Envoy received Australian registration VH-

The sleek lines of Airspeed's Envoy are illustrated by this company advertisement. During World War II a military variant, the Oxford, became Britain's most successful advanced trainer. (NASM)

On a number of flights, Ulm flew with P. G. "Bill" Taylor (right) as his copilot/navigator and employed J. Edwards (left) as radio operator. In 1934 Taylor became Charles Kingsford-Smith's navigator for the first west-east Pacific flight. (State Library of New South Wales)

UXY, and was shipped to Southampton where it was loaded on the Cunard liner R.M.S. *Ascania* for the journey to Canada. Ulm and Littlejohn accompanied their aircraft to Quebec, arriving on November 10, 1934.

Flying across country, via Detroit and Los Angeles to Vancouver, they carried out a series of flight tests to check the Envoy's fuel consumption. There were rumors that Ulm was not happy with the results. They failed to match the figures he had expected from the 350-hp Armstrong Siddeley Cheetah IX engines. Even so, they were more than adequate for the planned flight. In Vancouver they were joined by their radio operator/navigator, J. S. "Leon" Skilling, a ship's navigator who had served with the Orient Line but had no experience in aerial navigation. Following several training flights to accustom Skilling to the radios and aerial navigation, Ulm and his crew flew to Oakland for the final maximum-

load test. It was conducted on November 30 with the *Stella Australis* carrying its full crew and the maximum fuel load of 600 gallons. Afterwards Ulm told reporters, "She is in excellent shape and we can make the hop [to Honolulu] with no trouble at all."

Before leaving Australia Ulm had quietly established a new airline company and now, confident that the Envoy was capable of flying the Pacific, he announced to the press:

I expect Great Pacific Airways, of which I am managing director, to establish a service in the next two years. Planes, one a week between Sydney and Honolulu connecting with the steamer service between Honolulu and the United States, would reduce the transportation time of 21 days from San Francisco to Sydney to 7½ days.

In his Sydney office Charles Ulm (seated), George Littlejohn (right), and Cyril Westcott, a business associate, watch as navigator Leon Skilling pinpoints their Pacific route. (State Library of New South Wales)

Only a small crowd was at Oakland Airport for the *Stella Australis*'s departure on December 3, 1934. One of the last to bid Ulm good-bye was Amelia Earhart. The airwoman was preparing to sail for Honolulu from where, a month later, she would make the first solo flight to the mainland. Exuding the image of a professional, no-fuss airline crew, the three fliers were soberly dressed in dark suits and ties. The last thing they wished to recall was the image of the devil-may-care Dole barnstormers who had set out from the same airport seven years earlier. Just after 3:30 P.M. they climbed on board, started the engines, and minutes later were off on the first leg home. Depending on the winds they expected to reach Honolulu at about 7:30 A.M. the next day.

Littlejohn was at the controls for the first, relatively easy takeoff. Ulm's time would come on the more difficult island operations, particularly at Fanning Island where he had organized the construction of a special airstrip. With the massive overload of fuel the aircraft weighed 9,260 pounds—almost 50 percent above its normal operating weight. As the Envoy trundled across the airfield, slowly gaining flying speed, Ulm's mind must have gone back six years to when he and Smithy had made a similar takeoff in the *Southern Cross* and how his commander had wasted several hundred yards of precious runway. Ulm insisted that Littlejohn not squander an inch and start his takeoff roll at the very beginning of the airstrip.

The *Stella Australis* used most of Oakland's takeoff run, the 675-gallon fuel load obviously taking its toll on the aircraft's normally sprightly performance. From the right-hand seat Ulm carefully monitored his copilot. As the Envoy reached flying speed, Littlejohn eased it from the ground.

162

As Oakland mechanics make a final check of the Envoy, Ulm (second from left) and Skilling (far right) bid farewell to American friends. (State Library of New South Wales)

Shortly before climbing on board the *Stella Australis,* Ulm was wished good luck by Amelia Earhart. Less than three years later she too would vanish in the Pacific Ocean. (State Library of New South Wales)

The last photo taken of Charles Ulm, moments before starting on his ill-fated Pacific flight. (State Library of New South Wales)

With both engines running perfectly *Stella Australis* crept into a climbing attitude clawing for height over San Francisco Bay. Ulm reached down and hand-pumped the retractable undercarriage into the engine cowlings. With the decrease in drag, the Envoy accelerated to a slow but steady cruise climb. Airspeed limited was justifiably proud of its new hydraulically operated "Retractor" undercarriage system. It had been designed for their 1933 Courier, a single-engine forerunner of Ulm's aircraft, which was the first British aircraft equipped with the speed-increasing and fuel-saving feature.

As they slowly struggled to their cruising altitude San Francisco passed below: Nob Hill, Twin Peaks, and finally the Golden Gate fell astern. In his repositioned seat aft of the cabin fuel tank navigator Skilling busied himself with his charts. It was his responsibility to keep their course holding on the long, thin pencil line he had drawn across the featureless map to the specks in the ocean—for in relation to the vast Pacific, that was just about how large the Hawaiian Islands appeared. His track-planning accuracy and the pilot's course-holding ability had to be perfect. An error of just a couple of degrees would mean they would be 100 miles off course when they reached Hawaii and could miss the islands altogether. Provided that the weather stayed clear along the way, Skilling would be able to shoot the sun and the stars to help keep a check on their position. But the sextant could be a tricky instrument to use accurately on a relatively stable ship's bridge, let alone in the cramped confines of a bucking aircraft. It would take all his skill plus ideal weather conditions.

Thirty minutes out from the California coast they passed over the Farallon Islands, which gave Skilling one last positive check of their progress. From their position relative to the planned track he was able to assess the drift and ground speed. Armed with these, he could work out how the wind was affecting their progress and if necessary give Ulm and Littlejohn a new course to steer. By this time the two pilots would have been feeling more relaxed. The early stages of the climb were critical. Had they suffered an engine malfunction, there would have been insufficient time to operate the fuel dump, and the overloaded aircraft would have crashed. But with a safety buffer of altitude they now had the precious thirty seconds to dump the lethal fuel overload. Then, with luck, they should be able to hold height.

As the Farallons passed beneath, the men took a last look. Little did the trio realize they would never see land again. Between them and Hawaii lay 2,300 miles of open sea without a rock or a reef to break the surface with a vital clue for the navigator. When they eventually reached cruising level, Littlejohn throttled back the engines and set power for best-range fuel consumption. It gave a speed of 130 mph, well below the Envoy's normal cruising speed, but they were not concerned. As the flight progressed and they burned off the fuel overload, the speed would gradually increase.

Some hours out Ulm took command. It was planned that the two pilots would spell each other frequently to combat fatigue on the long crossing. Back in San Francisco radio operators kept a listening watch on the airway's channel logging Skilling's radio reports. Six hours and seventeen minutes after takeoff Skilling transmitted *Stella Australis*'s position as 900 miles southwest of San Francisco. Their speed had gradually increased to 150 mph and everything was going according to plan. The American added light-heartedly: "The boys are getting hungry and have started operating on the chicken sandwiches. The motors are working smoothly and we haven't got our feet wet yet."

The messages and replies were drawn-out affairs as long-range airborne radio was still carried out by Morse code with its time-consuming system of dots and dashes. Two hours earlier the Matson liner S.S. *Lurline* had seen the lights of the Airspeed as it passed high overhead. Sitting in his shack, the ship's radio officer had been listening for some time and had heard an earlier signal from the aircraft: "Making speed, weather perfect, engines sweet." That signal had also been picked up by an amateur operator on the California coast who had relayed the message to San Francisco.

The forecast for Hawaii was not as good as the weather the trio were obviously enjoying at that stage. It called for showers and variable winds. The lack of a predictable wind on the later stages must have been of concern to navigator Skilling, particularly if clouds prevented his obtaining a worthwhile star fix. Seven hours out, the aircraft came on the air again. This time the message was picked up by the operator at San Francisco's Mackay Radio Station. It was brief but to the point: "All O.K."

The liner *President Coolidge* was on her way to Honolulu and the ship's course put her close to the airmen's planned track. Her chief radio officer, Charles Scanlon, had decided to take the lonely watch through the early hours of the morning. At 3:55 A.M. local time, about sixteen hours after the plane's takeoff, a message cracked over his radio. The *Stella Australis* was calling him. They reported, "We are about over you now." The message was clear but Scanlon later recalled that it seemed strangely weak considering that the aircraft was apparently overhead. At that time the *President Coolidge* was only 400 miles from the islands. If the airmen could see her they must be in good shape to hit Honolulu in less than three hours. Everyone relaxed a little—they were almost there. In the cramped, darkened cockpit Ulm and his companions would have been breathing a sigh of relief. After 2,000 miles of featureless sea they now had a positive fix. But did they?

At about the time *Stella Australis* should have reached its destination, listeners were shocked to pick up Skilling's latest message: "We do not know whether we are north or south of the islands. Weather bad. Altitude 12,000 feet." It was obvious the airmen were worried. They should have been over the islands but had no land in sight. Fifteen minutes later a more urgent signal came: "Very little petrol left, need a beacon urgently but do not want to send out an SOS so tell them to snap it up."

With time running out Ulm had called for a radio signal on which to take a fix with the aircraft's primitive radio direction-finding system. A tragedy was inexorably developing and the oper-

ators at Honolulu's radio station tried frantically to help. They sent a series of long, continuous signals in the vain hope that Skilling would be able to pick up a radio bearing. Either the Envoy's receiver was not functioning or the aircraft was out of range. Skilling may have picked up some sort of signal for only minutes later he reported, "We are south of Honolulu but are heading back on course now." Whether that message was prompted by a radio fix or some visual clue will never be known. The momentary relief of Honolulu's radio operators was shattered five minutes later when Skilling transmitted: "Off course again in heavy cloud and strong winds. Petrol only for fifteen minutes. Can planes stand by?"

United States Navy and Army Air Corps authorities in Hawaii were advised to mount a search-and-rescue mission. It had happened before. There were many who still vividly recalled the tragedies of the Dole Air Race. The climax came quickly. Over the years Ulm's last messages have been reported dozens of times and the facts seem to have been confused. It is often stated that his final call came after the aircraft had force-landed and was made with the Envoy floating on the water. However, a transcript of the log of the Honolulu-based Globe Wireless Company published in the Brisbane *Courier* on December 8, 1934, is quite specific. At 9:38 A.M. local time Skilling tapped out the first of three heartbreaking signals: "We are just going to the water."

There was a break of 13 minutes before the second signal, and it seems obvious that during that period *Stella Australis* was making a slow descent from its last reported altitude (12,000 feet) down to the water. It was probably still under power for a part or all of the descent as it would have reached the sea much sooner if the engines had been stopped. It is probable that Ulm, estimating that he had only a few minutes fuel remaining, elected to use the last few gallons to position the doomed aircraft for the ditching.

The second message at 9:51 was brief: "We are turning into the wind," it said. Turning into the wind is the final maneuver before landing; thus it seems likely that the decision to ditch had been

165

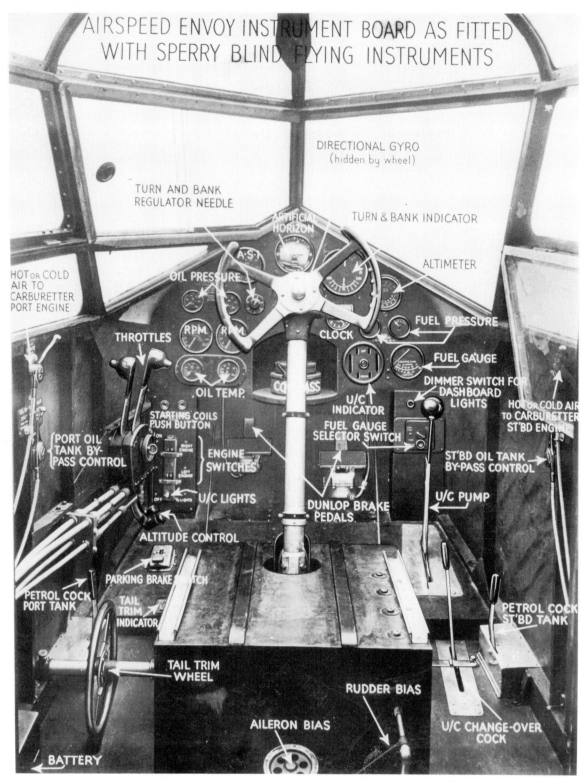

AIRSPEED ENVOY INSTRUMENT BOARD AS FITTED WITH SPERRY BLIND FLYING INSTRUMENTS

DIRECTIONAL GYRO (hidden by wheel)

TURN AND BANK REGULATOR NEEDLE

ARTIFICIAL HORIZON

TURN & BANK INDICATOR

A.S.I.

ALTIMETER

HOT OR COLD AIR TO CARBURETTER PORT ENGINE

OIL PRESSURE

FUEL PRESSURE

THROTTLES

RPM RPM

CLOCK

FUEL GAUGE

OIL TEMP.

COMPASS

DIMMER SWITCH FOR DASHBOARD LIGHTS

STARTING COILS PUSH BUTTON

U/C INDICATOR

FUEL GAUGE SELECTOR SWITCH

HOT OR COLD AIR TO CARBURETTER ST'BD ENGINE

PORT OIL TANK BY-PASS CONTROL

ENGINE SWITCHES

ST'BD OIL TANK BY-PASS CONTROL

U/C LIGHTS

DUNLOP BRAKE PEDALS

U/C PUMP

ALTITUDE CONTROL

PARKING BRAKE SWITCH

PETROL COCK PORT TANK

TAIL TRIM INDICATOR

PETROL COCK ST'BD TANK

TAIL TRIM WHEEL

RUDDER BIAS

U/C CHANGE-OVER COCK

AILERON BIAS

BATTERY

This photograph of the cockpit of the prototype Airspeed Envoy shows the sort of instrumentation Ulm and Littlejohn had for their Pacific flight. Note that the aircraft was originally designed for single pilot operation. (NASM)

The passenger cabin of the Envoy. In the *Stella Australis* these seats were removed and navigator Skilling was isolated at the rear of the aircraft by a huge cabin fuel tank. (NASM)

made. How long the engines would continue running would have been pure guesswork. They could continue to operate for ten seconds or ten minutes. Possibly Ulm turned into the wind in preparation for the final touchdown, and then just headed on until the fuel gave out—praying that they might see some sign of land and at least be able to radio a fix before they ditched. The Globe log seems to bear this out for it shows that the aircraft was transmitting for another nine minutes. At 9:54 came the last word message— Ulm probably told Skilling to send it while they still had time: "Come and pick us up. The plane will float for two days." A constant stream of SOS signals followed for the next six minutes. Then silence!

It seems certain that at some time during that final stream of SOS signals the Envoy's engines sucked the last dregs of fuel, sputtered, and stopped. The aircraft headed for the water with Skilling transmitting until the trailing wire antenna struck the sea and silenced the touch of his finger on the Morse key. A second or two later the aircraft hit the water. Whether the men and machine survived the ditching will never be known. The fliers' reports of heavy clouds and strong winds indicate that the sea was rough. If so, the wood-and-fabric aircraft could have broken up on impact and its crew died immediately. If they did find calm water, then maybe the trio survived the landing and waited, scanning the horizon, until their aircraft became waterlogged and sank without trace beneath the Pacific. How long that might have taken is pure guesswork. Depending on many variable factors it could have been minutes, hours, or days. If they survived the landing, the men most certainly regretted their decision not to carry a life raft. Preferring extra fuel to heavy safety equipment, Ulm had played the odds and lost. He had stated before the flight: "I don't think we would sink very quickly if we were forced down. That is the least of my worries."

A massive sea and air search was underway within hours of their last message. Rear Admiral Yarnell, commanding the U.S. Naval Base at Pearl Harbor, ordered twenty-three of his ships into the search area. Submarines, minelayers, and coast guard patrol boats scoured an area 300 miles in all directions from Honolulu. Eighteen Army aircraft and Navy seaplanes crisscrossed the sea. The problem was trying to predict just where the *Stella Australis* had come down. Lieutenant Stephens, a Navy meteorologist, explained to reporters: "We are handicapped as we don't know in which direction to search. I think they hit head winds and fell short of their goal, then turned back thinking they overshot the islands."

Opinion was that the Australian and his crew were down somewhere 200 to 300 miles east-northeast of Oahu. The search widened and was joined by large numbers of Japanese fishing boats around the islands. Eight hours after the aircraft went down the *President Coolidge* steamed into the area to help. After two days, 325,000 square miles of sea had been searched without a trace of the missing aircraft. Charles Kingsford-Smith, who had just completed an east-west Pacific flight in a Lockheed Altair, told reporters in Los Angeles: "If only my aircraft was not in the factory I would go to help. I think he may be short of the islands."

Back in Australia a stunned nation waited for news. The wives of the three airmen were to have been at Sydney airport to welcome their husbands after the triumphant Pacific crossing. Now they waited and prayed at the Ulm's Rose Bay home. Ulm's Sydney representative, Beau Shield, answering nonstop telephone calls for news at the company's office, optimistically stated:

I think the plane could float for days if not indefinitely. The aircraft's retractable gear design is ideal for a water landing. It would float with wings above the water, a bit nose down, but the empty fuel tanks would help keep it up. The batteries will probably be under water so there would be no radio signals.

Other pilots also agreed that Ulm might still be afloat. Everyone was guessing, clutching at straws, knowing that as long as there was the slightest hope the search would continue. Misinterpretation of the final word message—"Come and pick us up the plane will float for two days"—led to popular belief that the men were alive and in radio contact after the landing. But the experts knew that even if the airmen had survived the landing, and the batteries and radio were undamaged, the long wire antenna that trailed behind the Envoy in flight would be dangling uselessly in the water. Furthermore it was unlikely that Skilling could have rigged up a worthwhile emergency antenna in the waterlogged aircraft.

On the third day of the search, efforts were intensified in a southwesterly direction. The popular belief that the plane had landed short of the islands was radically changed by the theory advanced by Captain Doetsner, master of the S.S. *Maliko*. Doetsner's ship had been on the same course as the *President Coolidge* when Ulm had passed over the liner early on December 5. But the *Maliko* had been 150 miles closer to Hawaii. Doetsner believed that the airmen had sighted his ship and mistaken her lights for those of the *President Coolidge*. Additional weight was thrown behind the theory when the liner's radio operator reported that the signals from the aircraft's radio had been very weak when Skilling had reported overhead. They should have boomed through his receiver, but if Ulm had in fact been over the *Maliko*, *Stella Australis* was an hour's flying time past the liner and the signals would have been substantially weaker.

If indeed the airmen had mistakenly fixed themselves over the wrong ship, it meant that their expected time of arrival over Honolulu was in error by about one hour. In other words, they

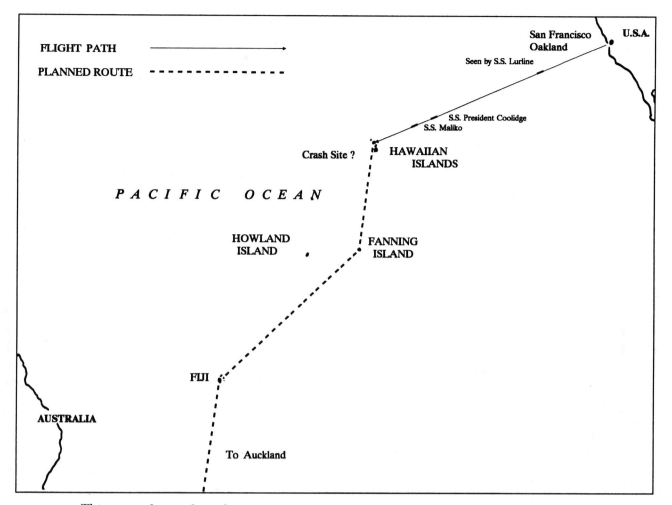

This map shows the relative positions of the liner *President Coolidge* and the merchant ship *Maliko*. It seems probable that misidentification of these ships at night led to the *Stella Australis*'s overshooting Hawaii.

overflew their destination an hour earlier than expected and, with the combination of darkness and clouds known to have been over the islands on that night, never sighted Hawaii waiting 12,000 feet below. An hour later, when Ulm and his crew descended below the clouds expecting to be over the islands, the *Stella Australis* was almost certainly already about 150 miles past Honolulu.

Amateur radio enthusiasts on both sides of the Pacific monitored their radio receivers throughout the drama. In Melbourne a short-wave "ham" picked up a message sent out by the Berlin National Broadcasting Service reporting that it had intercepted a signal from the *President Coolidge* stating that the airmen had been picked up. The German message was heard in England and the next day London's *Daily Express* reported that the lost fliers were safe. It was all a cruel mistake—misinterpretation and overeager journalism; the liner's actual message was that Ulm's last radio signals had been picked up on the ship's radio. The search continued.

A war of words developed in the newspapers when it was reported that aircraft mechanics who had serviced the *Stella Australis* in Oakland had

stated that the aircraft was not airworthy. They said that the aircraft's wood and fabric construction was not strong enough to support the fuel overload and that the fabric was sloppily attached to the airframe. Airspeed Limited immediately answered the charges. An official statement suggested that American aviation manufacturers had recently changed to the more costly aluminum skinning of aircraft and were prejudiced against the current British methods. Airspeed politely implied that the "Yanks" did not know what they were talking about, and stated that exhaustive testing had been carried out to prove the *Stella Australis* was capable of carrying the overload.

Believing that the American press was looking for an opportunity to denigrate British aircraft and thereby boost their own industry, Britain's Directorate of Civil Aviation requested a full report from Airspeed Limited. Hessell Tiltman conducted a searching investigation which proved that Ulm's Envoy had performed to the manufacturer's figures. The company had advised the Australian that the aircraft would remain airborne for 24.7 hours if it was flown at its best endurance speed. If flown for maximum range, at 150 mph and at a level above 10,000 feet, the aircraft would have an endurance of approximately 20.5 hours.

Ulm had taken the company's advice about setting engine power for maximum range as evidenced by the radio reports which referred to a speed of "150 mph" and a cruising level of "12,000 feet." From takeoff at Oakland until the radio signals ceased was a duration of 20 hours and 15 minutes—within a quarter of an hour of the company's maximum-range predictions. Clearly the aircraft performed well and workmanship was not a factor in the disaster. Ulm and his crew had simply become lost and run out of fuel.

Despite the loss of the *Stella Australis* and suggestions that it was not airworthy, Airspeed's Envoy became a successful feeder liner in Britain and its empire. Here the prototype cruises above Britain's famed transatlantic ocean liner R.M.S. *Queen Mary*. (NASM)

On the fourth day of the search violent gales swept the area. Radio experts now publicly announced that no message from the *Stella Australis* could have been sent once the aircraft was in the water. The search was winding down. Kingsford-Smith pleaded with authorities to continue it. In Australia Prime Minister Lyons announced that the government was providing £5,000 ($20,000) to fund a search by thirty seagoing fishing boats. He stated naively that "they will double the chances of finding the airmen." Lyons felt personally involved with the missing Australian. Only five months earlier Ulm had carried the prime minister on an airborne election tour in his Avro *Faith in Australia*. A week after the *Stella Australis* went down, the search was abandoned. Not a single clue to the aircraft's whereabouts had been found.

It was ironic that Australian newspapers reporting the news of the loss of the *Stella Australis* also carried headlines of another aviation story on the same page. Britain's Duke of Gloucester was at Archerfield Aerodrome in Brisbane to see off the Qantas airliner *Diana* on the first regular Australia-England mail flight. Since his entry into commercial aviation, Ulm had seen the international airmail routes as the catalyst to the establishment of international passenger services. He and Kingsford-Smith had tried to convince a skeptical government, and their *Southern Star* had pioneered the mail to England in 1931.

The mystery of the *Stella Australis*'s final resting place will probably never be solved. Reviewing the evidence, with the benefit of hindsight, it seems likely that Captain Doetsner was right when he suggested the airmen misidentified his ship as the *President Coolidge*. Had Ulm really been over the liner, just 400 miles from Honolulu and on track, it is highly improbable that he would have missed the island complex less than three hours away; he was too experienced a pilot. It was suggested following the tragedy that Skilling, inexperienced in aviation navigation, should not have been working behind the cabin fuel tank where Ulm could not visually double-check his maps and calculations. This could have had some bearing on their final demise. Yet if the fatal mistake was misidentification of the ship, anyone in the crew could have been responsible.

The *Stella Australis* probably flew over the cloud-shrouded islands, its crew excitedly anticipating to see Honolulu in an hour's time, around daybreak. Instead they ended up at least 150 miles past their destination, surrounded by open sea, and unable to get a worthwhile fix. It may be that in the last hour of flight they managed to pick up a radio bearing that indicated they were south and past the islands. Certainly it appears that they were backtracking for the last forty minutes before they ditched. But it was too late—they were too far away and they had too little fuel remaining. Even in the unlikely event that the fabric-and-wood machine survived the ditching without massive damage, it would have been only a matter of time before the sea found its way in and the sheer weight overcame the buoyancy of the empty tanks and wooden structure. Then, weighed down by its radial engines, the monoplane would have slipped nose first to the unfathomed bottom of the Pacific. Without a life raft, Ulm and his companions were doomed.

Before leaving on the great adventure, navigator Skilling wrote to a friend: "The chance we are taking in flying across the Pacific is no greater than we would take in crossing a busy street. Familiarity with fear breeds contempt. I believe there is a God and we continue to live in some mysterious way after death. We will die if it is our time." His estimate of their chances was undoubtedly optimistic. The element of risk was high on such a flight. Ulm, Littlejohn, and Skilling took a calculated gamble and lost. They belonged to that rare breed of men who could face a challenge with the philosophy that they would die if it was their time.

Following his death, several newspapers published articles suggesting that Ulm was not sufficiently experienced to have attempted the flight. Charles Kingsford-Smith was incensed at the reports. In an angry reply he said:

Charles Ulm was many things besides a great pilot and navigator. He was gifted and possessed in his unusual character and temperament many of the qualities of greatness. He had great business capacity, punch, and vigor and had he lived would have fulfilled his dream of becoming the head of a great, worldwide aviation organization, a position for which he was admirably suited. There is no saying to what goal his abilities would have taken him.

Had Charles Ulm's time not come in 1934 he might well have gone on to establish the first transpacific airline. In a note mailed home before leaving Oakland, Ulm reflected on his ambitious plan. Almost autobiographical, his words mirror the beliefs held by Pan Am's Juan Trippe—who was preparing to launch a similar service. Ulm wrote:

I am now on the eve of a tremendous adventure. I am tired as a result of working for this adventure, and whilst the outcome is still in the balance, I have no doubt in my own mind that I am standing on the threshold of vast possibilities of which I have dreamt, and for which I have worked for many years. In 1928, of course, Kingsford-Smith and I made the first transpacific crossing, but it is important to note that only in 1933–34 did aircraft design develop to the extent which brought a regular transpacific service within the realms of possibility. I now give it as my considered and emphatic opinion that it is economically possible to produce aircraft which can operate such a service, and furthermore, that after certain exploratory ground work has been done and bases established, that services can actually be inaugurated and maintained.

On December 14, 1934, the pilots of Honolulu paid the final tribute to Ulm and his crew. One hundred Army and Navy aircraft flew over the island and dropped leis off Diamond Head to honor their memory. The following month Juan Trippe established the Pacific Division of Pan American Airways at Alameda, on San Francisco Bay. Aviation was poised to enter the era of the fabled "clipper" ships of the air.

10

Kingsford-Smith and Taylor
Airmail Pioneering

In May 1935 the Tasman Sea was to be the scene of the last great flight made by Charles Kingsford-Smith and his beloved "old bus," the *Southern Cross*. Before retiring the aging Fokker, he decided to use it on one more promotional flight to interest the Australian government in his proposal for a regular airmail service to New Zealand.

Kingsford-Smith had turned his attention back to the Pacific the previous year, announcing that he intended to make the first east-west crossing of the South Pacific. His pioneering 1928 flight in the *Southern Cross* had brought the Australian airman fame but little financial reward. In addi-

Charles Kingsford-Smith, "Smithy" to his friends. Behind his fabled grin lurked a serious and highly professional airman. (Queensland Newspapers)

tion to the collapse of the airline he and Charles Ulm had started in 1930, the partners had suffered a second setback. Despite their pioneering the airmail route to England, the contract had been awarded to Qantas and Britain's Imperial Airlines. After the partnership had dissolved, Kingsford-Smith had been faced with bankruptcy and had returned to barnstorming to make ends meet. A brilliant pilot, he was no match for Ulm when it came to business matters. As their American navigator, Harry Lyon, had said about the Pacific flight, "Without Charlie Ulm we would never have got into the air."

Ironically, Kingsford-Smith was in the Australian capital, Canberra, giving $2 joy rides in the *Southern Cross* when he heard that he had been awarded a knighthood for "services to aviation." When a journalist asked "Sir Charles" if he would now give up barnstorming, Kingsford-Smith tersely replied: "Like hell I will. I've got obligations. There's food needed for my family, you know, and my wife depends on me to earn it."

Early in 1934 Sir Macpherson Robertson had backed Kingsford-Smith's entry in his MacRobertson Air Race from England to Australia. Keen to see an Australian win the race, the millionaire chocolate manufacturer had provided sufficient funds for Kingsford-Smith to purchase a single-engine Lockheed Altair. The news that he was to compete in an American aircraft caused a storm of protest in several Australian newspapers over his "unpatriotic decision not to use a British machine."

Plagued by bureaucratic red tape in getting his Altair an Australian Certificate of Airworthiness, the race start was only three weeks away when Kingsford-Smith was finally able to ferry the Lockheed to England. At the first refueling stop after leaving Sydney, serious cracks were discovered in the Altair's N.A.C.A. engine cowling. With insufficient time remaining to get a new one manufactured and still reach England in shape to start the race, Kingsford-Smith withdrew from the MacRobertson event. His withdrawal exacerbated the protests of his more vocal critics and, besides unfavorable newspaper reports, he received a number of abusive letters. Several contained white feathers—the traditional symbol of cowardice. Deeply hurt, Kingsford-Smith lashed out: "What the hell do these people know about the circumstances? . . . Nothing. Absolutely nothing. . . . I've done some foolish things in connection with the big race. I admit them. But I'm no squib [coward]."

Believing that he once again had to prove his courage to the Australian public, Kingsford-Smith announced his intention to make an eastbound crossing of the Pacific—thus becoming the first person to fly the ocean in both directions. Concerned about the dangers of Kingsford-Smith's undertaking the flight in a single-engine aircraft, the Australian newspaper *Smith's Weekly* sprung to his defense. In an editorial that began "Dear Kingsford-Smith" it said:

You say that you are making this Pacific flight to rehabilitate yourself with your fellow Australians. Such a flight carries with it tremendous risks alongside which the England-Australia route is a mere nothing. Need you take them? Australians do not demand such a gesture from you, They know you as the greatest airman the world has produced—from what you have done already.

However, there were other reasons for the flight. In an attempt to clear up his debts, Kingsford-Smith intended to sell the Altair upon reaching the United States, then concentrate his attention on starting a mail service to New Zealand. "The favorable publicity of a successful flight won't do any harm to my claims for the introduction of a trans-Tasman airmail service under my control," he explained.

On October 22, 1934, Kingsford-Smith and his new copilot/navigator, Patrick G. "Bill" Taylor, left Brisbane bound for Oakland via Fiji and Hawaii. Their Altair, which had been christened *Lady Southern Cross*, carried more than 500 gallons of fuel in its modified wing tanks. Half a world away the contestants in the MacRobertson race were thundering over Europe and the Middle East. Among them was Clyde Pangborn who, following his breakup with Hugh Herndon, had teamed with Roscoe Turner in a Boeing 247 airliner. The American pair was battling for the lead with a Douglas DC-2 entered by Holland's airline K.L.M. and three British de Havilland Comet racers. Undoubtedly the Australians would have preferred the camaraderie of the race to their lone combat with the great ocean, but they had little time to think about it as they concentrated on navigating to Fiji. After making a hair-raising landing at Suva's tiny Albert Park, the Australians faced strong crosswinds for their takeoff from Naseli Beach.

A first attempt was aborted when, as the Altair's tail came up, Kingsford-Smith had insufficient rudder control to prevent the wind from swinging them into the surf. A few days later the wind had dropped and the *Lady Southern Cross* took off safely on the 3,150-mile leg to Honolulu. Throughout the day Taylor's superb navigation kept them on course. In Hawaii radio operators recorded their position reports, plotting the airmen's steady progress toward the islands. With the night came tropical storms and thick clouds. Flying on instruments at 14,000 feet, Kingsford-Smith briefly switched on the landing light to try to assess the cloud situation. Moments after turning it off, the flight nearly came to an end as the Altair's speed decreased dramatically and it fell into a violent spin.

Taylor later recalled Kingsford-Smith yelling, "I'm sorry, Bill, but I can't get her out," before Taylor grabbed the duplicate set of controls in his cockpit and attempted to recover. Despite their combined efforts, the spin persisted for 8,000 feet before they eventually regained control. Even so, they were still unable to accelerate and the airspeed hovered just above the stall. It was only when Kingsford-Smith made a complete check of the cockpit instruments that he detected that the

Altair's wing flaps were fully extended. Somehow while fumbling in the darkness with the landing light switch, he had inadvertently lowered the flaps, and their drag had caused the aircraft to stall. Once the flaps were retracted the Altair again performed perfectly, and at dawn the Hawaiian Islands came into view. Taylor recalled: "I just sat there, filled with a curious sense of gratitude that we had been given the conditions to find these islands, that the engine had never shown a sign of failure in the 25 hours of flight; and the most wonderful sense of anticipation for our arrival at Honolulu."

Shortly after reaching Hawaii Kingsford-Smith offered to take the mayor of Honolulu for a flight over the city in the *Lady Southern Cross*. Soon after takeoff the engine failed and the Australian was forced to make a hair-raising downwind,

The scene at Wheeler Field, Oahu, for the arrival of Kingsford-Smith and P. G. (Bill) Taylor in the *Lady Southern Cross*. (NASM)

Arriving at Wheeler Field the *Lady Southern Cross* taxies to a group of waiting U.S. Army personnel. (NASM)

dead-stick landing. U.S. Army Air Corps engineers discovered that fuel had leaked away through a large crack that had developed in one of the tanks, and they were forced to remove the wings to make repairs.

On November 4, following a 15-hour flight, Kingsford-Smith and Taylor landed at Oakland Airport nearly 2 hours ahead of schedule. They had averaged 155 mph over the 7,312 air miles—55 mph faster than the *Southern Cross* six years earlier. Once again Kingsford-Smith was hailed as a hero. It brought him more world headlines

but no money. Expounding on the problem that faced many great pioneers, whose flying skill was not matched by their business acumen, Kingsford-Smith philosophized:

The successful aviator who performs some startling feat will always have the microphones and newspaper men around him. There will always be an excess of publicity, so that his name will spread to the ends of the world with the speed of radio. But when it all ends, and the captains and the kings depart, he is left

Charles Kingsford-Smith is bid fare-well by Lieutenant Sparhawk, a radio officer with the Army Air Corps, shortly before taking off from Wheeler Field. (NASM)

Kingsford-Smith taxies out in the *Lady Southern Cross* to take off for Oakland on November 3, 1934. Navigator Taylor sits high in the rear seat to get a better view over the Altair's bulbous nose. (NASM)

high and dry, stranded in a financial desert from which he must find his own way out.

The following month, Kingsford-Smith was in Los Angeles, unsuccessfully attempting to sell his Altair, when he heard the news that his friend Charles Ulm had vanished near Hawaii. After helping organize the fruitless search, he left his aircraft in California and returned to Australia to concentrate on forming a company to start a trans-Tasman airmail service. The New Zealand government was keen on the idea, but neither the Australian government nor private enterprise seemed interested in providing backing.

Early in 1935 Kingsford-Smith decided to use the *Southern Cross* to make one last promotional flight across the Tasman Sea before retiring the aging Fokker. Officially, its swan song was to be a special airmail flight in honor of the Jubilee of King George V and Queen Mary. Unofficially, it was a cleverly conceived plan to promote public support for a regular service. King George, an avid philatelist, had given his patronage by sending mail to Australia to be carried on the flight. Adding to the occasion, the Fokker was fitted with a special radio telephone linked to broadcasting stations in Australia and New Zealand. Millions would hear "Smithy" over the Tasman talking from the cockpit of his "old bus."

On May 15, 1935, minutes before taking off from Sydney's Richmond Airport, Kingsford-Smith joked: "Here I am, thirty-eight years old. Apparently sane and sensible, yet about to go off over the ocean again in the middle of the night. I am surprised at myself?" he said. Radio listeners would never have guessed that the pioneer's whole future now rested on one carefully stage-managed mail flight. If he could get the public 100 percent behind him again and the press back on his side, then national opinion might help sway the government. If not, his future looked bleak. Worry must have weighed heavily on Kingsford-Smith's shoulders as he watched 29,000 letters and 450 pounds of parcels being loaded aboard the *Southern Cross*. Yet he hid it behind his usual cheery grin.

By 11 P.M. the last of the mail was on board.

The hundreds who had turned up to watch the departure cheered as Kingsford-Smith and his crew climbed aboard. For the flight he had chosen his *Lady Southern Cross* teammate Bill Taylor as copilot/navigator. Their radio operator was John Stannage who had frequently flown with Kingsford-Smith for five record-breaking years.

Minutes later the three Wright Whirlwinds roared into life and Kingsford-Smith signaled the ground crew to remove the wheel chocks. The Fokker moved away from the lights of the parking area and took off into the darkness. It was a clear, bright night and the crowd watched as the aircraft's navigation lights disappeared into the east and the deafening roar of the engines dulled, then faded. Most rushed home to turn on their radios. That night listeners on both sides of the Tasman prepared to sit up, sharing with Australia's great pioneer airman the emotional experience of his last flight in his famous old aircraft. It would turn out to be a more emotional experience than anyone bargained for. Hundreds of thousands were to remain glued to their radios, awestruck, as one man's incredible courage saved the *Southern Cross* and its crew from disaster.

The first radio report was scheduled for thirty minutes after takeoff. It came up on the dot. Stannage told the vast radio audience that the *Southern Cross* was on course and flying smoothly. But he added, "The noise inside the cabin is terrific. Bill Taylor and Smithy are using their old system of communication—scribbled notes!"

At three in the morning Stannage was on the air again. New Zealand radio listeners were now also picking up his messages. He reported that Kingsford-Smith had just joined him in the cabin and that Taylor was flying the aircraft. Kingsford-Smith was "worried." A few minutes later another message: "Smithy says we are in for some dirty weather ahead, and Bill Taylor has just dropped a calcium flare—the third so far. The clouds are thick but I am happy to say I can clearly reach Bluff [New Zealand] on the radio. By the way, our speed is 95 miles per hour."

Taylor, sitting alone in the roaring darkness of the pilots' cockpit, had a nagging worry. The day before the flight he had walked into the hangar at

The three men who lived through the 1935 Tasman drama, from left: Taylor, Stannage, and Kingsford-Smith. Above their heads is the offending engine. Taylor's precarious walkway can be seen running from the engine, behind the propeller, toward the cockpit. (John Fairfax & Sons)

181

Richmond to find the *Southern Cross*'s center engine lying dismantled on the floor. The two men working on the motor were radio operator Stannage and Jack Percival, a journalist who had recently joined Kingsford-Smith's company. Taylor knew neither man had any formal engineering training. Horrified, he had approached Kingsford-Smith: "I am not an engineer and I have a strong dislike for pulling aeroplanes to pieces. Why don't we take *Faith in Australia,* her motors are in good condition and she's in better shape right through?"

Kingsford-Smith had dismissed his suggestion, saying: "Nothing wrong with the *Cross,* Bill. Never let me down yet." His refusal to consider using another aircraft was probably based on his desire to extract as much publicity from the flight as possible. To the Australian public his name was synonymous with the *Southern Cross,* whereas *Faith in Australia* had been flown by Charles Ulm until his death five months earlier. To use his dead comrade's aircraft would not have the same emotional impact on his audience; it might even have worked against him. Whatever the reason, he chose to ignore Taylor's advice. Kingsford-Smith may later have regretted his decision. Had he used Ulm's aircraft the drama that was to come probably would have been averted and it is likely he would have been awarded a trans-Tasman airmail contract.

As the aircraft moved steadily out across the Tasman the weather deteriorated rapidly. At 5:30 A.M. Stannage reported to Bluff that the sky outside was "Absolutely black and it is very cold. We are flying at 2,000 feet and are being knocked about by air pockets." As dawn approached Taylor was still at the controls and had finally relaxed. In his autobiography, *The Sky Beyond,* Taylor vividly recalled the next few minutes:

Lifting my eyes occasionally from the flight instruments I saw nothing unusual in the red glow of the exhaust rings. I sat relaxed and happy, flying into the dawn. But suddenly I noticed a change. Just one small spot on top of the exhaust manifold on the starboard [right] side of the center motor was glowing with a lighter, brighter color than all the visible parts of the exhaust ring. I looked quickly at the manifolds on the outer motors. The glow was steady and clean, with no light spots on the metal. I flew the aircraft by instinct so that I could fully concentrate on the exhaust of the center engine. The unusual light was certainly there. But since nothing could be done about it I kept a close watch while also checking the weather.

Moments later there were clear signs of trouble. The welded edge of the pipe had split, and through it the exhaust was blowing in a flickering slit of light. As I watched, the blow of the flaming exhaust was gradually forcing open the crack and bursting open the whole top of the manifold. At that moment Kingsford-Smith returned to the cockpit and took over. I pointed out the center manifold. We both sat fascinated but silent, watching the rapidly disintegrating pipe, until in a few moments the whole top section was blasted out by the flame, flicked away in the airstream and gone.

Kingsford-Smith's dream of a trans-Tasman service vanished with the glowing metal of the exhaust manifold which, as it was swept back in the rushing slipstream, passed through the arc of the right propeller. Had luck been flying with them it could have missed the two whirling wooden blades. But it was not to be. After having spent hundreds of hours over the continents and oceans of the world in his Fokker, the law of averages had finally caught up with Kingsford-Smith. This was the crossing he was not going to complete.

It was as if a huge jackhammer was pounding the aircraft. The right engine shook in its mounting and was in danger of wrenching itself from the aircraft. Kingsford-Smith closed the throttle and shut off the fuel. As the engine slowed, the pounding vibration changed to a sickening, irregular wobble. Then, as the windmilling propeller finally stopped, the aircraft lurched, then yawed with the drag of the dead engine. In a desperate effort to maintain height Kingsford-Smith rammed the throttles of the two remaining en-

The shattered propeller of the *Southern Cross*. (Queensland Newspapers)

gines to full power. He pushed on left rudder to counteract the yaw and to keep the nose straight. Three pairs of eyes were riveted on the dead engine. Pointing directly at them was the shattered stump of a propeller blade—a third of it was missing. Little wonder that it had thrown the engine out of balance. Turning their attention back to the altimeter, the two pilots saw the wavering needle slowly begin to unwind; there was insufficient thrust from the two remaining engines to maintain height.

They were 550 miles out in the Tasman—just short of the halfway point. For a moment Kingsford-Smith hesitated wondering whether or not to press on in the hope of reaching New Zealand. His company's future hinged on getting that mail contract. If they lightened the load, it was just possible they could nurse the ailing air-

plane across. However, once he weighed the gamble against the lives of his crew, Kingsford-Smith's decision became obvious. Sadly shaking his head he glanced at Bill Taylor. His copilot knew just how difficult the decision was. Slowly Kingsford-Smith put the Fokker into a gentle, sweeping turn and headed back to Australia.

The aircraft continued to descend, albeit very slowly. The crew had hoped that as they reached the denser air nearer sea level the crippled plane would find a level where it could hold height. A few minutes later it became obvious that this would not happen. After a short, shouted conference the two men agreed that they had about thirty minutes left before they reached the water. That would be the end, for even if they survived the ditching they carried neither a life raft nor life jackets. "Have to dump some weight. Shall I go ahead?" Taylor shouted over the deafening roar. "Anything except the mail," his commander replied.

During the cockpit conference Stannage had been busy on the radio. He sent out the news of the smashed propeller, and the radio audience listened as the drama unfolded: "Please inform all stations to stand by for information. . . . Smithy says we may not be able to hold height." As Taylor struggled back into the cabin he told the radio operator to start dumping overboard everything he could lay hands on. Everything, that was, except the precious airmail. First to go was a small pile of freight—women's hats earmarked for an Auckland retailer. Boxes of tools, the crew's luggage, seat cushions, anything movable went out the cabin door and plummeted down into the Tasman now less than 1,500 feet below.

Bill Taylor was doing some quick calculations. Based on their reduced airspeed of 60 mph he reckoned that it would take ten hours to reach the mainland. With the two operating engines burning 33 gallons of petrol per hour they required 330 gallons to get home; to this he added a safety margin in case they picked up head winds and arrived at a figure of 360 gallons. He opened the fuel dump valve to the main cabin tank and carefully jettisoned the excess fuel overboard. That was it. With the exception of the mail, there was nothing left to throw out.

Stannage went back to his radio and Taylor climbed back into the windswept cockpit alongside Kingsford-Smith. He stared long and hard at the altimeter. It had crawled down to 600 feet, wavered there for a while, and stopped. The two men turned to each other in jubilation—the *Southern Cross* was holding height. They reported later of feeling quite "lighthearted" at that moment. Kingsford-Smith had found just the right altitude to compensate for the lost engine. With rudders deflected just enough to overcome the yaw, and a shade of bank toward the dead engine, the crippled Fokker was holding height, direction, and a steady 60 mph.

The two men relaxed a little: they could reach the coast as long as the two remaining engines held up. However the Whirlwind engines, though reliable, were not designed to be run at maximum revolutions for long periods. They were ten hours out and the engines were old and tired. Added to this, Taylor could not stop thinking back to that dismantled nose motor being reassembled by Stannage and Percival.

Back in Australia the nation waited and prayed. The last message from Stannage had asked for all ships in the area to listen on the 600-meter band. At 7:10 A.M. Stannage informed listeners: "We have dumped a hundred gallons of fuel. Smithy says he hopes to be able to save the mail." Sydney Radio advised the airmen that the pilot vessel *Captain Cook* was sailing out along their track to meet them. H.M.S. *Sussex* had been ordered to sea and would be underway in three hours. Also *Faith in Australia* would fly out to escort them if a suitable crew could be found in time.

As the *Southern Cross* limped home there were still problems with the shattered propeller. The airstream intermittently forced it to revolve and drive the dead engine, setting up vibration and increasing the drag. Each time Kingsford-Smith had to raise the nose and reduce speed back close to the stall to stop the rotation. A hacksaw was among the few tools that still remained on board and Taylor decided to use it to trim the shattered propeller. He also hoped to cut an equal amount off the undamaged blade. Whipped by the wind, he leaned far out of the open cockpit until he reached well down the broken blade. However, the moment he applied pressure to begin sawing, the propeller started windmilling again. It was useless. A radio message had already been received from the Post Master General's Department instructing the airmen to dump the mail if it would help get them home. However, despite being unable to trim the offending propeller, the *Southern Cross* was still holding height, and Kingsford-Smith decided to try to save his precious cargo. At least if they brought the mail home he could arrange another flight and still convince the skeptics about a Tasman service.

They struggled on for five hours with Kingsford-Smith devoting his whole attention to keeping the aircraft from losing height. It was a knife-edge difference between staying up and losing height. Just a fractional variation in the aircraft's angle of attack, the amount of rudder, or the angle of bank and they lost height. This was real seat-of-the pants flying where the aircraft became an extension of the pilot's body and senses. This was a pioneer airman at his best, drawing on his years of experience and his uncanny knowledge of his aircraft: the indefinable quality called airmanship—the trump card of the true professional.

For copilot Bill Taylor it was five hours anxiously scanning the instruments and engines. He had been looking past Kingsford-Smith at the left engine for the thousandth time when he detected a faint but steady stream of blue smoke coming from the exhaust. He wrote of the chilling moment years later:

It was obvious in the clear air. It meant that the engine must be burning oil. There was no way to measure the oil left in the tank. Now with this alarming blue stream from the port [left] exhaust I had a vivid picture of a tank without enough oil to reach Australia. I could hardly keep my eyes off the oil pressure gauge. I said nothing about it to Smithy or John, because talking about it would not help, and in case they had not noticed the blue stream there was no point in passing on such depressing information when the situation was already very grim. If the port engine packed up there was no hope of staying in the air on one engine. Once again we seemed doomed to land in the sea. That horrifying prospect stirred me to thinking hard. There must be some way of getting oil from the useless starboard [right] engine into the tank of the port engine so that we could reach the coast.

Taylor sat quietly considering the alternatives. The only solution was to add more oil and that meant climbing out under the wing with the aircraft in flight. Worse still, with no spare oil on board the only source was the dead right engine. So that meant climbing out twice—once to fetch it and then once again to transfer it to the ailing left motor. What was most frightening was the realization that he was the obvious person to do it.

Should he attempt it now or wait until the pressure started to fall? Looking down at the streamlined strut he would have to cross to reach the engine, Taylor decided that the chances of slipping or just being blown off by the slipstream were much greater than the possibility of running out of oil. For the moment he would stay in the cabin. The risk was too great unless the oil pressure began to fall, in which case he would have little to lose as they were doomed anyway if reduced to only one engine. If he fell it would just mean a quicker and slightly earlier death.

Taylor kept his thoughts to himself. Noticing that Kingsford-Smith was obviously tiring under the strain of the hours of controlling the unbalanced aircraft, he suggested taking over from his commander. To his surprise Kingsford-Smith agreed. Initially Taylor found it very difficult to get the correct feel of the controls, but after a little while he got used to the strange flight angle and the minute margin for error required to maintain height. Kingsford-Smith was stretching and exercising his cramped muscles in the left-hand seat when Taylor noticed the needle of the left engine's oil pressure gauge flicker and very gradually start to fall. It was only a matter of time before the engine would lose lubrication and seize solid. Taylor directed his companion's attention to the gauge. Reassuming control, Kingsford-Smith throttled back the left engine then gave it several short jabs of power before opening back up to full power. The oil pressure had not returned to normal. His face creased with concern he looked across at his copilot. It was an expression that said it all: "No hope!"

Taylor climbed from his seat and went below into the cabin to advise John Stannage of the situation. He transmitted a signal immediately: "Port motor will only last quarter of an hour. Please stand by for exact position." For Bill Taylor the time had come to take the magnificent gamble. Stannage was aware of what was going on, and grabbing a thermos flask he, too, made a move to go for the oil. Taylor, who had by now removed his shoes, pulled his companion back and took the flask. He lashed a length of mailbag cord around his waist and told Stannage to attach it to somewhere in the cockpit. He then moved back up alongside Kingsford-Smith and almost casually shouted, "Going to have a stab at getting some oil."

The pilot shook his head. Apparently he had no knowledge of Taylor's plan. Before he could say anything Taylor stood up on his seat and put one leg out over the side into the airflow. It snatched at his leg and for a moment Taylor thought his plan was hopeless. Then, driven by some superhuman force, he felt for the narrow strut running between the fuselage and the engine pod. Stannage had attached the cord from the copilot's waist to the cabin framework. It was a futile gesture. If Taylor slipped, the cord would snap like string, and they both knew it. No words can better describe the terror of that first six-foot journey than can Taylor's:

I finally got my right foot on the strut, held fast to the edge of the cockpit with both hands, and managed to get my other foot out, and hang on in the airstream. The blast from the center motor screamed in my ears. For a moment I was panic-stricken. I stood on the strut with my shoulders braced against the leading edge of the wing and with a screaming hurricane threatening to blow my eyes out if I looked ahead. Then the panic passed and I felt no sense of height nor any fear of my tricky position. I just had to reach that oil. I edged along the strut, until at the full extent of my left arm to the cockpit edge, I found I could not reach the engine by stretching out with my right arm. I realized with horror that there was a short distance where I would have no handhold, but would have to move with only my feet on the strut and the back of my neck against the wing.

For a moment I felt quite defeated. It seemed almost certain I would never make it, but just be blown off the aircraft and fall in the sea. Then I thought, well I'm going into the sea anyhow; so it's better to take a chance on reaching the engine. I braced my neck well

against the wing, got a firm footing on the strut, and very carefully let go my handhold on the cockpit. Then moved sideways toward the engine. Those few seconds seemed an eternity and the distance endless. But I reached the engine mount and clung to it with both hands.

Kingsford-Smith struggled to maintain control of the *Southern Cross* with the extra weight and drag of his copilot added to the dead starboard engine. The oil pressure on the straining left engine was falling lower. Stannage stood on the empty copilot's seat and stretched out a hand holding an adjustable wrench. Taylor let go with one hand and reached for it. His fingers just met the wrench and with it firmly in his grasp Taylor climbed down to a position where he sat straddling the strut. With his left arm hooked around a tube and with both hands thus free to get the spanner into position, he tightened it on the head of the drain nut of the oil tank.

Slowly he applied pressure to the wrench shaft. If it slipped from the nut suddenly he might lose his grip of it and the wrench would fall into the sea. Worse still, he might overbalance and join the falling spanner. Thankfully the drain plug turned easily and was soon only finger tight. Now it was time to exchange the spanner for the flask. Holding on to the engine with one hand Taylor inched along the strut until his outstretched left arm made contact with Stannage's waiting hand. He felt the wrench taken from him, then saw the radio operator lean back out with the empty thermos. No relay team's baton pass could ever be as difficult as the handover of the large metal flask in the face of the 60 mph slipstream. Somehow they managed it.

Back down again, huddled next to the engine, Taylor removed the plug with his fingers and with his other hand jammed the flask up against the open hole. At first the oil was whipped away by the slipstream until he used his body as a shield and was able to fill it. Next Taylor had to replace the plug, one-handed, while the other held the precious oil close to his body. Finally he shuffled back along the strut until he was in range of Stannage's waiting arm. Some of the oil blew

This photo of Charles Ulm climbing down from the *Southern Cross* illustrates P. G. Taylor's heroism. Whipped by the windstream, Taylor performed a similar maneuver in midflight. (Queensland Newspapers)

away as the thermos was passed beyond the protection of his body to Stannage in the cockpit. While Taylor clung on, Stannage emptied the contents into a small suitcase, the only container of any description left in the aircraft. Then he passed the empty flask back out and the nightmare operation was repeated several times until the small case held enough oil to top up the failing left engine. Finally, with the radio operator's help, Taylor struggled back into the aircraft. For a few minutes he paused to recover from the numbing effect of the freezing slipstream until spurred on by a glance at the falling oil pressure gauge. It was hovering close to zero.

Clambering over Kingsford-Smith, Taylor attempted to climb out on the left horizontal strut. But this time he found it impossible to get his foot over and down. On this side he had to battle not only the slipstream from the nose engine but also that of the left motor. Their combined effect made it impossible to climb out. Twice he tried and twice he was beaten back gasping and cursing. After the second fruitless attempt Kingsford-Smith motioned to his copilot to wait. Somehow he managed to coax the Fokker up to about 750

feet. Then he throttled the left engine back to idle, leaving the aircraft flying on only the nose engine. It immediately started to lose height but there was enough time for Taylor to clamber out and repeat his nightmare crossing to the ailing left engine. Once he was clinging to it, Kingsford-Smith opened up the engine and slowly climbed. For Taylor the experience was terrifying.

Besides the slipstream of the aircraft, he now also had to contend with the added blast from the propeller and the shattering noise. He clung on for dear life as the *Southern Cross* fought for height and its life. Taylor looked down and saw wave tops skimming just a few feet below. Had he taken a few seconds more to reach the engine, Kingsford-Smith would have had no option but to open it up while Taylor was trapped between the fuselage and the engine. With nothing to grab on to, the blast from the propeller would have whisked him away!

Having regained height, Kingsford-Smith again throttled back the engine down to allow Taylor and Stannage to transfer the oil to the nearly empty port tank. Half the oil in the first flask was blown away before Taylor could empty it into the filler neck. Before they could repeat the process Kingsford-Smith warned his copilot to hang on as he climbed again. This time, as the engine roared back to life, Taylor saw Stannage giving a triumphant thumbs-up signal from the cockpit. Even with only half a flask of oil the pressure had improved!

Taylor's account, written nearly thirty years later, gave an insight to his emotional reaction to the ordeal:

> We were almost on the sea. I had flung myself down on the [engine] cowl again and the engine came in with a booming roar. I could see the surface of the ocean skimming a few feet below. I felt madly exhilarated and happy. I wanted to stand up and laugh and shout at the roaring mass of air that tore at everything around me. Then a sudden fear hit me as I realized I was letting go my hold. Suddenly the roaring stopped and I knew that Smithy had throttled back and I transferred about a gallon of oil into the tank. When Smithy had gained a few hundred feet again I moved safely back into the cabin. I collapsed inside, utterly worn out, but exhilarated. We could keep the *Cross* in the air.

Back at his radio Stannage told of the latest drama. He ended with, "Bill Taylor is the world's greatest hero." Throughout the long homeward flight radio stations on both sides of the Tasman followed the sensation-filled flight. Newspapers hit the street headlined SMITHY IN GREAT DANGER. Australia came to a virtual standstill as at home and at work crowds gathered around radios listening for the latest message. From some of Stannage's reports it seemed unlikely that the three men would make it. Just when it appeared their immediate problems were over he reported further complications. The build up in tension was like an expertly conceived thriller—there were even those who suggested the whole thing was a put-up job to gain publicity. Similar accusations had been made following an incident in 1929 when the *Southern Cross* was missing in the Australian outback for thirteen days. The idea was

preposterous. Even had they been able to engineer the broken manifold to strike the propeller, no amount of publicity based on public sympathy could make up for their failure to complete the vital mail service. The whole idea of the flight had been to convince the Australian and New Zealand governments of the company's ability to provide a fast and reliable mail service in order to gain government support.

Taylor had recovered somewhat from his ordeal and was back in the copilot's seat. He was a sorry sight, his eyes red and raw, fingers badly torn, and clothes covered in oil. Thirty minutes had gone by and he watched the oil pressure gauge in terrified fascination. Would he have to transfer more oil? How soon? How often?

Then it happened. The needle started to flicker and the pressure fell again. Until he saw it happen he had not been able to face up to the fact that he might have to repeat the terrifying ordeal. Taylor called Stannage up front—at least they had some sort of system organized this time. The collection of oil from the dead engine went without a hitch. The transfer to the left engine was achieved following the same procedure as before, with Kingsford-Smith alternately throttling the engine back, then clawing for height with Taylor hanging on for dear life. But this time as they were completing the top-up it became obvious that the ailing engine was starting to lose power. With Taylor still out under the wing, Kingsford-Smith decided it was time to call up his "ace in the hole." It was a bitter decision, but with Taylor risking his life to sustain an engine that was no longer giving full power, there was no alternative. Kingsford-Smith called to Stannage to dump the mail overboard. It saved the *Southern Cross* from the water.

With Taylor safely back in his seat, they carried on. The failing left engine was occasionally misfiring and could only be run at full throttle for short periods before a series of bangs from the exhaust forced them to throttle back. Fortunately most of the Fokker's fuel load had been used by this time and its decreasing weight along with dumping the mail helped compensate for the loss of engine power.

Listeners in Australia waited on the edge of their seats. Among the stream of messages came one that brought a wry smile. "What idiots men are to fly over the 'drink' . . . a nice comfy ship will do me in the future. If I ever get the chance to use one again." Stannage's message struck a chord with the press and was cabled around the world.

By 3 P.M. the fliers reckoned to be within sighting distance of land. For the last hour they had scanned the empty horizon in search of the S.S. *Captain Cook* but had not seen a single vessel. Their first sight of Australia was a thin purple ribbon on the western horizon. Kingsford-Smith called to the radio operator to come up front. Three pairs of eyes never left the dark ribbon until they had positively identified it as the coastline. Their progress toward it seemed painfully slow. Until then, with no reference point below on the open sea, they had not been aware of just how slowly they were flying. Their speed was less than most cars on the open highway.

The dying left engine was misfiring continuously and Kingsford-Smith was forced to throttle right back, letting it cool as they descended slowly toward the water. It would then respond for a while and allow them to fight back up a few hundred feet before it would overheat once more. The process was repeated again and again and then, about 25 miles from land, the telltale flicker of the oil pressure gauge again attracted their attention. Kingsford-Smith was loath to let his copilot risk his life again, reasoning that the engine would last long enough for them to ditch only a short distance from the coast. The *Southern Cross* should stay afloat long enough for them to be picked up. But the gallant Taylor would have none of it. For the third time he risked his life and kept the failing engine alive. With the oil pressure back up again, the *Southern Cross* staggered over Sydney's North Head at 4:45 P.M. and crawled toward Mascot.

A huge crowd was waiting to greet the fliers. As the Fokker approached, the crowd's pent-up anxiety was released and the arriving airmen were given a welcome "wilder than if they had just broken the record," as newspapers reported.

The drain filter housing from which Taylor extracted the lifesaving oil from the failed right engine. (TGJ)

With its shattered propeller stationary and the left engine backfiring almost continually, the *Southern Cross* flared over the edge of Mascot and made a "feather-light" touchdown. Even after nearly seventeen hours at the controls, most of them flying a crippled aircraft, Kingsford-Smith gave the crowd a superb landing.

For the next hour or so the trio were surrounded by the vast crowd signing autograph books and answering reporters' questions. They recounted how at times the Fokker had been so low that its wheels had almost clipped the waves—and showed salt smudges to prove their point. Kingsford-Smith announced that his copilot's courage deserved official recognition: "We wouldn't be here now if it hadn't been for him." Taylor was later awarded the Empire Medal, the

A 1930s montage showing the *Southern Cross*, with its shattered propeller, landing at Sydney following the trans-Tasman drama. The insets (left–right) show Taylor, Kingsford-Smith, and Stannage. (Queensland Newspapers).

highest possible award for civilian bravery. Following World War II Taylor would receive an even greater honor when he too was knighted for his contribution to Australian aviation. Besides pioneering the Indian Ocean from Australia to Africa in 1939, a few years later P. G. Taylor would also survey the South Pacific in a Consolidated Catalina (P.B.Y.) flying boat—establishing airline routes from Australia to Mexico and Chile.

When the last interview had been given and the last picture taken, the three exhausted men went home. Mary Kingsford-Smith, who had remained home throughout the nerve-wracking flight, was waiting for her husband. Kingsford-Smith more than anything wanted a hot bath and had been in the tub for more than an hour when visitors arrived. His wife went up to fetch him and found Smithy asleep in the bath with only his nose above water. "For the second time that day he came close to drowning," she recalled.

Six months later Australia's great Pacific pioneer was dead. As Pan American Airways prepared to dispatch its first transpacific airmail flight in the slipstream of the *Southern Cross,* Sir Charles Kingsford-Smith and his mechanic vanished over the Bay of Bengal. Sick, broke, still desperately trying to raise funds for his trans-Tasman airmail service, Kingsford-Smith was attempting to set a new speed record between England and Australia in his Lockheed *Lady Southern Cross.* Hearing the tragic news, his comrade Bill Taylor said: "He had the enlightened spirit of the born pioneer. Whatever the risks, the way into the unknown was always an irresistible invitation to him."

In the United States, where Allan Hancock and others had helped so much in Kingsford-Smith's first transpacific flight, Jimmy Doolittle wrote:

Smithy was one of the finest gentlemen it was my good fortune to know. He was a pioneer who made great contributions to the progress of aeronautics. He is truly one of the outstanding names in the history of aviation. His loss is a tragedy, not only for Australia, but for the world.

Smithy's mechanic, Tommy Pethybridge, inspects the damaged propeller following the *Southern Cross*'s safe arrival in Sydney. Six months later Pethybridge was with Kingsford-Smith aboard the Lockheed Altair *Lady Southern Cross* when it vanished in the Bay of Bengal. (Queensland Newspapers)

11

Pan Am's Gleaming Clippers
The Final Conquest

AIR ROUTE NETWORK ACROSS THE PACIFIC IS VISION OF PAN-AMERICA'S CHIEF.... CALIFORNIA-CHINA HOP MAY BLAZE THE TRAIL FOR REGULAR SERVICE. These headlines in *The Washington Daily News* on February 4, 1935, came just two months after the tragic loss of Charles Ulm's *Stella Australis*.

Like Ulm, the visionary president of Pan American Airways, Juan T. Trippe, had long dreamed of a transpacific airline. But rather than a hastily contrived ship-and-plane service, Trippe's plan was the result of years of research and development and was aimed at providing a total Pacific

November 22, 1935. The *China Clipper* sets out from San Francisco on Pan Am's inaugural transpacific service. Beneath the M-130 the suspension cables are being hung on the Golden Gate Bridge, and in the background is the partially completed Bay Bridge to Oakland. (NASM)

network. Indeed, the map accompanying the February 4 article depicted island-hopping routes to Japan, China, the Philippines, New Zealand, and Australia. However, unlike Ulm's plans to use ocean liners for the critical leg between Hawaii and California, Trippe already had aircraft in production that would fly his passengers over the 2,400 mile barrier. Trippe said in the article:

In approaching the new engineering problems involved in conducting transoceanic services across the Pacific, we have been greatly aided by the practical experiences of four years' operations directly across the Caribbean Sea, still the longest overwater air transport service in the world.

Juan Trippe's consuming passion with airplanes went back to 1917 when he took a leave of absence from his studies at Yale to join the Navy.

Pan Am founder Juan Trippe chats with Charles Lindbergh in Panama following the introduction of the airline's Miami-Panama Ford Tri-Motor service in 1929. Employed as a consultant, Lindbergh gave advice that helped shape the airline for thirty years. (NASM)

Trained as a bomber pilot, he eventually returned to Yale determined to pursue a career in aviation. But unlike most demobilized military pilots, Trippe was not interested in stick-and-rudder barnstorming or battling across America carrying airmail. He saw the airplane as the people carrier of the future, a miraculous machine that soon would replace transcontinental trains and trans-oceanic passenger liners. His vision was to build an airline that would shrink the world until the continents were but a day apart.

The determined young entrepreneur took the first step in 1923 when he purchased seven war-surplus Navy seaplanes and formed Long Island Airways—a charter service that ferried the rich to their East Coast summer resorts. Four years later, by contrived mergers, incisive corporate maneuvers, political lobbying, and calling on wealthy Yale friends for backing, the shrewd twenty-eight-year-old was president of Pan American Airways, Inc., and had a government airmail contract between Key West, Florida, and Havana. By 1939 Trippe had parlayed that two-airplane, 90-mile airmail service into the largest airline in the world. Its greatest achievement was to be the conquest of the Pacific.

Trippe surrounded himself with talented young men like Dutch-born Andre Priester, whose planning and crew-training skills quickly earned him the reputation of "the wizard of operations." When it became obvious that trans-oceanic success hinged on new navigation techniques, Trippe hired a brilliant engineer, Hugo Leuteritz, to invent new radio navigation systems. To survey and advise on new Pan Am routes, and to route-test new aircraft, he recruited Charles Lindbergh.

By 1931 Pan American's network encircled the Caribbean and most of Central and South America. With air routes stretching 20,308 miles to twenty countries, Trippe's airline was the world's largest in terms of route miles. Throughout the Caribbean and Latin America, Pan American's aircraft and immaculately uniformed crews had become an unofficial ambassador, a highly visible symbol of Washington's Good Neighbor Policy. In June of that year, as Pan Am's twenty-two-seat Consolidated Commodore flying boats ranged across the Caribbean and south to Buenos Aires, Trippe made known his ultimate goal.

Though already awaiting delivery of brand new thirty-eight-seat Sikorsky S-40 flying boats for his lucrative Canal Zone routes, he wrote to aircraft manufacturers asking them to submit designs for an even more advanced airliner. His specifica-

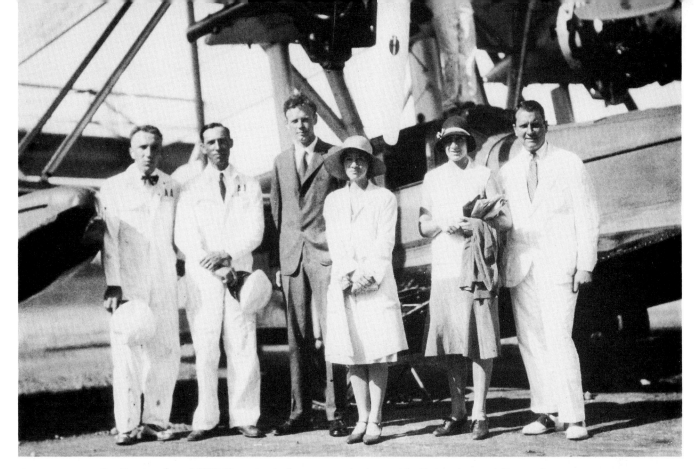

In September 1929 Pan Am's long association with flying boat airliners began with Igor Sikorsky's S-38. Lindbergh (third from left) and Trippe (right) were accompanied by their wives when Lindy inaugurated the S-38 service to Paramaribo, in Dutch Guiana. (NASM)

tions called for a high-speed, multiengine flying boat with a range of 2,500 miles against 30-mph head winds. It must carry a crew of four and at least 300 pounds of airmail. Trippe was preparing to bridge the Atlantic and Pacific oceans.

A month later Charles Lindbergh and his wife left New York in a single-engine Lockheed Sirius floatplane to survey a route to China. Trippe believed that the key to transpacific mail and passenger operations lay with a northern route similar to that followed by the Army's 1924 World Fliers. Accordingly Lindbergh was instructed to investigate a land-hugging airway via Canada, Alaska, the Soviet Union, and Japan. Completing the remarkable journey, Lindbergh reported that the northern route was viable. However, the plan had to be dropped when the Soviet government, which had not then been formally recognized by the United States, refused permission for exploration of its territory.

With the northern route no longer a proposition, Trippe had no alternative but to plan an island-hopping route across the Pacific. To achieve this meant finding a passenger aircraft capable of carrying a profitable payload over the 2,400-mile overwater barrier between the mainland and Hawaii. He was aware that such an aircraft would also enable Pan Am to fly the Atlantic—potentially the world's most lucrative route. As early as 1928 Trippe had commenced negotiations with Britain's Imperial Airways, but with the Atlantic run still tangled in international bureaucratic red tape, he decided to concentrate on the Pacific. That dream was now in the hands of the six aircraft manufacturers who agonized over meeting his seemingly impossible requirements.

Two companies eventually submitted bids. Igor Sikorsky, who had pioneered the concept of big multiengine airliners before fleeing the Russian

Although Igor Sikorsky's S-42 flying boat lacked the range to carry a profitable transpacific payload, it was an ideal workhorse for Pan Am's Pacific survey flights. (NASM)

Revolution, proposed a thirty-two-seat S-42 flying boat powered by four 700-hp Pratt & Whitney Hornet engines. Although its range was only 1,200 miles with a full passenger load, it could cover nearly 3,000 miles if the payload was reduced to 800 pounds. The second bidder was Glenn Martin, who had designed an elegant forty-one-seater powered by four 850-hp Pratt & Whitney Twin Wasp engines. With a gross takeoff weight of 52,000 pounds—11,000 more than the S-42—and a range of 4,000 miles in the airmail-only configuration, Martin's M-130 seemed the obvious choice. However, at around $420,000 (approximately $6 million in today's money), the M-130 would cost $180,000 more than the S-42 and it would take a year longer to be delivered. Trippe placed orders for both machines: three

M-130s and ten S-42s. Although the S-42 was clearly more suited to Pan Am's Caribbean routes, he planned to use one to survey the Pacific while awaiting delivery of the first M-130.

Pan Am's first S-42 was tested by Charles Lindbergh, who found its maximum range to be about 2,540 miles. As this was insufficient to provide an adequate safety margin on the leg to Hawaii, additional fuel tanks were ordered for the second aircraft. The prototype was named the *Brazilian Clipper* and was put into service on the run between Miami and Rio de Janeiro in August 1934. Since introducing its predecessor, the S-40, Pan Am had decided that all its aircraft would carry the Clipper name, in honor of the fabled tall-masted Yankee clipper ships that had once sailed the world's oceans. Satisfied that he would soon

Designer Igor Sikorsky and Charles Lindbergh in the passenger cabin of the S-42. Lindbergh flight-tested the prototype and recommended the installation of additional fuel tanks. (NASM)

have an aircraft capable of crossing the Pacific, Trippe approached Postmaster General James Farley for an airmail contract. However, at this stage, Pan Am only received assurances that the Post Office Department was "interested."

Capt. Edwin C. Musick was chosen to command the modified S-42 *Pan American Clipper* on the Pacific survey flights. A former civilian instructor with the Army Air Service, Musick had joined the company in 1927 and was chief pilot of the Caribbean Division. Since the first S-42 had gone into service, Musick had conducted a series of rigorous tests, including a 2,500-mile nonstop dress rehearsal for the flight to Hawaii. In March 1935, satisfied with the modified S-42's range and performance, Musick and his crew ferried it from Miami to Pan Am's new Pacific Division base at Alameda, near San Francisco. There test-

ing and crew training continued. Pan Am's proposed route stretched 8,120 miles from San Francisco to Manila. Refueling stops were planned at Honolulu, Midway Island, Wake Island, and Guam. The company was still negotiating for landing rights in Hong Kong to link with the China National Aviation Corporation's mainland routes (Trippe had already acquired a majority interest in this Chinese airline). Musick's first survey flight was to encompass only the critical leg to Honolulu.

Before it began the airline service, Pan Am was also faced with the mammoth task of building refueling and passenger facilities on its mid-Pacific steppingstones. Years after, explaining the incredible logistics involved to members of Britain's Royal Aeronautical Society, Trippe related:

We decided to set up complete bases at all five points in a single expedition. On March 27, 1935, the S.S. *North Haven* left San Francisco on a four months' assignment. Aboard her had been shipped two complete villages, five air bases, a quarter million gallons of fuel, forty-four airline technicians, a construction force of seventy-four, food to feed them for months and, literally, 1,018,897 other items of equipment and material. Before the *North Haven* had reached Midway in early April a specially fitted Sikorsky S-42, the *Pan American Clipper,* took off on a round-trip survey flight to Honolulu. Within the next few months, as each succeeding island base was set up, this same plane conducted, step by step, surveys of the remaining stages of the route.

Only the first of the *Pan American Clipper*'s four survey flights produced a serious operational problem. On the 18-hour outbound leg Musick averaged 130 mph and reached Honolulu a mere one minute behind schedule. However, on the return journey the S-42 was buffeted by severe head winds. With its ground speed reduced to less than 100 mph it appeared that the flying boat might not reach the coast. When Musick eventually landed safely on San Francisco Bay they had been airborne 21 hours and the tanks were virtually dry. Lessons learned on the survey flights were passed on as modifications for the three M-130s, mainly concerning improvements to the navigation and radio equipment.

It was also decided to eliminate as much night flying as possible due to the difficulties experienced in avoiding turbulent cumulonimbus cloud during the hours of darkness. Thus, with night stops at each port of call, the final schedule called for a six-day crossing involving about 60 hours actual flying. It was a leisurely pace when compared with today's 15-hour jet service. Nevertheless in 1935 it represented a massive saving in time—being only a third of the time taken by the fastest transpacific ocean liner.

The first Martin M-130 was delivered in October 1935, and Musick and his crew began training on the new aircraft. Two weeks later Pan

Capt. Edwin Musick and his Sikorsky S-42 *Pan American Clipper* shortly before departing from Alameda on the first survey flight to Hawaii on April 16, 1935. (NASM)

American received the welcome news that it had been awarded the vital transpacific airmail contract at the rate of $2 per mile. Preparations began for the first revenue service. As the hotels being built on Midway, Wake, and Guam were not yet completed, the flight was to carry airmail, freight, and company staff only. The lack of mid-Pacific passenger facilities also would give the crew an opportunity to complete a number of shakedown flights on the difficult route. On November 2 the M-130, named *China Clipper,* made a 2,400-mile practice flight from Miami to Puerto Rico and back—the range between San Francisco and Honolulu. Six days later it took off for California via Acapulco, Mexico. Arriving in San Francisco, Musick and his crew heard the sad

Hawaii-bound, the *Pan American Clipper* passes through San Francisco's Golden Gate. Below the Sikorsky, work is underway on the towers of the now-famous bridge. (NASM)

Off Diamond Head on April 17, 1935, the *Pan American Clipper* completes the first survey mission. The flight to Hawaii took eighteen hours and nine minutes. (NASM)

Though slower than the S-42, Glenn Martin's M-130 carried sufficient payload for Pan Am to commence transpacific services. This cutaway drawing illustrates the locations of crew, passenger, and cargo compartments. (NASM)

news that pioneer Pacific flier, Sir Charles Kingsford-Smith, was missing over the Bay of Bengal on a flight between England and Australia. Within a space of only ten months the two Australian airmen who had led the way in the *Southern Cross* had vanished at sea.

On November 22, 1935, twenty-five thousand people crammed the shore around Alameda for the departure of the *China Clipper*. Thousands more waited along the San Francisco waterfront to watch the flying boat depart across the bay. Nowhere along the route was the departure of the first service anticipated with more excitement than in Honolulu which, like much of the world, listened on the special international radio hookup. Even though eight years had passed since the Army's *Bird of Paradise* had brought the promise of an air link with the mainland, Hawaiians had not forgotten the exhilaration of the flight of the *Southern Cross* and the tragedy of the Dole Derby. As the celebrations to mark the *China Clipper*'s departure from Alameda got underway, Hawaii prepared to celebrate. As if the gods were sending a spectacular acknowledgment of the event, the active volcano Mokuaweoweo erupted, sending smoke and sparks towering over Hawaii Island.

On the flag-draped pier at Alameda, Postmaster General Farley read a message from President Franklin D. Roosevelt. "This is a century of progress that is without parallel, and it is our just pride that America and Americans have played no minor part in the blazing of new trails," it said in part. Moments later a stagecoach, the mail carrier of earlier days, delivered 110,000 letters for the *China Clipper* service. Weighing 1,897 pounds, they represented Pan American's first Pacific payload. Stepping up to the microphone, Juan Trippe soberly addressed the crew lining the jetty alongside their Clipper. "Captain Musick, you have your sailing orders. Cast off and depart for Manila in accordance therewith." As the band struck up "The Star-Spangled Banner," the great gleaming flying boat taxied out into the bay.

The takeoff didn't quite go according to plan, as Second Engineering Officer Victor Wright recalled years after in the *Alameda Times Star*. On the thirtieth anniversary of the flight he wrote:

After leaving the waterfront ramp Captain Musick circled on the water a few times to warm up the engines and then headed up the bay heading toward the looping wires of the San Francisco–Oakland bridge, then being built. As we left a convoy of escorting planes closed in behind us. It had been our intention to fly over the bridge, but Musick quickly saw that with the engine cowl flaps open he wouldn't be able to get enough speed to clear the wires, so

Standing next to the mail sacks, Postmaster General James A. Farley supervises loading of the transpacific mail aboard the M-130 *China Clipper* for the inaugural service to Manila. Juan Trippe (hatless, second from right) looks on. Captain Musick is at the top of the ramp flanked by the first officer, Capt. R. O. D. Sullivan. (NASM)

he nosed the Clipper down at the last moment and went under the bridge cables, threading his way through the dangling construction wires. We all ducked and held our breath until we were in the clear. I think the little planes must have been as surprised as we were, but they all followed us right through.

As the *China Clipper* climbed slowly out over the unfinished Golden Gate Bridge, Emory Bronte watched thoughtfully from a balcony on the University Club of San Francisco. Saying a quiet prayer, perhaps, he recalled his dramatic flight in the *City of Oakland* eight years earlier. The prayers that were offered for the men aboard the *China Clipper* were not in vain, for, other than the somewhat spectacular departure, the flight to Hawaii went like clockwork. The Martin's seven crew members quickly settled down to their carefully preplanned tasks. Besides Musick, who was in command of the flight, there were two other pilots: Capt. R. O. D. Sullivan was flying as first officer and 2dO George King was the junior pilot. Fred Noonan was navigation officer, Wilson Jarboe the radio officer, and C. D. Wright the first engineering officer. On this vital flight the *China Clipper* was in the hands of one of the most talented crews in airline history. No less than five of the men held airline transport licenses, three were aeronautical engineers, three were licensed radio operators, and two were master mariners. Furthermore Sullivan, Noonan, Jarboe, and C. D. Wright had already flown with Musick on several of the S-42 survey flights.

With no passengers on board, the airmen could afford the small luxury of wearing comfortable clothes for the 21-hour flight to Hawaii. Once clear of the coast they got out of their formal navy blue uniforms. "I wore a pair of red pajamas and bedroom slippers and the rest of the crew were just about as informal. We were sure a strange looking bunch of trail-blazers," Victor Wright recalled. Two hours out, Second Officer King, appointed flight correspondent for United Press, radioed the first of his "in-flight" dispatches. A few hours later the newspaper presses of the United States were printing his lyrical story. Un-

der a giant front-page banner depicting the flying boat and its route to Manila the *San Francisco Chronicle* reported:

ENGINES DRONE STEADILY. MEN GO ABOUT DUTIES LIKE CLOCKWORK. By George King, Second Flight Officer, aboard the *China Clipper* en route to Honolulu. As the sun goes down casting a flaming mantle over bulbous clouds beneath, scattered strips of cumulus high above the circular world sink into impenetrable blackness. A cloudy ceiling above shuts off the stars and the clouds below shut off the Pacific Ocean 7,000 feet below.

Throughout the night, flying mostly between layers of cloud and punching into stiff head winds, Musick and Sullivan fine-tuned the engines—ensuring they were getting the maximum air miles for each gallon of fuel they used. On the flight deck there were numerous conferences between pilots, engineers, and navigator Noonan as they compared fuel checks with the aircraft's progress. Maintaining the aircraft dead on track, Noonan took seven celestial sightings and the radio log showed forty-one radio direction bearings taken on various ships and ground stations in California and Hawaii. Besides making routine progress reports to land stations, the fliers were also in radio contact with ships along the route. At the midway point they reported their position to the U.S. Coast Guard cutter *Itasca*.

To combat fatigue, the crew was split into watches (teams). Horace Brock, who joined the Pacific Division the following year, described the routine that Pan Am had devised for the long haul:

While domestic pilots were limited by law to 8 hours a day and 85 hours a month, we flew up to 24 hours in a day and were limited only to 250 hours in three months. Of course, a Pacific crew was a multiple crew; everyone stood watches, four hours on and two off, but there was no way to get out of the environment. It was just as tiring off duty as on.

The next morning, cruising at 10,300 feet, they sighted the peaks of Hawaii Island and the towering column of smoke from the erupting volcano looming above a low bank of cloud. Musick ordered his crew back into uniform and shortly thereafter began descending into Honolulu. Approaching Diamond Head, the flying boat was joined by a formation of sixty military aircraft, which escorted it to Pan Am's new base on the Pearl City peninsula. At 10:19 A.M.—just one hour behind schedule—the *China Clipper* touched down on the placid waters of Pearl Harbor. ALOHA, GALLANT CLIPPER OF THE SKIES, trumpeted one local newspaper, echoing the feelings of Hawaii.

Through the night the Clipper was loaded with forty-two crates of fresh fruit, vegetables, and turkeys for Thanksgiving dinners for the Pan Am employees working on Midway and Wake. Also loaded were cartons of equipment and spares, and sixteen thousand letters for Manila. With a reduced fuel load required for the 1,296-mile run to Midway, the *China Clipper* could also carry passengers, and Pan Am took advantage of the opportunity. When the aircraft departed the next day, fourteen employees—relief ground staff for Midway and Wake—became the service's first unofficial passengers. They gazed in awe at the aircraft's interior. It was like a mini-hotel with its luxurious lounge–dining room, three separate passenger compartments, fully equipped galley, and toilets. Clearly Pan Am Clippers were going to set a new standard for airborne luxury.

The flight to Midway was also routine. With clear skies and a glittering chain of reefs and islands to follow, the aircraft completed the flight in 13 hours and 30 minutes, arriving on the lagoon just one minute late. The next day's flight across the International Date Line to Wake Island was not such a simple navigational exercise. Much of the flight was conducted over a dense cover of low cloud. Even though the island base was equipped with a radio direction finder to provide the aircraft with bearings, the equipment was still notoriously unreliable and no crew worth its salt would dare rely on radio alone to find its way. Their midocean target was actually a small

circular reef linking three tiny sand islets. Barely poking higher than the Pacific surf, its total land mass was less than three square miles. There was no land within 1,000 miles and the Martin did not have enough fuel to backtrack to Midway once it had passed its "point of no return."

Although taking octant (aerial sextant) sights of the sun enabled the navigator to easily determine the latitude, there was little to assist in determining the longitude, which indicated how far they had traveled along their course. Thus, on this leg in particular, Noonan navigated in earnest, putting into practice the techniques he had set up after conferring with Harold Gatty, Wiley Post's navigator on his first world flight. The Australian navigational expert was yet another of the bright young men whom Trippe had signed up as consultants to the airline. One of the navigation methods Gatty introduced to Pan Am was Francis Chichester's "theory of deliberate error," a technique once used by sailing ships that Chichester had developed to locate minuscule Lord Howe Island on his trans-Tasman flight in 1931. It was a standby procedure for locating Wake, as a former Clipper pilot Horace Brock recalled in his book *Flying the Oceans:*

> If we had serious doubts about our position, we would get a sun line when the sun was low in the sky in the late afternoon, as we were nearing Wake, and then advance the line to have it run through Wake on the chart. Then we would make a definite turn to the north or south and dead reckon up to the line, so to be reasonably sure we were either north or south of Wake. Then we would turn to fly down the line till we made landfall. It was sometimes nerve-wracking. Radio bearings would have made it all so easy—had good ones been obtainable. Often they were not.

Having relied mainly on dead reckoning and sun shots for much of the flight, the *China Clipper* got a welcome fix when, with the clouds breaking up, it passed over the Matson liner *President Lincoln,* which was en route for Japan. Later as they neared Wake all eyes in the cockpit scanned the horizon for a sight of pale water—the most visible indication of the underwater reefs and sand shoals that surround most Pacific atolls. Musick and Sullivan followed company routine of sticking to the course that Noonan had clipped on the instrument panel. No matter what change in water color or shadow they might see just off the bow, the rule was that there was to be no change in the compass heading until someone made a positive identification. On this occasion they were receiving bearings from Wake, and 12

hours and 26 minutes out of Midway, touched down inside the reef.

To the Pan Am ground crew arriving for the first time Wake must have been a depressing sight. Instead of the tropical palms and flowering bushes one expects on a Pacific isle, Wake was covered with dense undergrowth and stunted trees. Indeed it was so totally devoid of fresh water and worthwhile vegetation that it was later to become the site of an early experiment in hydroponic gardening. By 1939 passengers would dine

The cockpit of the M-130. In the center of the instrument panel, clearly visible to both pilots, is the blind-flying display surmounted by an early type of gyroscopic artificial horizon. (NASM)

ALOHA, GALLANT CLIPPER OF THE SKIES, headlined the Hawaiian newspapers. The *China Clipper*'s crew were feted as heroes. (NASM)

on fresh vegetables grown in weak solutions of mineral salts. By then Pan Am's Wake Hotel would be an oasis, surrounded by manicured lawns and flowering shrubs. Guests would play tennis, swim in a pool, and view the lagoon's coral gardens though glass-bottomed boats.

The *China Clipper*'s next leg, a low-level flight to Guam, was a far cry from today's high-flying jets, as engineer Victor Wright recalled. He wrote: "Even though the Clipper performed best at 8,000 feet we tried various altitudes to make the most of the trade winds, which were now pushing us along. As an indication of how flying has changed—at 1,200 feet we found it so warm and comfortable that we opened all the windows." Approaching Guam, radio operator Jarboe used a trick to get a cross bearing from a Japanese radio station on an island 50 miles north of their route. Sending out a "CQ" signal, the international code requiring listening stations to answer, Jarboe took a bearing while the Japanese operator replied. "We couldn't use that too often, though, because in 1935 the Japanese weren't interested in helping anyone establish an airline across the Pacific," Wright explained.

CHINA CLIPPER GIVES GUAM MAIL FROM U.S. IN FOUR DAYS, Guam's Associated Press correspondent cabled the world on November 27, following the

205

A flotilla of small boats welcomed the *China Clipper* in Manila Bay. They circled dangerously close as the flying boat tied up at Pan Am's mooring stage. (NASM)

China Clipper's arrival. At Guam Musick discovered the only planning error of the flight. Someone in Manila, confused by the date change caused by crossing the International Dateline, had scheduled the flying boat's arrival for November 29. With special welcoming ceremonies already planned, there was no alternative but to lay over in Guam for two days.

Shortly after 6 A.M. on November 29, Musick lifted his M-130 safely from rough water in Guam's Apra Harbor. Fourteen uneventful hours later he landed in Manila Bay. A crowd estimated to exceed a quarter of a million lined the waterfront at Luneta Park. Minutes after mooring, as formations of military planes circled overhead, the flying boat was surrounded by a fleet of small boats and ferries. The celebrations were astonishing. The crewmen were led through a massive floral arch, then treated to a ticker-tape parade through a city decorated especially for the occasion. Manila's *Tribune* newspaper produced a special pictorial issue headlined CLIPPER COMPLETES EPOCHAL FLIGHT. Besides including details of the *China Clipper*'s 59-hour-48-minute flight time Pacific crossing, it recorded Musick's speech at the official welcoming ceremony hosted by Philippines President Manuel Quezon. Showing that he could turn a phrase almost as neatly as he could his flying boat, Musick gave a stirring address. Toward the end he paraphrased the years of effort that Juan Trippe and his team had put into the transpacific mission, stating:

Today's flight is not the result of a simple process. Five years of ceaseless planning, designing and construction, training and practice have advanced aviation to this point where today it is possible for us to span an ocean, where hereto air transport service only crossed narrow channels. The rich reward of sweeping away that age-old barrier of distance between the new world and the old, between East and West, has been the inspiration through which this great achievement has been made.

At the conclusion of his speech Musick handed President Quezon a letter from President Roosevelt to officially mark the opening of the transpacific airmail service. The Filipino President gave Musick a letter to carry back to President Roosevelt on the return flight.

The following year more than a thousand travelers had applied for tickets on Pan Am's first transpacific passenger service. With the M-130 still restricted by the fuel required on the San Francisco–Hawaii sector, only seven seats were available. The first transpacific ticket went to R. F. Bradley, the aviation manager of Standard Oil of California. The others went to four businessmen and two women who declared themselves "world travelers." Ultimately the lack of seat capacity was not to prove a major problem as the $799 one-way fare between San Francisco and Manila (about $10,000 today) kept demand low. Those who could afford the fare were to experience luxurious aerial cruising that became legendary on Pan Am's Clippers. Even Hollywood was to be caught up in the romance of flying boat travel, adding to the glamour with a film entitled *China Clipper* starring Humphrey Bogart as the aircraft's skipper. No other airlines would match Pan Am's Clipper service until several years later, when Imperial Airways and Qantas combined to

A quarter of a million Filipinos lined the shores of Manila Bay to watch the arrival of the first transpacific airline. (NASM)

A San Francisco shop window, displaying bird of paradise flowers flown overnight from Hawaii, advertises Pan Am's New Pacific service. (NASM)

R. F. Bradley, manager of the Standard Oil Company of California's aviation department, proudly holds the first transpacific passenger ticket issued by P.A.A. Displaying a model of the *China Clipper* is the airline's San Francisco traffic manager, V. A. Kropff. (NASM)

Passengers disembark from an M-130 at Pan Am's Pearl Harbor base. (NASM)

introduce their Short S-23 Empire flying boats.

When the first passenger service commenced from Alameda on October 21, 1936, the reliability of the M-130s had been tested by a series of airmail flights, and the hotels had been built at Wake and Midway. Captain Musick was again in command as the *Hawaii Clipper* took off from San Francisco Bay. His crew now included male flight attendants to pamper the passengers. In the dining lounge five-course meals were served on bone china, with flashing silverware and spotless linen. For the long haul to Hawaii there were changing rooms and sleeping berths—all the luxuries of an ocean liner. From Hawaii, with fuel requirements reduced, four extra passengers were carried. The six-day crossing was completed without incident and the return flight reached San Francisco on November 11. Pan Am's third M-130, the *Philippine Clipper,* made a special flight to Hong Kong on October 23, 1936, to cel-

ebrate the awarding of landing rights at the British colony. On board were Juan Trippe and his wife. A regular Manila–Hong Kong link was to begin in April 1937 using a Sikorsky S-42 named the *Hong Kong Clipper*.

To prepare for future passenger increase, and the planned Atlantic service, Pan American Airways had already placed an order with the Boeing Aircraft Company for six seventy-four-passenger flying boats, the first to be delivered early December 1937. They were a far cry from Boeing's first aircraft, the 1916 B & W floatplane, which had operated New Zealand's earliest airmail service. The company had recently designed a new long-range B-15 bomber, and when asked to develop a flying boat, Boeing engineer Wellwood Beall suggested: "Take the [B-15] wing and put a hull under it." Boeing did just that and came up with a stunning double-deck flying hotel that promised a cruise speed of 175 mph over a distance of 3,500

When a jetty was not available, passengers and crew disembarked by launch. (NASM)

The spacious forward passenger cabin of the Martin M-130. (NASM)

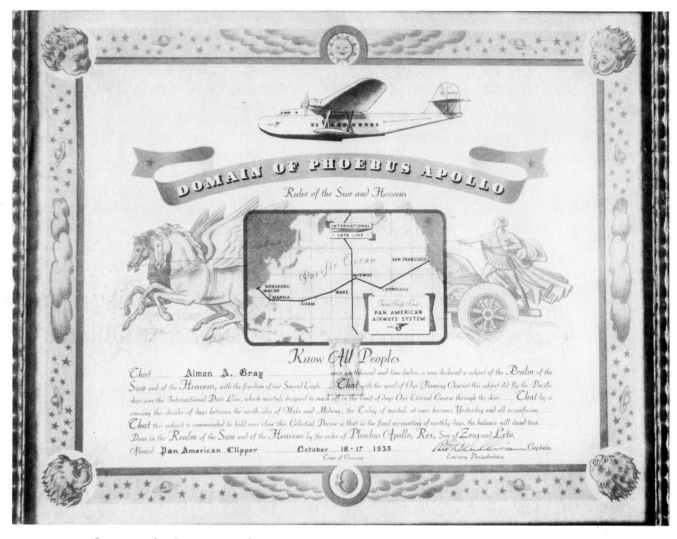

Crossing the International Date Line, passengers were presented with special certificates. This one, signed by Capt. R. O. D. Sullivan, was awarded to a comany employee carried on the S-42 *Pan American Clipper*'s final pacific survey flight. (NASM)

miles. Weighing more than 41 tons fully loaded, its Wright Double Cyclone engines had more than twice the power of the Martin and could be serviced in flight by walkways inside the giant wing. Named the B-314 Clipper, it would become the largest passenger aircraft of its day and the most successful flying boat ever built.

Juan Trippe also saw the Boeing 314 as the key to running a profitable passenger service in the South Pacific. With the route now established to mainland Asia, and with Japan too involved in its war with China to consider a Tokyo service, Trippe had turned his attention to Australasia. It had always been his intention to include the South Pacific region in his airline network. However, Britain's Imperial Airways had by then combined with Australia's fledgling international airline Qantas to service Australia via the Middle

To Emory Bronte

On the tenth anniversary of his pioneering 1927 flight to Hawaii, Emory Bronte was a passenger on board the *China Clipper*. The *Honolulu Advertiser* presented the airman with this photo montage. (NASM)

East. The British government was not keen to see Pan Am flying into Australia unless reciprocal landing rights were given for Imperial Airways to fly to Hawaii. When this was refused by the United States government, Australia bowed to British pressure. Although an obvious candidate for an extension of the Imperial Airways–Qantas service, tiny New Zealand had not yet been included in Imperial's Empire route. With no trans-Tasman service to link it with Australia, the New Zealand government jumped at Trippe's offer to become the terminus of Pan American's South Pacific network.

On March 17, 1937, Pan Am's pioneering Captain Musick took off from San Francisco in a special long-range Sikorsky S-42B to survey the route to Auckland, New Zealand. After refueling at Honolulu he flew to Kingman Reef, an atoll midway between Hawaii and American Samoa, where the steamer *North Wind* was stationed with fuel and supplies. From there the S-42B flew on to Pago Pago, Samoa, finally reaching Auckland on March 29. It made the return journey to Honolulu the following month. Unfortunately, Boeing was running a year behind schedule on the new flying boats, and with the three Martins

In February 1939 the brilliant Boeing 314 flying boats began Pacific operations. This artist's impression shows the double-deck design, which set a new standard for passenger comfort and space. Following World War II, Boeing's double-deck concept was incorporated into their piston-engine Stratocruiser and eventually their 747 jumbo jet. (NASM)

The world's greatest flying boat, the Boeing 314, on liftoff. Able to carry a profitable payload more than 3,500 miles, it put Pan American Airways at the leading edge of transoceanic flying. (NASM)

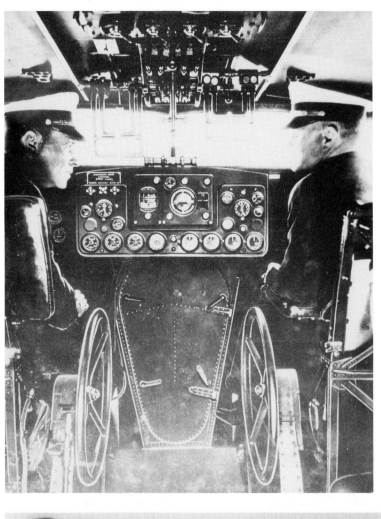

The flight deck of the Boeing 314. Flying boat crews used the more nautical term "control bridge." (NASM)

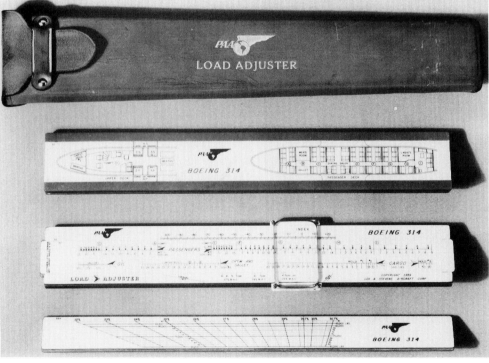

To assist in the critical task of loading the Boeing 314, Pan Am turned to slide-rule technology. Today's major airlines use computers to perform weight and balance calculations. (NASM)

In April 1937 the S-42 *Hong Kong Clipper* began a new service linking Manila with Hong Kong. (NASM)

already committed on the northern run, Pan Am was forced to begin a mail-only service using the long-range Sikorskys. On December 23, 1937, the *Samoan Clipper* operated the first airmail service to New Zealand.

On the second run, in January 1938, Pan Am suffered its first tragic loss in the Pacific. Musick was at the controls of the S-42B *Samoan Clipper* when it radioed that it was returning to Pago Pago with an oil leak in one of the engines. A later message was received advising that Musick was intending to lighten the Clipper by dumping some of the fuel load. Nothing more was heard from the crippled flying boat. A search found only floating life jackets and an oil slick at the crash scene. It was later surmised by investigators that the Sikorsky had exploded in flight while dumping fuel—probably from the siphoning gasoline being ignited by an engine's exhaust pipe.

The sad news was cabled to all Pan American Pacific stations by Divisional Manager Clarence M. Young. Advising that the aircraft had suffered a "sudden fire of undetermined origin," Young called for a five-minute suspension of all operations, other than responding to emergencies. Musick was idolized by the airline's staff and Young's

On March 29, 1937, Captain Musick completed Pan Am's first survey flight to New Zealand. Elated at the prospect of finally getting an international airline service, crowds lined the shore as the special long-range Sikorsky S-42B dropped anchor in Auckland Harbor. (Whites Aviation)

Captain Musick's ill-fated S-42B NC-16734 *Samoan Clipper* exploded in flight near Pago Pago in January 1938. (NASM)

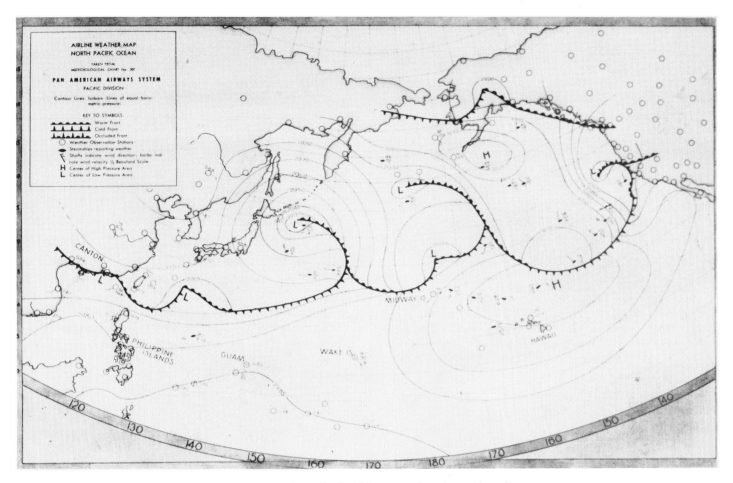

Pan American Airways introduced a highly specialized weather forecasting service for its transpacific flights. Route weather maps (above) were updated by radio throughout the flight. (NASM)

five-minute operational "silence" was to allow everyone across the Pacific to honor the pioneering pilot. Young's message ended:

It is intended solely as an effort on the part of those of us who have been privileged to be associated with Captain Musick and the members of his crew to express in some measure our deep sorrow and our great loss which has befallen not only ourselves but the entire air transportation industry throughout the world.

Following the loss of the *Samoan Clipper,* the U.S. Department of Commerce withdrew its authorization of Pago Pago as a landing site, and operations to New Zealand were suspended pending delivery of the new Boeings and selection of a less tenuous route. The airline suffered

an even more crippling setback six months later when the *China Clipper* vanished without a trace between Guam and Manila. Besides its crew of nine, six passengers were lost.

The results were devastating. For more than two years Pan American Clippers had calmly bridged the ocean with a precision that had made crossing the Pacific seem almost routine. Its aircraft and crews seemed almost invincible. Not even the tragic loss of Amelia Earhart and her former Pan Am navigator Fred Noonan while crossing the Pacific in July 1937 had shaken public confidence in transoceanic air travel. The two airline catastrophes, however, coming only six months apart, were another matter. Passenger business fell off sharply. Furthermore, with only two Martins left, services had to be severely reduced. With losses on the Pacific route nearing $100,000 a month, Pan Am held on grimly await-

In 1937 the *China Clipper* made a special flight to Catalina Island. On board was the aircraft's designer, Glenn Martin, and his mother. A quarter of a century earlier Martin had made the 60-mile return flight from the mainland in a wood and wire seaplane, thus making America's first tentative step across the Pacific. (NASM)

ing the delivery of the more profitable Boeings. Coincidentally Trippe renewed his efforts to commence Atlantic operations.

Pan American weathered the storm, and on February 22, 1939, the first Boeing B-314 *California Clipper* replaced the Martins on the northern Pacific route. Four months later the brilliant Boeing had also opened Pan Am's long awaited Atlantic service. On July 12, 1940, another B-314 reopened the airmail service to New Zealand following a new route via Los Angeles, Honolulu, Canton Island, and Noumea, New Caledonia. On its second flight the brilliant Boeing began carrying passengers to New Zealand. By October 1941 Charles Kingsford-Smith's steppingstone

islands of Fiji had been added to Pan American's network.

On December 7, 1941, the B-314 *Pacific Clipper* was en route from New Caledonia for Auckland when RO John Poindexter received a dramatic message. The Japanese had bombed Pearl Harbor and the *Pacific Clipper* was instructed to remain in New Zealand awaiting new orders. In Auckland the Boeing's commander, Capt. Robert Ford, received orders from Pan Am's New York headquarters informing him to return to America "the long way round"—thus avoiding the possibility of being intercepted by Japanese aircraft over the Pacific. Twenty-five days later, after circling home via Australia, India, Africa,

Above: P.A.A.'s hotel on Midway Island was one of three hotels constructed by Pan Am. The soil for the lawn had to be shipped from Guam. (NASM)

Above: The rotating beacon at Wake Island. (NASM)

The aerial system of the long-range radio direction finders that were built on Pan Am's Pacific island bases. (NASM)

and South America, the *Pacific Clipper* landed unannounced in New York harbor.

On Wake Island the M-130 *Philippine Clipper*, though strafed by Japanese aircraft, managed to escape carrying a staggering load of seventy Pan Am personnel. One courageous employee, Waldo Ranquist, elected to remain behind to help the wounded and was captured when the Japanese overran the island. On Guam eleven Pan Am base staffers were eventually captured hiding out in the hills. All, including Ranquist, survived the war in Japanese prison camps. Midway escaped with minor damage until June 4, 1942, when Pan Am's luxurious hotel and base facilities were de-

stroyed in the pivotal engagement of the Pacific war—the Battle of Midway.

With the war bringing commercial operations to an end, Pan Am's flying boats were adapted for use as military transports. Flown by airline crews, the Boeings transported military personnel and cargo on safe routes across the South Atlantic. The two remaining M-130s operated a service for the Navy between San Francisco and Honolulu.

The war produced new technology. Refined to meet military needs aviation moved into the jet age. With large modern airfields available almost everywhere, four-engine land planes replaced all but a handful of tired flying boats, which ended

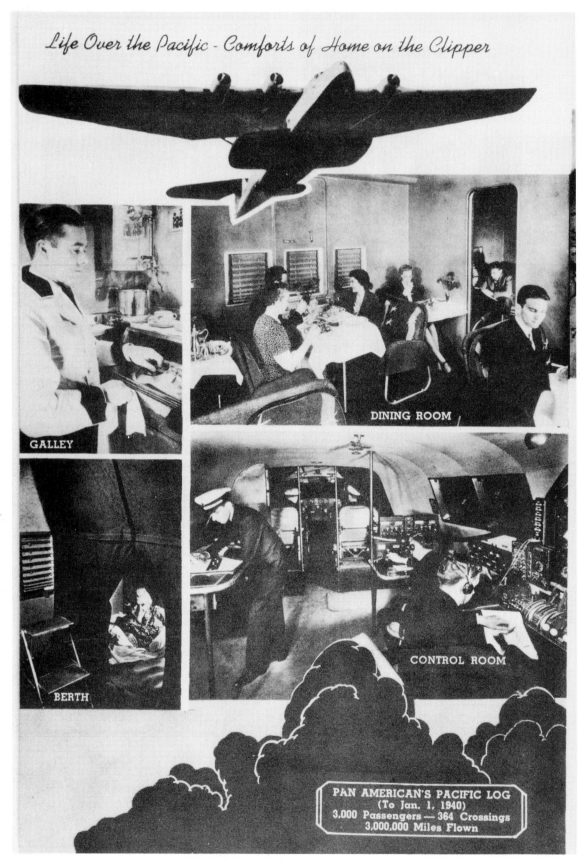

In 1940 Pan Am produced this brochure celebrating three million air miles and three thousand passengers on Pacific operations. It includes photos of the M-130 and the Boeing 314. (NASM)

their lives flying to remote little islands. In quick succession, high-flying pressurized piston airliners were replaced by the first four-engine jets. Hardly had passengers become accustomed to the novelty of 130 people whisking across the Pacific in a Boeing 707 before Pan Am introduced the revolutionary Boeing 747 jumbo jet in 1970 carrying three times the number. With the jumbo jet came the era of cheap mass air travel, and across the Pacific ranged international airlines—flag carriers of nations around its rim. Among them Pan Am, Qantas, Japan Air Lines, even tiny Air New Zealand symbolized the struggle and sacrifice of their early Pacific pioneers.

Today Pan American's Clippers no longer command the Pacific. In 1985, after a decade of trimming its massive network to remain competitive, Pan Am sold its lucrative Pacific division to United Airlines. Its autocratic founder, Juan Trippe, was no longer at the helm, having resigned in 1968 after forty years of building the world's largest airline. He has been called "the man who shrank the earth." An overstatement, perhaps, that could equally be applied to European visionaries who in the 1920s established other great international airlines. However there can be no argument that Trippe, with his great gleaming flying boats, was "the man who shrank the oceans," nor that his greatest achievement was Pan American's brilliantly conceived and executed conquest of the Pacific.

Kingsford-Smith and Ulm had pointed the way. Their daring flight, like Lindbergh's Atlantic crossing, had been a catalyst, a signpost of aviation's future promise, showing the way and holding world attention until aircraft design caught up with the pledge. Such men were the pioneers who defeated distance over the world's greatest ocean. However, in its broadest sense, the conquest was not complete until the public, without fear, climbed aboard Pan American's great Clippers to be transported in unequaled luxury to the far corners of the Pacific Ocean.

Each new Pan Am Clipper set a further standard in passenger luxury. From top to bottom: dining in the Sikorsky S-42, the Martin M-130, and the Boeing 314. (NASM)

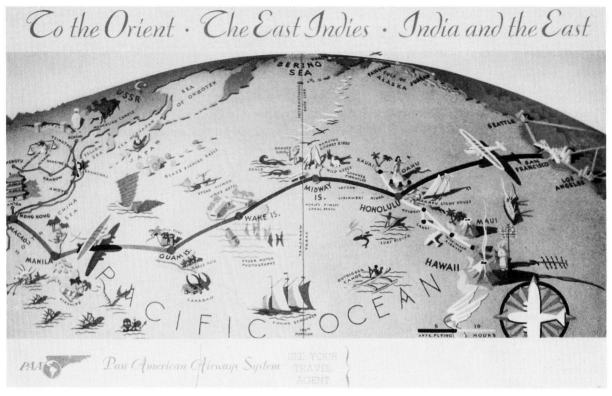

An entertaining and informative route map used to promote Pan Am's transpacific service. (NASM)

Pan Am celebrated the beginning of its Boeing 314 service in 1939 with this evocative brochure. (NASM)

Only the Atlantic Ocean remained to be added to the Pan Am network when this brochure was published in the late 1930s. (NASM)

The cover for the Wilbur Wright Memorial Lecture, given by Juan Trippe to Britain's Royal Aeronautical Society in 1941, illustrates the airline's network six months before America entered World War II. (NASM)

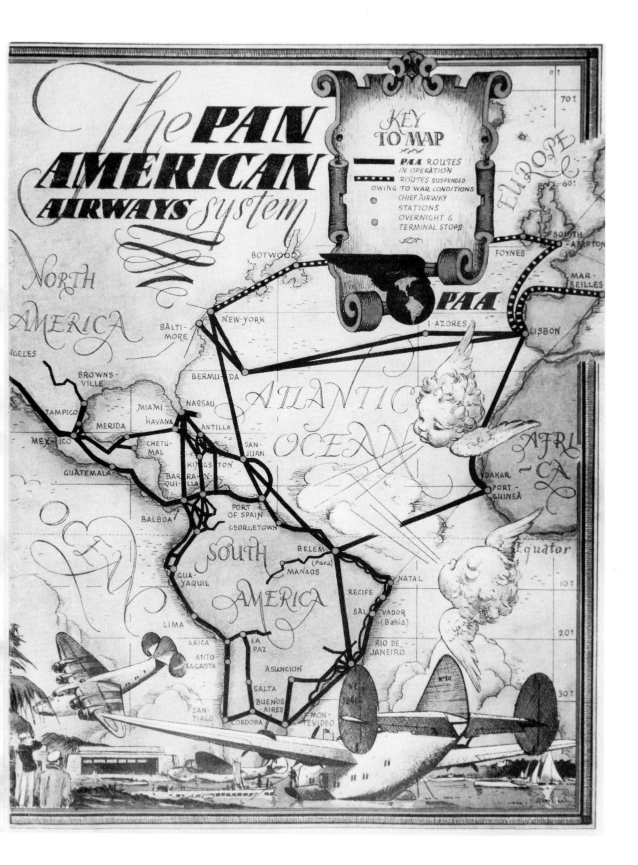

12

Amelia Earhart
Missing in the Pacific

We are in a line of position 157–337 [degrees]. Will repeat this message on 6210. We are running north and south. We have only a half hour's fuel left and cannot see land." The message came loud and clear over the radio of the U.S. Coast Guard cutter *Itasca*. The airwoman's voice betrayed anxiety. Quickly the operator switched to 6210 kilocycles and waited for her call. It never came. Her silence was shrouded in the crackling static of interference out over the vast Pacific Ocean.

It was July 2, 1937—a day that would never be forgotten by generations of Americans. Amelia

Amelia Earhart examines the loop antenna of the Bendix radio compass that was installed in the Electra. Its performance, and her ability to interpret its readings, were to be critical on the transpacific flight to Howland Island. (NASM)

Earhart, the darling of American aviation was missing. She and her navigator, Fred Noonan, would never complete their flight around the world. The mystery and the long fruitless search had begun. Two generations later the mystery surrounding her disappearance remains unsolved and, for some, the search still continues.

Amelia Earhart's association with flying the Pacific went back to January 1935 when she made a solo flight from Honolulu to Oakland in a Lockheed Vega. Not only had she been the first pilot, man or woman, to fly solo over the daunting 2,400-mile route, but she had done it in the remarkable time of 18 hours and 16 minutes. Amelia Earhart had described the flight, conducted in perfect weather, as a "joy ride." She wrote: "Contrasted to the Atlantic crossings, it was a journey of stars, not storms; of tropic loveliness instead of ice." Sadly she would find conditions less idyllic next time she challenged the Pacific.

Few pilots gained greater world attention than

Amelia Earhart. Born in Kansas in 1898, she used the airplane to promote the cause of women. Greatly influenced by her mother, an early feminist, she studied medicine until deciding to become a pilot after attending an air meet in 1920.

Equipped with a new license, Earhart tried to find work, but there were no flying jobs for an inexperienced female. She had become a social worker when, in 1928, she was hired as a crew member for a transatlantic flight. However delight turned to disgust when she realized her presence was merely a publicity gimmick. Not allowed to do any of the flying, Amelia Earhart felt "like a sack of potatoes." Nevertheless she became the first woman across the Atlantic and rocketed into the headlines. Her strong resemblance to Charles Lindbergh led to Earhart's being dubbed "Lady Lindy"—a sobriquet she detested.

In 1931 she married publishing magnate George Putnam, who became her manager. The following year, determined to earn her public adulation, she flew solo across the Atlantic. Trying doggedly to prove that women fliers were equal in ability to their male counterparts, she made numerous other long-distance flights. Writing, lecturing, counseling on women's careers at Purdue University, she used her fame to promote women's rights. "Amelia has become a symbol of a new womanhood," one journalist wrote.

By 1937 she was the world's best-known airwoman. But what was personally important to Amelia Earhart was the knowledge that the hero worship she now generated had been earned. She was no longer Lady Lindy, the false hero concocted by a clever press agent and abetted by the news media following her 1928 transatlantic passenger flight. Nor was she merely a woman who flew. She had developed into a superb pilot whose skill and courage were respected by her aviation peers. Undoubtedly much of her success had been due to her husband's wealth. But his money only assisted in providing her record-breaking equipment. Even the most chauvinistic of airmen could not deny that wealth had no bearing on skill and courage. In the cockpit, profligate women pilots faced the same dangers as impov-

erished airmen, battling the elements over the desolate oceans of the world.

Amelia Earhart's circumnavigation of the world was to be her last flight. When asked why she was making the flight, she replied: "Because I want to." However, her autobiography, *Last Flight,* published by George Putnam following her death, illustrated that the reasons went much deeper than just the desire to be the first woman to complete such a flight. She wrote:

> Here was a shining adventure, beckoning with new experiences, adding knowledge to flying, of peoples—of myself. I felt that with the flight behind me I would be more useful to me and to the program we had planned at Purdue. Then, too, there was my belief that now and then women should do for themselves what men had already done—thereby establishing themselves as persons, and perhaps encouraging other women toward greater independence of thought and action.

The aircraft chosen for the flight was a modified twin-engine Lockheed L-10 Electra. Lockheed's sleek ten-passenger airliners had been in service since 1934. Designated the 10-E (Earhart), modifications to the specially built aircraft included more powerful 550-hp Pratt & Whitney Wasp S3H1 radial engines, removal of the passenger seats to accommodate extra fuel tanks in the cabin, and blanking out the passenger cabin windows. It was equipped with the latest blind-flying instruments, a Sperry autopilot, a Bendix radio compass, and both voice and Morse code radios. The purchase of the aircraft was assisted by research funds provided by Purdue University, where Earhart used it to conduct high-altitude tests. With a fuel capacity of 1,150 gallons, it had a theoretical range of 4,000 miles when flown at 4,000 feet and at a true airspeed of 145 mph—sufficient for the longest legs of her proposed flight.

Amelia Earhart took off from Oakland on March 17, 1937, heading west on a 27,000-mile globe-girdling route that followed close to the equator. She had two navigators on board: ma-

It was a transatlantic flight in this float-equipped Fokker that accelerated Amelia
Earhart's flagging aviation career. Though only a passenger, the press promoted
the young airwoman as "Lady Lindy." (NASM)

In 1935 Amelia Earhart made the first solo crossing from Hawaii to the American
mainland. Sitting on the wing of her Lockheed Vega after arriving at Oakland,
she was mobbed by a huge crowd. (NASM)

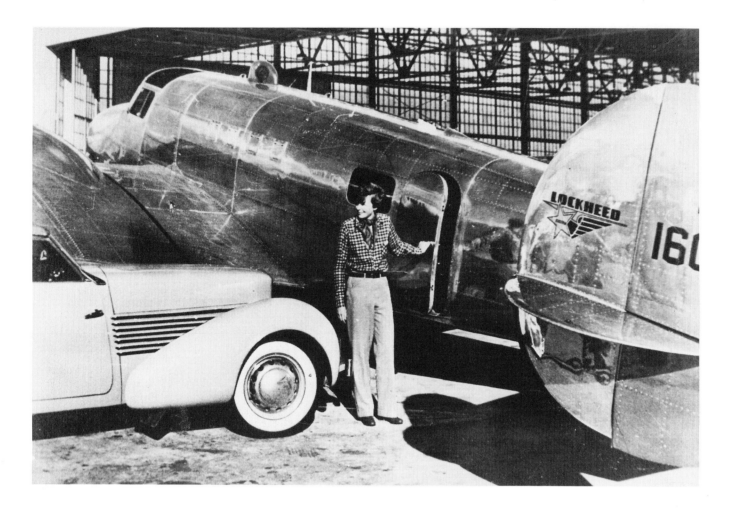

The trappings of success. Amelia Earhart with her Cord Cabriolet car and the Lockheed 10-E (Earhart) Electra provided by Purdue University. Note that the airliner's passenger windows were covered on this specially produced aircraft. (NASM)

rine navigator Capt. Harry Manning and Pan Am's Pacific expert Fred Noonan, who had lost his airline job because of a drinking problem. Realizing that a lone pilot could not fly and perform the exacting navigation required to island-hop across the Pacific, Amelia Earhart had developed an unusual compromise which would allow her to complete the flight alone. She explained: "I planned to drop Noonan at Howland [Island] and Manning in Australia. At the time we said here would be the occasion where it would be the males who'd do the walking home."

An hour out, the Electra overtook Pan Am's Hawaii-bound Clipper service. For both Amelia Earhart and the Clipper's captain, Ed Musick, this was the first time that either had seen another plane during a transoceanic flight. After an uneventful 15-hour-and-47-minute flight the world fliers landed at Wheeler Field, setting a new speed record for the route. However the flight ended three days later when, bound for Howland Island, the Electra blew a tire early dur-

ing its takeoff run from Honolulu. The strain caused the whole right landing gear to collapse and the aircraft was severely damaged. The crew emerged unhurt. "I'll be back," Amelia Earhart told reporters, as she and the crippled Lockheed sailed back to California.

Three months later the plane had been repaired and was ready for a second attempt. Following her abortive takeoff in Hawaii, Earhart had removed some equipment to reduce the Electra's weight. One item was the 250-foot-long trailing antenna that was normally used for radio communications and obtaining directional bearings on the frequencies most commonly used by ground-based radio stations. This strange deci-

On the leg to Hawaii, during her first around-the-world attempt, Amelia Earhart carried three crewmen. From left: Paul Mantz, Harry Manning, and Fred Noonan. (NASM)

Amelia Earhart at the controls of the Electra. Despite intensive training from Paul Mantz, the airwoman was still relatively inexperienced in multiengine operations when she began the world flight. (NASM)

sion appears to have been based on Earhart's aversion to winding it in and out in flight, and the fact that neither she or Noonan was skilled in the use of Morse code. Instead they had elected to rely entirely on the aircraft's fixed antenna, even though it had less range. For the second attempt Earhart had changed the route, deciding instead to head eastward, thus leaving the Pacific crossing till last. Following the Honolulu crash, Manning had dropped out, and Earhart decided now to carry only one navigator, Fred Noonan. He would be on board for the whole flight.

The pair left the American continent from Miami on June 1 heading southeast toward the equator. Before leaving she told newsmen: "I have the feeling that there is just about one more good flight left in my system, and I hope this trip is it." She planned to be back home for the Independence Day celebrations on July 4, or at worst for her thirty-ninth birthday party planned for July 24.

Their flight took them over Africa and Asia. At Bandung, Java (Indonesia), they were held up for three days as Dutch airline mechanics worked on malfunctioning "long-distance flying instruments," as Earhart reported in a long-distance phone call to her husband. AMELIA DELAYED IN JAVA, the newspapers reported on June 27, although for once she was outheadlined by another American woman. The previous day Britain's Duke of Windsor—the man who gave up a throne for love—had married America's Wallis Simpson. As the duke and duchess set out on their secret honeymoon Earhart and Noonan finally got airborne for Darwin in northern Australia, where they landed with radio problems. Stanley Rose, the young Australian radio engineer who repaired the equipment, recalled the fliers shipping their parachutes home from Darwin in a final attempt to minimize the load for the Pacific crossing. He was also appalled to note that they had removed the aircraft's trailing antenna. The next day the pair flew to Lae, New Guinea, for the final dash across the Pacific. The first transoceanic leg would be 2,556 miles from Lae to tiny Howland Island—the most grueling of the entire flight.

At Lae they topped up the fuel tanks to the 950 gallons that they estimated would get them safely to Howland with a little more than two hours' reserves. Undoubtedly they would have preferred a full 1,150-gallon load but were clearly concerned about trying to lift excessive overload off Lae's 3,000-foot airstrip. At Lae they were delayed a day by strong head winds along their route. Furthermore, due to radio difficulties, Noonan was unable to reset his two chronometers—the accuracy of his celestial navigation depended on his time being exactly correct. Noonan's inability to check his navigational clocks added to his problem of locating a destination that was a mere speck of sand and coral—1½ miles long and ½ mile wide! The Electra was to be the first aircraft to land on Howland Island's newly constructed airstrip.

Even with a first-class navigator on board it would have been an incredible feat to find the island by celestial navigation and dead reckoning alone. If they were only one degree off their course Earhart and Noonan would miss their target by 40 miles. Even if Noonan's calculations were exactly right, it was impossible for a pilot to read and hold a compass heading on such a razor's edge of accuracy—particularly over such a long distance. Aware of these hazards, Amelia Earhart had enlisted the aid of the U.S. government. The Navy fleet tug *Ontario* was positioned halfway along their route and the Coast Guard ship *Itasca* was anchored at Howland. Besides normal voice communications, the *Itasca* was equipped with a radio direction finder and had a beacon that could be picked up by the aircraft's Bendix radio compass. Furthermore it had been arranged that the *Itasca* would act as a visual beacon by making smoke. Once the Lockheed came within range, the ship could guide it in. Even if the plane was a little off course it would not matter . . . or so it seemed!

At 10 A.M. on the morning of July 2 they took off from Lae. In Greenwich Mean Time—generally used by navigators on long flights—the time was exactly 0000 hours (midnight). They estimated that the flight to Howland Island would take exactly 18 hours.

"Miss Earhart's Wasp-motored Lockheed Electra plane made a difficult takeoff with ease, but it was only fifty yards from the end of the runway when it rose in the air," reported the *New York Herald Tribune*. In a second, radioed report headlined ABOARD THE CUTTER "ITASCA"—OFF HOWLAND ISLAND the paper told its readers:

United States sailors and Coast Guardsmen set watch tonight along one of the loneliest stretches of the earth's surface to guide Amelia Earhart on the longest, most hazardous flight of her career. The *Itasca* and the *Ontario* awaited word of her takeoff from Lae for Howland Island, an almost microscopic bit of land representing America's frontier in the South Pacific.

During the early hours of the flight, the Electra, using its radio call sign "KHAQQ," reported by radio every 30 minutes to operators in Lae. Seven hours out they reported that the weather had deteriorated and they were experiencing increased head winds. Their position report indicated they were achieving a speed over the water of only about 128 mph—considerably less than planned. But the pair seemed unconcerned. All was going well and Amelia Earhart advised that the engines were operating perfectly. Through the night radio operators on the *Ontario* and the *Itasca* listened for the Lockheed's scheduled reports, but heavy static interference made reception impossible. A contributing factor was Earhart and Noonan's decision to remove the Lockheed's trailing antenna.

At 1215 hours G.M.T. Amelia Earhart's transmissions broke through for a moment. Her only intelligible words were "cloudy and overcast." Spirits soared, the fliers were safe and coming in. With renewed efforts the operators broadcast homing signals for the pilot to pick up on her radio compass. But for an hour nothing more was heard. However, no one was greatly concerned, for at this stage, the aircraft was still 1,000 miles out and at extreme radio range. Another garbled message was heard. The pilot was calling for a homing signal, but again, they were unable to establish two-way communications. At 1745

hours G.M.T., as the sun rose at Howland Island, the *Itasca*'s radio operator heard another snatch of Earhart's voice reporting they were "200 miles out and no landfall." Thirty minutes later she broke through loud and clear reporting: "We are approximately 100 miles from *Itasca,* position doubtful. Please take a bearing on us and report in half an hour. I will transmit into the microphone." The seamen swung their ship's direction finder in vain. For some reason he could not lock onto her signal.

For another hour intermittent calls were heard, but it appeared that the fliers were not picking up the *Itasca*'s radio nor the signal beamed to the aircraft's radio compass. At 1912 hours G.M.T. Earhart called again: "We must be right on top of you but cannot see you. Our gas is running low. Have been unable to reach you by radio. We are flying at an altitude of 1,000 feet. Please take a bearing." The *Itasca* acknowledged her message and immediately transmitted a homing signal. The radio operators made several calls over the next 10 minutes but again the Electra was not receiving them. The ship was still unable to take a bearing on the aircraft's transmissions. Something was radically wrong, for at that range it should not miss the plane.

Again the airwoman's voice came booming through the static: "KHAQQ to *Itasca*. We are circling but cannot hear you. Go ahead on 7,500 now." Frantically the operators switched frequency and sent a homing signal on 7,500 kilocycles. For a moment it seemed to have worked. She called back: "Receiving your signal but unable to get a minimum . . . please take a bearing on us." By "minimum" the airwoman was referring to getting a bearing with the aircraft's radio compass. When its rotatable antenna was pointing at the *Itasca*'s radio beacon, Earhart would hear a minimum or silent signal. It worked on a reverse, but similar, principle to turning a handheld transistor radio to get the best reception from a broadcast station.

At 2000 hours G.M.T. the Electra had been airborne for 20 hours. The *Itasca*'s crew realized that the confused fliers were nearby, circling and attempting to use their radio compass. It seemed the fliers must be within spitting distance of Howland Island yet for some reason could not sight the small twist of sand. Perhaps because it rose only a few feet above the sea and was impossible to spot from their low altitude? That problem would have been compounded by their scanning directly into the morning sun.

At 2025 hours G.M.T., 12 minutes after the Electra's fuel should technically have run out, Amelia Earhart's final urgent message was heard. The *Itasca*'s operators later reported their belief that she must have been very close because it was so loud. They also noted that her voice was high-pitched and tinged with alarm. Her reference to a 157–337 degrees "line of position," some researchers believe, indicated that the fliers had finally picked up a reading on their radio compass but were not sure whether they were north or south of the station. If this was the case, with insufficient fuel remaining to solve this ambiguity of location, the pair resorted to flying a search pattern north and south along the position line.

However there is another explanation of Earhart's use of the unusual "line of position" terminology, rather than the common aviation expression "position line." It is quite probable that she was relaying the words used by her navigator. During his transpacific flying for Pan American Airways, Noonan and the airlines' navigation consultant, Harold Gatty, had instituted Francis Chichester's island-finding navigational technique of "deliberate error." Chichester's technique had been adapted from an early sailing manual and used the term "line of position." It is unlikely that the desperate fliers had sufficient fuel remaining following sunrise to use Chichester's complete method. This would have involved putting the Lockheed well north or south of their destination—thus solving the problem of which way to turn once they reached the "line of position." However, it seems certain that with the *Itasca*'s direction finder and his own radio compass not working, Noonan took an astro shot of the rising sun and worked out a "line of position." The problem the fliers then faced was which way to turn to head for Howland. There would have

been little recourse but to search in both directions along the line. This theory is reenforced by the statement "We are running north and south" in Amelia Earhart's final message.

Following meticulous research, noted British aviation historian and former R.A.F. navigator Roy Nesbit is also of the opinion that Noonan used a sunrise astro shot. Furthermore he believes that the problem was probably exacerbated by Noonan's simple oversight of neglecting to allow a "dip correction" to compensate for the aircraft's cruising altitude of 1,000 feet. Nesbit's findings were recently published in the prestigious *Aeroplane Monthly*. He wrote:

One might have expected Noonan to have known this, but he was primarily a marine navigator and he was probably mentally exhausted after working solidly for eighteen hours. If he had made this oversight, it would have resulted in the Electra flying up and down a position line at least 35 miles to the west of Howland Island.

Whatever the case, the 157–337 degrees position line came too late to help them locate Howland Island. Nothing more was heard from the Electra. It was probably only a matter of minutes after the final message that Earhart and Noonan ditched in the Pacific. Even if they managed a faultless landing, the Lockheed would have probably sunk very soon after—contrary to the erroneous belief of the time that metal aircraft could float for days. However it is more likely that Earhart and Noonan would not have survived the forced landing because it was later established that the seas in the area were rough at the time. This would have made a safe touchdown virtually impossible.

Soon after losing radio contact with the plane, the *Itasca* sent out a message telling the world that Amelia Earhart was missing. Within hours a fleet of naval ships set out from Pearl Harbor and San Diego. But it was several days before they reached the area. Meanwhile a stunned world listened to the radio for news. Within hours of the plane's disappearance, hopes had soared when

Earhart and Noonan take off at Caripito, Venezuela, from an airport operated by Pan American Airways and the Standard Oil Company. (NASM)

Earhart and Noonan at an unidentified airport as they head eastward around the world. (NASM)

One of the last photos taken of Amelia Earhart as she and Fred Noonan chat with well-wishers during their flight. (NASM)

three naval operators reported picking up a Morse code message which said: "Can't last much longer. Plane is sinking." Then, as a massive search slowly got underway, other garbled messages were received indicating that the pair had crashed on a reef and were well.

At first the messages reenforced the public's desperate hope that their hero was still alive and awaiting rescue. However, from the outset the experts were skeptical that radio signals could have been sent from the downed aircraft. Then, as the signals continued, the authorities became certain that they were the work of the warped minds of hoaxers, the ghouls who frequently came out of the woodwork when such events oc-

curred. On July 4, with a cloud hanging over the United States' Independence Day celebrations, newspapers dashed the nation's hopes. The *Baltimore American* reported on a press conference held by Amelia Earhart's husband and search officials: "Putnam, grim-faced and communicating his views rarely, expressed his belief that the messages had not come from Miss Earhart's plane. The Coast Guard was more emphatic in its disparagement of the atrocity of the many signals claimed to have been received."

A desperate and distraught George Putnam even enlisted the aid of woman flier and family friend Jacqueline Cochran, who was noted for her powers of extrasensory perception. She put

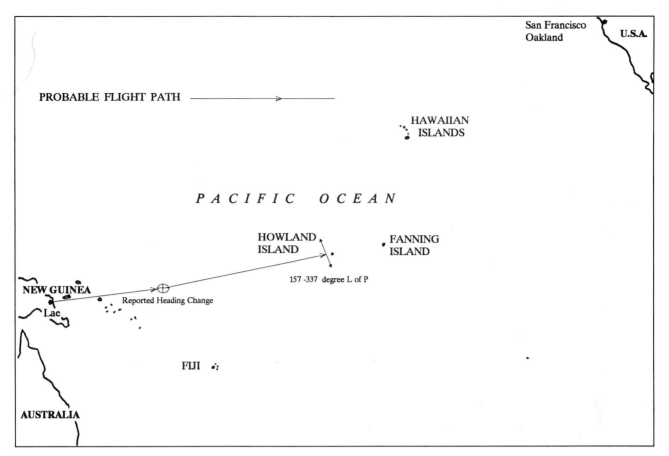

The circle represents the only positive fix given by Earhart and Noonan. Thirteen miles west of the Nukumanu Islands and slightly south of the direct track, it indicated that they were experiencing unexpectedly strong head winds. Most serious researchers believe that the pair were searching along a 157–337 degree line of position, about 30 miles short of Howland Island, when they ran out of fuel.

Besides cranks making fake radio calls purporting to come from the downed fliers, someone sent the authorities this ghoulish message on a charred stick. It read: "To my husband—I have crashed 250 mls from Hawaii—N.W. Our motor . . . into flames—Sharks are about me. A.E. (NASM)

Navy Planes Halted By Storm In Search For Amelia, Noonan; Fears Grow

ROUTE OF EARHART FLIGHT
Circle near the right marks Howland Island, where the famous aviatrix and her navigator are believed to have overshot their mark.

Storm Turns Back U. S. Planes In Search For Miss Earhart

Continued from First Page.

U. S. S. Colorado, which dashed toward Howland from Honolulu, was not expected to reach the vicinity before Monday night or Tuesday. The Colorado is equipped with three planes, one of which made a brief strike from her decks today, only to be forced back by the furious storm.

Raging Storm

The aircraft carrier U. S. S. Lexington, carrying 54 planes, was ordered by Washington to leave San Diego early tomorrow to join the search.

Wrong Message

Fear For Plane

Last Message

Searchers said they had reason to believe the last message from the plane came at 1:45 A. M. today.

KHAQQ SOS, KHAQQ SOS.
KHAQQ SOS.

Said Mrs. E. S. Earhart, Amelia's

Storm Diminishes Hopes For Rescue

HONOLULU, July 3—(A. P.)—Chances for the rescue of Amelia Earhart and her navigator, Fred Noonan, diminished today when storms turned a big naval flying boat away from the search.

Searches Area

President Keeps In Close Touch

HYDE PARK, N. Y., July 3—(A. P.)—President Roosevelt kept in close touch with the Navy Department today seeking information on the fate of Amelia Earhart.

Gets 30 Years

Bandit Caught Here Sentenced in D. C.

Synod Leaders Fined By Nazis

BERLIN, July 3—(A. P.)—The first of the trials of members of the Prussian Council of the Confessional Church was at end today with two synod leaders, Pastors Niesel and Von Arnim Lieben, fined with marks. Pastor Gerhard Jacobi and Dr. Ehlers were released.

Huge Aircraft Carrier Ordered Into Search

SAN DIEGO, Cal., July 3—(A. P.)—Facilities of the Naval Air Service were thrown into the search for the missing plane of Amelia Earhart and her navigator, Fred Noonan, today when the huge aircraft carrier Lexington was ordered to prepare for a South Seas cruise, which might last for weeks, with 54 planes aboard.

WILL THIS BOAT SAVE HER LIFE?
Miss Earhart is shown inflating the collapsible rubber lifeboat she carried for such emergencies.

Amelia's Own Story Before Hop

Continued from First Page.

Buys Dictionary

Forded River

Plane 'Biscuit Box'

Dominican Convent Procession Today

WIRE NEWS IN BRIEF

NATIONAL

FOREIGN

MARYLAND

Says World Fair Holds Sway Daily In Washington

By ARTHUR "BUGS" BAER

Husband Finds Wife In Gas-Filled Room

$300,000 Blaze At Rockaway

Amusement Area Fire Blamed On Racketeers

NEW YORK, July 3—(A. P.)—Five roared through a square block of Rockaway Beach's amusement area today and 14 Boardwalk buildings valued at $300,000 were razed.

For days America's newspapers were filled with reports concerning the search for Earhart and Noonan. To give its readers some hope, the *Baltimore American* featured a photograph of the airwoman with the Electra's tiny life raft. (NASM)

her mind to the problem of finding her missing friend and told Putnam that the two were alive and that the Lockheed was still floating. In desperation navy vessels fruitlessly searched the area Cochran described. After 16 days the search was finally called off. Ten ships and sixty-two aircraft had covered an area of 200,000 square miles. Not even an oil slick had been sighted.

There was criticism that the one vessel capable of mounting an immediate rescue was not allowed to head into the search area. The *Itasca* had set sail within hours of losing contact with the plane but was recalled by Washington to hold at Howland and act as tender for seaplanes flying in from Hawaii. Unfortunately the seaplanes were delayed for several days by severe storms. When the *Itasca* was finally released, and the search had reached significant proportions, 8 days had passed during which the storms had also struck the area around Howland Island. By that time any traces of the crashed Electra lay beneath the Pacific.

Following the tragedy there were many people who refused to believe that their hero was dead. In the absence of indisputable proof, many wild and improbable theories were advanced concerning her fate. The most popular was that Earhart and Noonan were on a clandestine government mission to photograph Japanese military establishments in the Pacific. During World War II a number of clues supposedly surfaced proving that the fliers had been captured by Japanese soldiers. Over the years writers of countless books and articles have kept the aura of mystery alive. Some claim Earhart survived the war in a Japanese prison; others that she and Noonan were executed on Saipan. Even today, there are people who believe that Amelia Earhart still lives, that she was smuggled back to the United States disguised as a Catholic nun and lives anonymously in New Jersey still guarding the secret of her covert mission.

Besides Roy Nesbit, several other fliers have tried to solve the problem of Earhart's disappearance and put the mystery to rest. The most noted—and dedicated—is Capt. Elgin Long, an airline pilot, navigator, and trained crash investigator. Having spent years researching every minute detail of the flight, he ran critical tests on the range and performance of the direction-finding equipment used by the Electra and the *Itasca*. From the tests a vital clue emerged explaining why the ship's direction-finding equipment had failed to lock onto Amelia Earhart's booming transmissions. By experimenting with identical equipment, Captain Long established that it had been turned on hours too early. By the time the Electra was within range, the equipment's inefficient lead-acid batteries were too flat to allow it to operate correctly.

Like most other professional fliers, Elgin Long finally came to the conclusion, based on his exhaustive investigation, that Amelia Earhart's Lockheed simply ran out of fuel close to Howland Island. He believes that the plane's remains probably lie somewhere within a 30-mile radius of its tiny target. However, for those who need to believe in the immortality of heroes and heroines, the mystery remains unsolved and the search continues.

Amelia Earhart would have preferred that her millions of admirers, particularly women whose cause she espoused, remembered her best for the reasons she gambled her life against the vast Pacific. She once wrote: "Women must try to do things as men have tried. When they fail, their failures must be a challenge to others."

We will never know exactly what happened near Howland Island on July 2, 1937. The secret is locked for eternity on the bed of the Pacific Ocean. However we do know that Amelia Earhart fulfilled a last wish she once expressed to her husband: "I don't want to go; but when I do, I'd like to go in my plane—quickly."

The stunning Tachikawa A-26's two 1,000-hp Nakajima engines gave it a top speed of 273 mph. For maximum range it cruised at 186 mph. (Robert C. Mikesh)

Epilogue

A Matter of Japanese Honor

Changchun, China, July 2, 1944

I t was a strange machine. An all-metal twin-engine monoplane, it faintly resembled the Japanese bombers that were desperately fighting a losing battle against the Allied forces that island-hopped the Pacific toward Japan. But there the resemblance stopped. Its superbly streamlined fuselage and remarkably long, gliderlike wings indicated that this machine was not built for war. Rather it had all the trademarks of a purpose-built, long-range record breaker. Incredible as it may now seem, in the dying stages of World War II, Japanese airmen were about to stage their own quasi conquest of the Pacific.

Six airmen watched as the ground crew pumped a staggering 3,052-gallon fuel load into the aircraft's wing tanks. Then, after exchanging salutes with an Imperial Japanese Army officer, the six climbed aboard and took off easily following a ground roll of only 4,400 feet. If all went well over the next three days they were about to fly, nonstop, for more than 11,000 miles.

The project had its beginning during the 1930s following the unsuccessful attempts by Japanese airmen to fly nonstop across the Pacific. Following the loss of the Junkers W33 *Hochi Nichi Bei* all further attempts had been officially suspended. However, in February 1940, as Pan American's Clippers ranged across the Pacific, the Tokyo newspaper *Asahi Shimbun* came up with a plan to set world aviation back on its heels. To mark the 2,600th birthday of the Japanese Empire, the newspaper announced that it was sponsoring construction of an aircraft to make a goodwill flight from Tokyo to New York City. For good measure the aircraft would then fly nonstop to Buenos Aires.

The plan sparked intense interest among Japanese aviation circles, not the least from a group of army officers. They had already unsuccessfully approached several aircraft companies with the impossible task of designing a superbomber that would be capable of carrying a heavy load of bombs and possessing a range of 10,000 miles! Japan still perceived Russia as its greatest threat, and the army was keen to have a bomber that could devastate Russian cities far to the west. Like the other aircraft builders, the Tachikawa Aircraft Company had told the army officers that a 10,000-mile range requirement for a heavily loaded bomber was totally unrealistic. However, when approached by the *Asahi Shimbun*, Tachikawa agreed to design a long-range aircraft for the special flight. Without the need for a bomb-load on the goodwill mission, Tachikawa was confident it could produce a machine with adequate range. Hoping to benefit from the design technology that would be incorporated in the *Asahi Shimbun*'s airplane, the army also became involved in the project.

The newspaper's specifications called for a minimum range of 9,325 miles, a cruising speed of at least 186 mph, and an ability to cruise at around 20,000 feet where it might benefit from the high-speed jet streams. An all-civilian team headed by Dr. Hidemasa Kimura worked on the design, which centered around a high-aspect ratio wing with a laminar flow aerofoil. These two features were employed to minimize drag. Seventy percent of the wing's internal area was to carry the massive fuel load, which would more than double the aircraft's 15,955-pound empty weight. Early plans called for two of the aircraft to be completed by November 1941, but delays put them behind schedule. With the outbreak of the Pacific war the project was canceled and the uncompleted machines were put into storage.

In the summer of 1942 the army ordered Tachikawa to resume production of the A-26. It had been decided that the aircraft's range would make it ideal for special missions between Japan and Germany. First flight tests were conducted late in 1942. Powered by two 1,000-hp Nakajima engines, similar to those used in Japan's famous Zero fighter, the A-26 handled superbly. A top speed of 273 mph was achieved at 15,000 feet and the desired fuel flows were established at an economical cruising speed of 186 mph. Other than minor oxygen flow problems within its sealed high-altitude cabin, the radical machine met or surpassed all its design expectations.

On June 30, 1943, one of the A-26s took off from Fussa, near Tokyo, on a clandestine flight to Berlin. Besides a crew of five it carried a Colonel Nakamura who it appears had a special mission in Germany. To avoid interception by Soviet fighters on a northern route over Russia, the A-26 was dispatched first to Singapore, where it refueled for the long flight over the Middle East and southern Europe to Berlin. On July 7, somewhere over the Indian Ocean, contact was lost with the A-26. The reason for its loss was never established. Severe tropical storms were known to be in the area. It is also possible that the unarmed aircraft was shot down, as British war records disclose that an unidentified Japanese plane was destroyed over the Indian Ocean on the same date.

The remaining A-26 languished until the spring of 1944 when, as U.S. Marines landed on Saipan and China-based Army Air Force B-29s began raiding northern Kyushu, the strange decision was taken to use it to set a new world distance record. Why, with the war situation deteriorating rapidly, the Japanese should use valuable resources on such a venture has not been fully established. Whatever the reason, it was an opportunity for *Asahi Shimbun* and the men who designed and built the revolutionary A-26 to prove that their aircraft was capable of conducting the flight for which it had been designed. Even though there would be no world headlines, they would know the Japanese technology had finally rivaled the United States and Europe. Was it, perhaps, a matter of honor?

Clearly it was suicidal to contemplate flying the mission over the originally planned course to New York and Buenos Aires. Instead a secret closed circuit was chosen, far removed from the war, over Manchuria. The aircraft was flown to Hsinking (now Changchun) 250 miles north of the Korean border from where it was to circle over a 537.5-mile course until it had flown a distance exceeding the Tokyo-New York flight. Japanese records are sketchy concerning its crew of military and civilian airmen. They record that Komata and Tanaka were the two pilots, Shimozaki and Morimatsu were the engineers,

The cockpit of the A-26 was sophisticated for its day. Between the pilot's control wheels the autopilot control panel is visible. This system failed during the record flight. (Robert C. Mikesh)

Habiro was radio operator, and Sakamoto was to record details of the record attempt.

Following takeoff the aircraft's weight of 36,800 pounds limited its ceiling to 10,000 feet. However, as fuel was consumed the aircraft was able to climb until it finally reached 20,000 feet. Throughout the flight, as weight decreased, the power was reduced to maintain the minimum required fuel flow. The autopilot had failed early in the flight and the two pilots took turns at the controls. With no air circulating in the sealed cockpit the crew had problems staying awake by the second day. Their discomfort was exacerbated by the oxygen masks they were forced to wear. Although sun streaming into the cockpit made the interior uncomfortably warm, condensation from their breathing formed ice on the windows and metal frames.

By the start of the third day aloft the A-26 had flown 8,550 miles in 48 hours. On the ground a team monitoring the flight disagreed with the crew's assessment of the fuel remaining. Later in the day the officer in charge of the ground team ordered the airmen to land at the completion of the nineteenth circuit. It seems likely that he believed the error in fuel calculation was due to the crew's becoming too exhausted to concentrate fully. In the early evening of July, 4, 1944, the A-26 landed safely after a flight of 57 hours and 11 minutes. It had flown a staggering 10,248

The ground crew loads cylinders of oxygen aboard the A-26. (Robert C. Mikesh)

The crew of the record-breaking A-26 is bid farewell by the mission commander prior to taking off on the record-breaking flight in July 1944. (Robert C. Mikesh)

The A-26 takes off at Hsinking to simulate the nonstop flight from Tokyo to New York. Its gliderlike high-aspect ratio wings are clearly evident. (Robert C. Mikesh)

miles. Furthermore, when the tanks were checked it was found that 211 gallons of fuel remained—enough to have flown an additional 1,120 miles! The actual distance the Japanese airmen had flown exceeded the Great Circle route distance to New York by more than 3,000 miles—not to mention the reserves that remained in their tanks. Their unofficial world record was not announced. The country's military leader, Gen. Hideki Tojo, had other things on his mind. Facing inevitable defeat, he was to resign two weeks after the flight.

Following the end of the war, Tachikawa's brilliant A-26 was among a number of Japanese aircraft shipped to the United States to be studied by aviation experts. No one was aware of its stunning record flight, and sadly, it was later reduced to scrap. In September 1946 its record was eventually exceeded by the Lockheed P2V-1 *Truculent Turtle* which flew 11,227 miles across the Pacific from Perth, Australia, to Columbus, Ohio. On August 12, 1960—thirty-three years after the purchase of a replica of Charles Lindbergh's Ryan NYP started its crusade—Japan finally conquered the Pacific. The trial-and-error years of tragedy and frustration were forgotten in the celebrations marking Japan Air Lines' inaugural nonstop DC-8C service from Tokyo to San Fran-

245

The spoils of war. The A-26 bearing U.S. markings was one of several Japanese airplanes test-flown and shipped to America. (Robert C. Mikesh)

cisco. Fifteen years later another airline event was to recall the efforts *Asahi Shimbun* and its A-26.

On November 12, 1975, the Boeing Aircraft Company arranged a special transpacific flight to demonstrate the intercontinental ability of its new 747-SP long-range jumbo. The "Special Purpose" jumbo was the brainchild of Pan American Airways. As with its fabled B-314 Clipper flying boats, the airline had again turned to Boeing for a solution to a special need. This time Pan Am required an airliner to carry a full payload nonstop across the Pacific between New York and Tokyo.

When the 747 landed at Haneda Airport after a 13½-hour flight, reporters clustered around one of its 181 V.I.P. passengers. They were eager to hear the verdict on the nonstop flight from seventy-one-year-old Dr. Hidemasa Kimura—the man who thirty-five years earlier had produced an aircraft capable of connecting the two cities with 4,000 miles to spare. Closing his eyes momentarily, as if thinking back to his miraculous A-26, he mused: "It was a long wait," then, smiling brightly, added, "but a very comfortable ride."

The A-26, with all markings removed, was painted black before being shipped to the United States. It appears that no one realized its significance, and it was later reduced to scrap. (Robert C. Mikesh)

On November 12, 1975, the prototype Boeing 747-SP, demonstrating its intercontinental potential, made the first nonstop transpacific flight between New York and Tokyo. (NASM)

Sources

Allen, Oliver E. *The Airline Builders*. Alexandria: Time-Life Books, 1981.

Allen, Richard S. *Revolution in the Sky*. Rev. Ed. New York: Orion Books, 1988.

Chichester, Francis. *The Lonely Sea and the Sky*. London: Pan Books, 1967.

Cleveland, Carl M. *"Upside-Down" Pangborn*. Glandale: Aviation Book Co., 1978.

Cohen, Stan. *Wings to the Orient: Pan American Clipper Planes 1935–1945*. Missoula, Mont.: Pictorial Histories Publishing Co., 1985.

Crouch, Tom D., ed. *Charles A. Lindbergh: An American Life*. Washington, D.C.: Smithsonian Institution, 1977.

Davies R. E. G. *A History of the World's Airlines*. London: Oxford University Press, 1964.

Davies R. E. G. *Airlines of the United States since 1914*. London: Putnam, 1972.

Davies R. E. G. *Pan American Airways: An Airline and Its Aircraft*. New York: Orion Books, 1987.

Davis, Pedr. *Charles Kingsford-Smith*. Sydney: Summit Books, 1977.

In 1990 Qantas began operating Boeing's new long-range 747-400s on its nonstop Pacific service. Depending on the fuel load required, the incredible 450-ton giants can carry up to 400 passengers. (Qantas)

Earhart, Amelia. *Last Flight*. New York: Harcourt, Brace, 1937.

Ellison, Norman. *Flying Matilda*. Sydney: Angus and Robertson, 1957.

Horvat, William J. *Above the Pacific,* Fallbrook, Calif.: Aero Publishers Inc., 1966.

Joy, W. *The Aviators,* Sydney: Shakespeare Head Press, 1965.

Kingsford-Smith, Charles and C. T. P. Ulm. *The Flight of the Southern Cross*. New York: Robert M. Mc-Bride and Co., 1929.

Kohri, K., I. Komori and I. Naito. *The Fifty Years of Japanese Aviation: 1910–1960*. Tokyo: Kantosha Co., 1961.

McNally, Ward. *The Man on the Twenty Dollar Note*. Sydney: A. H. and A. W. Reed Pty. Ltd., 1976.

McNally, Ward. *Smithy*. London: Robert Hale, 1966.

Messimer, Dwight. *No Margin for Error: The U.S. Navy's Transpacific Flight of 1925*. Annapolis: Naval Institute Press, 1981.

Nozawa, Tadishi, ed. *Encyclopedia of Japanese Aircraft*, Vols. 3 and 6, Tokyo: Shuppan-Kyodo, n.d.

Rogers, Ellen. *Faith in Australia*. Crow's Nest, Sydney, Australia: Book Production Services, 1987.

Scheppler, Robert H. *Pacific Air Race*. Washington, D.C.: Smithsonian Institution Press, 1988.

Taylor, Sir Gordon. *The Sky Beyond*. Boston: Houghton Mifflin, 1963.

————. *Pacific Flight: The Story of the Lady Southern Cross*. Sydney: Angus and Robertson, 1935.

Thomas, Lowell. *The First World Flight*. London: Hutchinson, 1926.

Turner, P. St. John, *Pictorial History of Pan American World Airways*. London: Ian Allan, 1973.

"The Flying Schoolma'am and the Dole Birds." *The Bulletin*, San Francisco, 1927.

Aeronautical Chamber of Commerce of America Inc., *The Aircraft Year Book*, various editions. New York: Aeronautical Chamber of Commerce of America Inc. and other publishers for the Aeronautical Chamber of Commerce, 1924–1940.

Besides numerous research reports, papers, and documents in the archives of the Smithsonian Institution's National Air and Space Museum, extensive use was also made of articles published in editions of the following:

Magazines

Aerial Age, Aero Digest, Aeronautics, The Aeroplane, Aeroplane Monthly, Aerospace Historian, Air and Airways, Air Corps News, Aloha, American Aviation Historical Society Journal, Australian Flying, FAA World, Flight, National Aeronautics, National Geographic.

Newspapers

United States: *Chicago Tribune, Enquirer* (Philadelphia), *Honolulu Advertiser, Honolulu Star-Bulletin, New York Herald, New York Times, Oakland Tribune, Post-Enquirer* (Oakland), *San Francisco Chronicle, San Francisco Examiner, San Francisco Post, Sunday Star* (Washington), *The Bulletin* (San Francisco), *Washington Post, Washington Herald, Wenatchee Daily World.*

Great Britain: *Daily Express, Daily Mail, The Times* (London).

Australia and New Zealand: *Argus* (Melbourne), *Auckland Star, Courier* (Brisbane), *Queenslander* (Brisbane), *Telegraph* (Brisbane), *Smith's Weekly* (Sydney), *Sydney Morning Herald.*

Index

Page numbers in *italics* refer to illustrations.

251